Heref Withi Memory

Compiled by the Herefordshire
Federation of Women's Institutes

Published jointly by
Countryside Books, Newbury
and the HFWI, Hereford

First Published 1993
© Herefordshire Federation of Women's Institutes 1993

COUNTRYSIDE BOOKS
3 Catherine Road
Newbury, Berkshire

ISBN 1 85306 247 2

The cover photograph shows Lugg Meadows in about 1900
and is from the collection of Hereford City Museums.

Designed by Mon Mohan
Produced through MRM Associates Ltd, Reading
Phototypeset by The Midlands Book Typesetting Company,
Loughborough
Printed in England

Contents

Acknowledgements

My sincere thanks to all those W.I.s who spent so much time and effort in compiling their collections of memories for this book, and for presenting them so beautifully typed (thus saving me a lot of hard work!) and to Mrs Sonia Taylor of Eardisley W.I., whose line drawings illustrate *Herefordshire Within Living Memory* so delightfully.

I've had a great time reading through all this fascinating material and studying all the wonderful old photographs which were submitted, and I have also enjoyed speaking to the many members who telephoned me with their queries.

I hope the publication of this book will reward our 'authors' for their prodigious efforts, recording for posterity, as it does, their own and their families' recollections of times past.

Paddy Ariss
Co-ordinator
Pembridge W.I.

List of Contributing Institutes

Contributions have been received from the following Herefordshire Women's Institutes:

Aston Ingham, Ballingham & Dist., Bartonsham, Belmont & Dist., Bishops Frome, Bishopswood, Bodenham, Bredenbury, Brilley & Michaelchurch, Brockhampton, Bullinghope & Dist., Burghill & Tillington, Clifford & Dist., Colwall, Cradley, Dilwyn, Dinedor, Holme Lacy & Dist., Dorstone, Eardisland, Eardisley, Eastnor, Edwyn Ralph & Dist., Felton & Preston Wynne, Fownhope, Foy, Hampton Bishop, Holmer, Huntington (Hereford), Huntington (Kington), Kimbolton, King's Caple, Kingsland, Kington, Ledbury, Leintwardine & Dist., Leominister, Linton, Little Hereford, Llanwarne & Dist., Longtown & Dist., Lyonshall, Madley, Marden, Mathon, Much Birch, Much Marcle & Yatton, Newton St Margarets, Orleton, Pembridge, Pencombe & Little Cowarne, Peterchurch & Dist., Peterstow, Preston-on-Wye, Putley, Ross-on-Wye, Shobdon & Dist., Staunton-on-Arrow, Stoke Prior & Dist., Stretton Sugwas & Dist., St Weonards, Sutton St Nicholas, Titley, Tupsley, Weobley, Withington and Woolhope.

Foreword

At the end of the 20th century, Herefordshire remains predominantly rural and, with only a short length of motorway in the south east, most people still travel to, rather than through, this beautiful county. Nevertheless time does not stand still in Herefordshire, and the constantly changing pattern of our modern agricultural industry has resulted in changes in the scenery. We have lost many of the old apple and pear orchards and hop fields for which the county was famous, and with them have gone the old way of life, old crafts and pastimes.

It is important that memories of former times are recorded for the benefit of future generations of Herefordians and for our visitors. We hope this record of life in Herefordshire in the early and middle decades of the century will provide a fascinating glimpse of our social heritage.

Shirley Eastwood
County Chairman

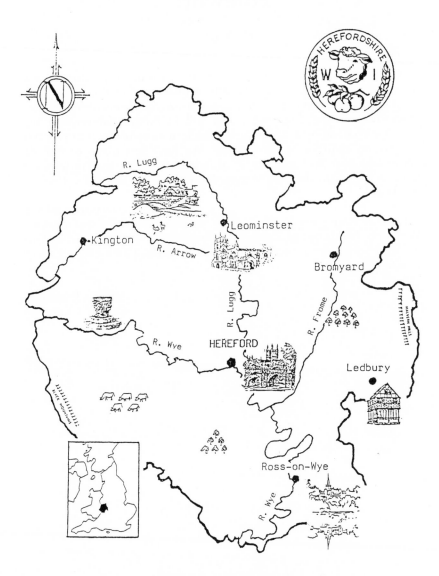

Herefordshire

TOWN & COUNTRY LIFE

SOME TOWNS AND VILLAGES REMEMBERED

Whistling errand boys on the streets of Hereford, the Midsummer Meadows of Leominster, or the days when we knew everyone in our village and could stop and chat over the garden gate and catch up on all the local news. Not so very long ago, but these memories are an introduction to a world now gone forever.

A TASTE OF HEREFORD

'I was born and grew up in the city of Hereford. One of my earliest childhood memories, in the mid 1920s, was the sound of the street cry of the "rag and bone man". Once a week he pushed his cart along the road where I lived and loudly shouted for rags and bones. I am not sure about the bones, or what he did with them, but people in the road brought out pieces of cloth, jamjars and all kinds of bits and pieces, which nowadays would be thrown in the rubbish bin. In return they would be given a few coppers. The medicine bottles brought a better reward, they could be taken back to the chemists, and when I was older I used to supplement my pocket money that way.

There were many callers at the door in those days. Our milkman came twice a day in a float, pulled by a pony, and filled the jugs from his measure, dipped in his large can. That way we were assured of fresh milk, because, of course, there were not any refrigerators. The milk jugs were covered with little beaded muslin circles and, in summer time, were put in a "safe" in the cellar. The baker boy also called several times a week, coming to the door with his big basket containing a selection of freshly baked cottage and tin loaves.

In some ways, we were quite spoilt. My mother would visit her favourite dress shop – there she would choose one or two dresses, and then, if she was undecided, they would be sent "on approval" so that she could try them on in her own home. They would be delivered in a big box by a boy on a bicycle, whistling as he cycled down the streets. All the errand boys whistled, quite often songs from the Great War, which people still talked about and remembered.

However, a new generation was arriving with the faster rhythm of the "Charleston" and the "Black Bottom". The ladies had their hair cut short, and raised their skirts to the knees. The flappers had arrived, and the pace of living increased rapidly in every way. Life was never the same again in the little cathedral city of Hereford.'

'A visit to Hereford was a holiday treat for my brother and myself. We travelled the 35 miles from our Shropshire village by train, stopping at every little station and halt, which was a delight to me, as I loved looking at the little platform gardens, ablaze with colour.

Once in Hereford, we made straight for High Town, busy with traffic in those days, in order to look at the big shops. My brother was fascinated by the strange concave windows of Edwards the furriers, whilst I admired the display of exotic hats in King's. Our favourite store, of course, was Greenlands, with its arcades and thick carpets, and dignified assistants. I remember that in the toy department was a little stuffed bird in a cage, which moved and sang when you inserted a penny.

The aroma of roasting coffee beans in High Street always led Mother into Marchant's grocery store to buy some coffee, while we waited impatiently to reach Eign Street and the Continental Café, for lunch. We loved going there, because they had wonderful ice cream sundaes in tall glasses.

After lunch there was the matinée at the Odeon cinema. I don't remember anything about the films, but I remember vividly the cinema organ. In the interval it would suddenly appear, as if by magic, from below floor level. The organist would play popular music for about ten minutes, then bow and wave, and disappear as mysteriously as he came.

Our day out ended with tea in the cinema restaurant. These magical visits ended in 1939, when life changed for most people. After the war, we were, alas, grown up!'

'In Attwood Lane, Holmer, was an old cider works run by Bonner and Durrant. Mr Durrant lived at The Priory House in Holmer Road adjoining the racecourse. On Easter Monday we used to go to Hereford Races. The horses crossed in front of The Priory House, over the A49 road, around the gasworks and back across the road again by Spring Gardens onto the racecourse. Peat was put on the road and the traffic was stopped, and in between races men raked the peat ready for the next race.'

A WALK ROUND PETERCHURCH

'The area stretching from the old village hall down to the rear of The Boughton Arms surrounding the present petrol station was the

11

Quiet and empty of traffic – Kington High Street in the early years of the century. On market day the streets were full of animals, shoppers, farmers and dealers.

site of Peterchurch Market from the first quarter of this century until it closed in the late 1950s. Market day was Monday and in the early days it was a very mixed stock trade run by the auctioneers Montague Harris of Abergavenny.

The majority of animals were either walked to the market along the drover's lanes or driven in by horse and cart. At the ewe sales up to 400 sheep would be brought in from the Black Mountains. Occasionally stock would be transported to and fro by the Golden Valley Railway and the weighbridge at the station in Peterchurch was used to weigh stock when that became obligatory. The hut remains to this day.

Together with the normal stock items of cattle, pigs and sheep, folk would buy and sell dogs, horses, timber, galvanised sheets and assorted farm implements. Both the Midland and the National Provincial Banks used to open up temporary branches on market days; the Midland used High House and the other took over a room at The Boughton Arms which stayed open all day. Mr Wilson, a dentist from Hay, found it profitable to journey to Peterchurch every Monday in the 1930s to pull teeth.

On certain days, in connection with the market, fairs were held, mainly in May and November with all kinds of sideshows, etc. Hiring of casual labour for farmwork was a feature of these fairs and available men would signify which aspect of farming they were best suited to by displaying an appropriate "badge". For example, a horseman or waggoner would have plaited straw pinned to his lapel and a shepherd would wear a piece of wool.

The amount of stock for sale declined as transport made it easier for farmers to sell their animals in the larger markets of Hereford and Abergavenny, although even in the early days these markets were used by the Golden Valley farmers. Stock such as cattle or sheep would be walked to Clehonger on Tuesdays and rested overnight. Early the following morning they would complete the journey into Hereford for the weekly sale on Wednesdays. It was also quite common for women to walk to Hereford Butter Market with a large basket of eggs or trussed poultry and return with goods purchased in Hereford from the proceeds of their sales. In the mid 1930s the market in Peterchurch became more specialised selling only cattle, with occasional ewe sales, the largest of which was on the first Monday of October each year. Around 1953, Chadwicks of Abergavenny took over from Montague Harris holding monthly sales of store cattle, but the heyday of the market was over; it became unprofitable, and finally closed in 1956.

Moving closer to the centre of the village one comes to the site of Emmanuel Jones' cobbler's shop made of corrugated iron sheets, attached to the rear of The Boughton Arms. Manny used to charge a shilling for most shoe repairs, which was expensive in those days before the First World War, but it is said he did a good job. He used to sell cigarettes and tobacco – presumably so that people could smoke while waiting for their only pair of shoes to be repaired.

High House on the opposite side of the road, as well as being a temporary bank, has been used for many commercial purposes through the years. In 1902 George Llewellyn had a blacksmith's shop behind the house. It was the custom with George that anyone wanting a horse shod on the spot paid him a shilling first, whereupon George would disappear into The Boughton Arms for a quick drink. He would then reappear and shoe the horse, charging the going rate; this was known as "rising the latch". His wife supplemented this living with Bed and Breakfast, and hiring out horses and traps.

The butcher's shop used to be the Corner Stores – grocer's, fishmonger's and fruiterer's, they boasted ice cream a speciality. The Imperial Stores next door was another general stores around 1905, but the competition from Lane's Store became too great and the grocery business ceased. It was a dressmaker's for a while after that, and later Mrs Pratt used to sell newspapers there.

One has now reached the heart of Peterchurch village, which was known as The Square. The Boughton Arms being in one quarter, diagonally opposite (where the DRG Plastics factory is now) was once Tyneham Garage selling petrol and oil and repairing motor cars. Before that, Herbert Pikes had a cycle shop and agency. He was a "Jack of all trades" – not only did he sell and repair bicycles, he was a carpenter and wheelwright, and an undertaker who also used to dig the graves. Apparently he did not like boys and would not allow them to enter his domain, according to Jack Reece; however, Jack won him over, being a frequent visitor with articles from his father's farm to repair, and he used to help Herbert in the carpenter's shop making coffins etc. Jack recalled one day, having made a superb bow from the branch of a certain yew tree, he was walking through the churchyard when Herbert Pikes, who was slightly the worse for drink, made fun of Jack's bow and arrow, saying it was of no use and bet him two shillings and sixpence he could not fire the arrow over the church roof. Jack went one better and fired it over the cock atop the steeple – and Herbert graciously handed over the halfcrown.

Herbert's father John owned the shop next door to Miss Appleyard's post office in the first years of this century. It is now part of the DRG Offices, but the place where the letter-box was situated still remains. Mail used to arrive at 7 am prompt from Hereford by horse and trap; five postmen and women were employed to deliver the letters and parcels. One man remembers that, as a lad, his round took him to Hinton, up Long Lane to Snodhill and back via Fine Street, three and a half hours each day for six shillings a week.

Across the road, where the Golden Valley Stores and post office is now, used to be the main blacksmith's shop owned and run by the most famous smith of all, Albert Leighton. He was known to one and all as "Haddock and Treacle", this apparently being his favourite concoction.

The house next door was a newspaper shop, and the shop next door to that was a butcher's. The owner, Mr Cresswell, and later his sons, used to bring meat out from Hereford in a horse and cart early in the morning and sell it in the village. The actual shop was up some steps on the outside of the building, and underneath was where the Cresswells kept the horses and cart. Old man Cresswell would allow other people to leave their horses there for a while, providing they were good customers. The shop later became the first youth club in the village, known as "The Steps", by which one entered.

Albion House was the former domain of the famous Charles Edwin

Lane. C E Lane's Store was known for miles around, and was the largest general store in Herefordshire. A whole book could be written about this one aspect of commercial Peterchurch. Few stores in the area could compete with his prices and none with his range of goods. The first mention of the store comes in *Kelly's Directory* of 1867. With the advent of the railway and improved bus services his trade increased, reaching a peak after the First World War. A devout chapel man, Lane was also a local benefactor; at one time he had 32 orphans from the Hereford Dr Barnado's home employed as delivery boys.

Lane also employed tailors and seamstresses who could make a dress for a lady in an afternoon or a suit for a gentleman in a day. He claimed to have a choice of over 3,000 boots and shoes in his shop, and his special insurance policy protected one from damage caused by German zeppelins. Ladies had a choice of corsets including the new Long Waist, Double Busk, Fitu, CB etc in dove, black, grey and white, from one shilling to ten shillings and sixpence. In his watch and clock department he boasted that "nobody yet slept through the noise made by Lane's Wonderously Cheap Alarum Clocks". His Annual Presentation Almanac which he distributed free to his customers not only contained lists of all his stock items but many household and medical hints, for example, "To prevent the hair from falling out, sponge the head lightly every day with cold tea. A simple cure for eczema is had by rubbing half a pound of pure lard and two ounces of flour of brimstone into the affected parts. To render shoes waterproof, rub on melted beeswax and mutton suet, or to rid a house of the smell of paint simply plunge a handful of hay into a full pail of water and stand in the room."

Charles Lane's son Reginald used to ride around all the local farms, smallholdings and cottages in the area collecting orders for grocery and other items. It was strictly cash with the order, and by the end of the day his bag would be full of sovereigns, notes and silver, so he carried an old revolver to protect himself from would-be thieves. The orders so obtained would be made up in the shop and delivered either by horse and cart or by the delivery boys on foot.

In the early 1920s C E Lane retired and went to live in Dorstone; the store at Albion House was sold to G & W Griffiths Ltd, who renamed it Golden Valley Stores. It continued through the Second World War, and for some time the post office was housed there, but it never achieved the same fame and prosperity. Like many other village stores in rural areas it was impossible to compete with the new supermarkets springing up in the towns.'

LEOMINSTER CHILDHOOD

'I was born, as was my mother, at the family home, The Chequers, in Leominster, a half-timbered black and white coaching inn, still little altered upstairs with wide uneven floorboards and a little twisty stair to the attics where was found, a few years ago, a lady's side-saddle dating from 1750, now on loan to the museum. I thought I knew every nook and cranny of those attics, wonderful fragrantly-dusty hiding places among the stored apples.

The Burbage plots in those days extended right up to The Grange where now the sterile car park lies. Grandfather's superb garden was enormous (to a child), growing every flower and vegetable imaginable. His runner beans were his pride, each one having to measure a straight 24 inches for him to be pleased.

There were barns and stables and pig sties and, beyond, a long way from the back door and up a narrow alleyway, the lavatory – the only one. It was terrifying to have to go there in the dark with a flickering candle, imagining all sorts of monsters lurking in the outbuildings. In the bedrooms were flower-festooned potties which, mercifully, someone else dealt with.

When the circus came to town, some horses were always stabled with us, but one occasion I vividly recall was when they tried to get an elephant down the side passage through a door which one can still see. The thing got stuck and they had to pour melted lard down its flanks to ease it out before it pulled the shaking house down!

Grandfather brewed his own beer, and many's the time I was lifted up to see inside the two great vats in the "brewus" and to help stir the pungent, bubbling gunge with the huge paddles.

Do you remember when the fields along the river bank, where we splashed and fished for tiddlers, really were the Midsummer Meadows? Halcyon days when the grasses were shoulder-high to a child, full of wild flowers, poppies and clovers, buttercups and cornflowers, white moon-daisies and, among them, a lovely fairy-like grass with little brown bobbles which we called Quaker grass. Eaton Hill above was a seemingly huge, dense and mysterious wood, with tiny streams, masses of primroses – these were picked in great bunches to fill jamjars for the church porch at Easter – wood anemones and bluebells in the spring and a little ruined castle nearby where we played out romantic but entirely innocent fantasies.

The innocence of childhood indeed! The depths of depravity to which we sank were scrumping in the apple orchards, terrified lest the farmer with the gun would catch us and tell Grandfather; knocking on doors in Etnam Street and running like mad into

The Grange and – perhaps worst of all – spending half the Sunday school penny in Mr Morris's sweet shop on the way to church.

Years later, and time changed all that. The river was canalised to control flooding, the meadows were cut, and they and the lovely hill devastated by the plough to grow cereals – not very successfully, for the river still floods. The headlands are gone and the footpaths vanished, while the hillside is nothing now but scrub and bramble where the primroses struggle valiantly to return.

As for innocence – well, that seems to have gone for ever. Today's children are so very different. Will their memories be as happy as mine, I wonder?'

PUTLEY CAMEOS

'Granny and Grandad Brookes lived at Putley Mill from 1890 to 1911 and my mother was born at the Mill Cottage in 1893. When the Mill House was built they moved there. In addition to being the miller, Grandad was also the parish overseer. Sometime in 1910, he fell out with the Squire over water rights, so built the Twynings where they went to live after leaving the mill. All the locals called the new house "Robsack Castle" because they said William Brookes gave short weight in the flour sacks to afford to build the Twynings.

Granny Brookes was a real part of my childhood. I can remember on dark winter Sunday evenings we used to walk to church with her down the Mill Lane and across the Church Meadow. She would carry a candle lantern which flickered and threw enormous weird shadows across the grass. It never gave enough light to prevent us falling over the sleeping cows and always blew out when we reached the churchyard.

Granny used to do all the washing up and cut the bread and butter – these were her two jobs. She used to stand at the sink with a pair of long-legged knickers draped over her shoulders because they didn't fall off like a shawl! For the last ten years of her life she never went out. Not because she was ill, she just didn't like going out, although as a young woman she would walk to Ledbury and back before breakfast to fetch the yeast.

My mother was always known as Pudding Brookes, not because she was plump but for the large wedges of bread pudding she used to eat. She married Norman Taylor at the end of the First World War in 1918. He was one of ten children of Harry Taylor who was Squire Riley's farm manager. Harry was responsible for planting all the fruit plantations in Putley. My mother never quite got over her annoyance that her wedding day was dwarfed by Miss Ursula Riley, who should have played the organ for the ceremony, eloping with one of her father's workmen. Not only was the organist missing, but far worse people could talk and think of nothing else but Miss Riley's departure.

The greatest pride of my mother was that her family had the first flush loo in the parish, even before the Squire. They also had the first car in the village – a Rover two-seater with a dicky seat, plate wheels and pneumatic tyres. There was great distress when the car had to be sold to buy a lorry (Model A Ford) to transport fruit to Ashperton station.

Next to the Twynings lived Miss Innes whose family did all the washing for the Rileys. You couldn't move in the house for drying clothes. On wet days they often had to stay up all night to get the laundry finished. Miss Innes, who was also the ladies' maid always seemed to be wielding the goffering iron. In the 1930s Miss Innes' uncle came to live with her. He was a serving soldier at the battle of Lucknow in 1857. I remember he gave a talk in 1938 when he was 99 years old on the relief of Lucknow, on the day that Edward VIII abdicated. The cottage was renamed Lucknow Cottage.

Mrs Baggot lived next door, always resplendent in her starched bonnet. She stood at the gate all day talking to the customers visiting the bakery, shop and post office next door.

Mrs Matty, my grandmother's sister-in-law, kept the shop. From the counter there was a long board to the half (stable) door. You didn't actually go in the shop. You stood by the door and she would push the groceries down the board with a long stick and scrape the money back. We children used to order lots of things and when she pushed them down, we would run away. Granny Brookes threatened us with dire punishments but that never really stopped us.

Bill Matty was the baker and blacksmith. The smithy was down the yard adjoining the shop. Three blacksmiths worked here; William Lloyd (also part time postman), Jim Cox and Bill Matty. As children we used to go and blow the bellows and watch the coals glow. The big shire horses that worked the land used to stamp and strike sparks off the cobbles with their hooves.

Further along the road were some cottages on one side and then the New House where the Tobys farmed on the other. I remember hop picking here – walking over the fields on long hot September days to the hopyard. We pulled the bines down into the crib and picked the hops. Our hands were soon black and our arms scratched by the rough bines. The unmistakable smell of sulphur and hops flavoured our sandwiches. Twice a day the busheler would come with the horse and dray, shouting as he came, "Clean 'em up." We picked out as many leaves as we could and the hops were then measured in a bushel and tipped into a sack. We were paid by the number of bushels we had picked – four bushels for a shilling. When we walked past the kiln, we liked to be taken in to see the hops drying although the roaring sound from the engine running the fans for the drying was rather frightening. Sometimes we called in at the house, and one day old Mrs Toby was making gravy when the cat jumped up on the table. She hit it on the head with the gravy spoon and the cat dropped dead.

Mr Gladwyn from Abbots Place used to ride around on his bicycle with two cans of milk hanging from the handlebars. He called at houses and ladled out the milk into people's jugs.

When I was five (1927), I started at Putley village school. This was a Church of England school and the teachers, Miss Toy and Miss Perkins were Church of England nuns. They wore calf length brown habits and brown head gear. We walked the mile up to the common with Iris and Joyce Williams, wearing our aprons with hankies pinned on the bodice with a safety pin. There were two rooms – the Juniors in one and nine to 14 year olds in the other. These rooms had big fireplaces with open fires and on cold winter days there used to be a big pot of cocoa which was ladled into cups for us. No cocoa has ever tasted so good.

Miss Toy who taught the older children, nearly always had a cane in her hand. She would hit you on the fingers as she walked past if you were inattentive or doing something wrong in your book. Miss Perkins was gentle and kind. She once gave me sixpence for being the first to finish knitting a vest.

Mrs Maund kept the shop on the common and we would buy a halfpenny worth of lemonade crystals and take them to the stream to make lemonade from the stream water. Sometimes Mrs Preece was there. When they had killed a pig, she would take the chitterlings down to the stream to clean and wash them. As she had a great liking for cider, occasionally the chitterlings escaped downstream and she would say, "Ther's another bugger gone. Let un go!"

In the school dinner hours we played Fox and Hounds through the woods. Time often slipped by and we would be late for afternoon school and in trouble and have to stay in after school to make up the time. When I started at school we wrote on slates with chalk and we had a sand tray in which we drew biblical scenes. I can remember chanting tables and learning the collect for the week.

The parson, Rev Bernie, used to come twice a week to take scripture lesson and would question us to make sure we were listening. On Ascension Day and Good Friday the whole school would walk to church and then we would have a holiday for the rest of the day. At one service, which was particularly long, the

19

organist dozed off and woke up and played Amen in the middle of the sermon.

The school was also used as the community meeting centre for the village before the hall was built. The Women's Institute would meet there. The Miss Rileys held the main offices of President and Secretary. They would bring their own silver tea pot and tea service, leaving the other members to use the enamel teapot and crock cups. There were also penny readings. You paid a penny and were read to by local dignitaries such as Charles Masefield (the Poet Laureate's brother), Rev Bishop and Squire Riley from edifying classics such as Dickens, Walter Scott and Eliot.'

LIFE ON THE ESTATE

'My father was estate foreman to Sir Joseph Verdin. Every working day he had to go to the castle at six o'clock to report the day's happenings. My brother and I were allowed to stay up until he returned.

I remember trucks of coal being carted from Moorhampton station every autumn to heat the castle, which was a very cold house.

In the Park, women in white starched aprons and cotton caps regularly brushed the gravel paths to keep them tidy. They were also allowed to gather acorns for their pigs and young fronds of ferns which were boiled and also fed to the pigs.

There was a machine like a giant mincer which was used to kibble the corn for the pheasants. When the pheasants were small, the keepers had to sleep in an old railway carriage on site to protect them from predators – two legged and four legged!'

'Lord Bateman took a great interest in Shobdon village and his estate workers. He left a sum of money, the interest of which was to be used to help finance the further education of any child of the village, on application. Every Christmas there was a party for the village children, and Lord Bateman presented each child with sixpence. He was also the school benefactor, and financed it. Once a year he visited the school and examined the pupils; he always wore black and white plus-fours and a cap. When he died, a message came down for the village postman to visit the Court. On his return, he carried a parcel. This contained Lord Bateman's cane and the plus-fours. A present resident of Shobdon made these into a skirt, which she still has. Lord Bateman left no heirs and the estate was broken up, and many villagers were offered their homes. The post office was on sale for £400 – this was at a time when local wages were 30 shillings a week.'

CHURCH AND CHAPEL

Sunday was a true day of rest for most people and a day for visiting relatives – but most of all it was set aside for church, chapel and Sunday school. Country life seemed to breed larger than life characters, including the local vicar or preacher, but he was held in esteem by his parishioners. The Sunday school outing has remained a pleasant memory for those who had few opportunities to travel.

A DAY OF REST

'Sundays were always kept as a day of rest. No work was done on the farm with the team of horses, and only essential work with the animals was permitted.

My father would not allow us to knit or sew on Sundays. All shoes had to be cleaned on Saturday as we all attended morning service and Sunday school the next day. We would wear our best clothes which were strictly kept for Sunday wear for some time, and then relegated to second best. We did not have many clothes.'

SUNDAY TEA WITH GRANNY

'My maternal grandmother, or Granny to us, lived in Haven Lane at Dilwyn, in a black and white cottage, known to everyone now as Moore's Cottage. Most Sundays we were summoned to Granny's for tea, with some trepidation because we were scared stiff of her! Yes, we loved her and respected her, but she could scare the living daylights out of us if we dare put a foot wrong.

So, having had our Sunday dinner, and the washing up done, we would be scrubbed clean and dressed in our Sunday best. Then off we would set – if the weather was not too good we would walk up the lane, but if it was a nice day we would walk up over the Banky (the footpath is still there, with a signpost now) past Hilltop, then "over the top" to Haven Lane, which saved our legs a little. On arrival at Granny's we would hang our coats etc in the proper place, then be made to "sit down, keep still, and be quiet" so the grown-ups could catch up with the news! Granny had a basket chair, and she would be sat there in *her* Sunday best. She was always dressed in black, with a pure white apron, freshly laundered by Aunty Margaret (with a flat iron which was heated by placing a grid on the open fire. There was no electricity supply at Haven Lane then, so everything was done the hard way).

After a while Aunty Margaret would sense that the children had had enough of sitting still, and suggest that we help her prepare tea. One of us would accompany her to the well, to draw water for making the tea. She would never allow us to do this alone, as it was quite a dangerous operation. Having safely accomplished this, the big black kettle would be filled and hung over the fire to boil – this could take quite a while, as it was a huge kettle.

So off we would go into the back kitchen (or scullery). Aunty M would slice bread, and we would butter it (farmhouse butter!); during the winter it would be rock hard, so had to be put in front of the fire to soften. Then the lovely home-made jam would be put into a glass dish. The cakes were then removed from their tins – fruit cake, sponge cake, scones etc – all baked by Aunty M in the coal oven (no mean task as there were no such things as thermostats; to see how hot the oven was – just open the door and hold a hand inside for a second to test how hot it was, and that was it. The resulting products were marvellous). Occasionally a tin of fruit would be opened, and sometimes (mostly high days and holidays) there would be a tin of *salmon* – that really was something!

After all the food preparations, the best tea service would be produced, a snowy-white cloth would be put on the table, then the food was carried in and placed on it, by which time the kettle would be boiling, ready to make the tea in a big brown pot. We would all gather round the laden table and enjoy our tea. After which in summer we would be allowed outside for "an airing" and a game of some sort, or maybe to pick a posy of wild flowers for Granny. Also, the menfolk would be "gardening", talking about it only, as in most households Sunday was a day of rest – for the *men* at least! During this time Mum and Aunty M would be doing the washing up, and Granny dozing in her chair.

Then it was time to say "Goodnight, God bless", and head for home, with Aunty M walking with us a little way to "send us". If it were dark, we would enjoy trying to make spooky noises to scare each other. Needless to say, Aunty M would join in the fun.'

CHURCH PEWS AND CHARITIES

'Whilst in some churches families had their own, named, pews, this was not the custom at Aston Ingham. The rector's family always sat in the front pew. Others, by common usage, tended to sit in the same place each week and were quite offended if a stranger sat in "their" pew by mistake. Sunday best was always worn and one memory is of one lady of the upper strata of the village who wore a long grey taffeta dress with a black bodice and a hat, summer and winter alike. She would sweep into the church just before the start of the Communion service, never at the beginning of worship. Hats were always worn and at Easter the little girls would have a new straw bonnet. If the family could afford it a complete new outfit would be purchased.

Aston Ingham had three charities all of which were set up during the 18th and 19th centuries and which are still in existence today. Villagers remember receiving a new shilling piece from the Booth Charity as a reward for good attendance at school. Later on the money was used to buy books as prizes. The Garrold Bread Charity was a great event as the money was to provide a loaf of bread for each poor family, to be distributed on Candlemas, ie 2nd February. Cottage loaves were baked in a brick oven locally and each family collected theirs from the school. Later the village hall became the distribution point. Nowadays, the bread is still made in the village. The size of the loaf has shrunk considerably and distribution takes place on the Sunday nearest to 2nd February from church.

The third charity, the Stocke Charity, provided ten free places at the village school until the 1944 Education Act. The money now is a very small amount and is combined with the other charities.'

'A goodly number walked to Pembridge church in the mornings, and the indoor and outdoor staffs of the big houses were expected to attend service too, the maids, demure in black, sitting behind their mistresses. At least until the 1920s, youngsters were trained to curtsy to their elders and betters when they met.

At Christmas time bread was fetched from the church porch by the needy; and in March and September there was another distribution of bread (under the will of Alice Trafford, dated 1701, £5 worth of bread was to be given to selected families at Christmas).'

'One charity which has survived into the late 20th century is the Brilley Chantry Bequest. Although now a mere shadow of its former value it is still distributed at the New Year to "those in need" as defined by the vicar and two other trustees. Originally it was as a result of a bequest in the mid 17th century for the rent from a cottage and seven and a half acres of Poors Land at Brilley. To this was added £1 annually from an estate called Woolton. The value of the rents increased very slowly over the years and in 1839 it was £3, which the then vicar, Rev Rice-Price, administered in the form of two cwts of coal to each of 21 needy poor.'

'There was a great celebratory service held in Madley church on 6th February 1955 to mark the coming of electricity to the village. The Bishop of Hereford was to preach. However, the service had to begin by the light of candles, because the main fuse had burnt out. The Bishop suggested they first sing a hymn that everybody knew, and then he would straightway give his sermon, in order to give the engineers time to carry out repairs. Before he was halfway through, the church was flooded with light, and the service of thanksgiving was carried to a joyful conclusion.'

DRESSING UP

'It was always hats and gloves for church in the evening. The boys waited outside on their bicycles to accompany young ladies home. Riding two on a bike was fun – those were the days!'

LARGER THAN LIFE

'In 1906 George Henry Powell became rector of Dorstone. People remember him in his tweeds, plus-fours and old trilby hat, with his dogs and shooting stick, every inch the squire. He had the ability to communicate with everyone, and if a man was working in the fields he would walk up and down with him for several turns. If he was fishing in the river Dore, the train driver on the Golden Valley line would stop his train and ask what he had caught. When the biggest fish was produced, Bennet, the driver would cry, "By gob, it's as big as a bullifant!" He would then give the parson a lift to further down the river.

He was a father figure, squire, doctor, lawyer and parson all rolled into one. He would not accept payment for funerals, and at weddings would take seven shillings and sixpence from the groom and return it to the bride.

At the end of his first sermon in Dorstone church, his father's old gardener clapped his hands and said in a loud voice, "Well done, Master George."

George Powell retired in 1953. He lived a further five years and his death marked the end of an era.'

'Rev Worsey, vicar of Bodenham from 1905 to 1944, has been described as one of the most popular clergymen in the county. He is remembered for organising the Red Cross and other sales during the First World War, when as much as £200 (an enormous sum at that time) was raised each time. He also laid in an emergency stock of coal during the war so that his poorer parishioners could have it when needed. In 1919 he sold the whole of Bodenham Glebe because he did not consider it right that a church minister should be a landed proprietor. At this time the church was short of money and the proceeds of the sale were invested by the church authorities so that a fixed annual income was secured for the living.'

'The vicar at Weobley was visiting his parishioners, and tied his trap at the carpenter and wheelwright's shop. When he came back he said, "You are doing the job our Lord started."

"Yes," came back the reply from the carpenter, "but He gave it up for a better job preaching!"'

'George Griffiths was a member of the choir at Hampton Bishop church for 40 years, starting in 1877. He was also clerk and sexton, and for many years a member of the Guild of Bellringers. He was secretary of three Coronation celebrations in the village. He was a basket maker by trade, although this was not well paid; he owned a withy bed in Hampton Bishop and made baskets for the locals and hampers for the council.

When told by the vicar that electric light was now in the church, he said he would go out with his old lamps which he kept clean and in working order. He died in 1951.'

'St Peter's church at Withington stands in the centre of the old part of the village, and can be seen for miles around, its elegant spire topped by a gilded weathercock pointing heavenward. Bellringers visit the church, travelling for many miles in order to ring the peal of six in the church belfry. Mrs Marion Lister and her husband, who lived in Church House, used to wind and look after the church clock. In common with many in those days, jobs like this one were done for love, not payment. Mr Lister would wind the clock every Saturday afternoon, that being his half-day off from work, but unfortunately the clock's works did not quite last for a full week, so Mrs Lister would climb up to the clock chamber and give the huge handle a few turns to keep it ticking over until the Saturday afternoon. Mr Lister would set the clock to Big Ben, and put bricks and half-bricks on the pendulum to make the correct weight in order to keep the clock to the right time. People would set their watches by St Peter's church clock. When the clocks had to be put forward and backward in the spring and autumn, husband and wife would go into the church and at exactly midnight make the necessary adjustments. Mrs Lister says how very eerie it was, when moonlight or torchlight cast flickering shadows on the walls, and especially once when a bier was standing in the aisle supporting a coffin, awaiting a funeral the next morning.'

OPEN AIR BAPTISM

'Up until the beginning of this century, open air baptisms used to take place at Little Dewchurch. There is a stream flowing through the churchyard and into the field opposite, and although a mere trickle at times now, was then quite a swift running stream which collected in a pond in the field opposite. It appears that the custom of total immersion took place there, according to the recollections of some of the older inhabitants.'

CHAPEL DAYS

'I spent my early Sundays, from the time I was dedicated until I was married in 1960, attending Oldway Baptist chapel at Fownhope.

I went to Sunday school and Sunday service at a very early age – morning service, Sunday school in the afternoon and service again in the evening. On occasions it was boring but according to my father it was "the done thing". Nothing else was done on a Sunday. I wasn't allowed to knit, sew, cut my nails, wash my hair etc. He had been brought up this way by his parents and I had to follow suit.

There were some happy times – the annual anniversary which was held in May, and the Sunday school anniversary which if I remember correctly was held in July when everyone that went to Sunday school had to take part reciting a verse, reading a piece from the bible or singing – I usually sang because I was the one with the "lovely little voice". There were great preparations for this until it was word perfect, but there was usually a little hiccup. Once I stood up to recite my well-rehearsed verse and couldn't remember a word. I looked up at the ceiling and said, "Sorry, I can't remember it", but with a little prompting it came back and I sailed through. We had the usual trip to the seaside when a bus was hired and we took our swim things and picnic lunch and then had afternoon tea at a cafe which had been pre-booked in advance – that was the highlight of the day; then it was back to the bus and home, singing songs and hymns on the way. As I grew into my teens I joined the choir, helped with the Sunday school and also played the organ when Mrs James the usual organist was unable to attend.'

'When I was a child in the 1940s we looked forward to May and the anniversary at Llanrosser chapel in Michaelchurch Escley. We lived in the next valley and walked there across the fields, a distance of about three miles.

There was an afternoon session when the Sunday school children sang and recited, not always in tune but they did their best. The highlight of the day came next, with tea out of a big teapot, fish paste sandwiches cut from very long loaves, and lots of cakes. The evening session followed, with the adults singing solos, duets and quartets, interspersed with recitations. This went on long past midnight. The long walk home followed; we were very tired, with aching legs, needing adult encouragement to put one foot in front of the other.'

'When we were kids we never missed the chapel anniversary or their harvest festival, and looked with envy at the person who could afford to buy the bunch of grapes – we usually bought apples with our tuppences, though we had an orchard full of fruit!'

A CENTURY OF COMMITMENT

'The story of the founding of the Eardisley Primitive Methodist chapel in Brook Street is quite well known owing to the family continuity.

By the early 1860s the Nonconformist movement was strongly established in this area, but it needed men and women of the strength of character of John Saveker and his wife Elizabeth to achieve a foothold in the village where his grandfather had survived an assassination attempt. John Saveker was born on 26th September 1837, being one of a family of nine children. Very early in his life he was apprenticed to a saddler and was sent to London as an assistant in an army saddlery establishment. He returned to the family home at Eardisley to set up business and there married Elizabeth Underwood of Dilwyn who he had met as a local evangelist. Before her marriage she had travelled the greater part of England and Wales on religious work, but was particularly well known in the Western counties and South Staffordshire. She had a great reputation as a preacher with a natural talent and ability that carried her congregations along with her, moving them to both tears and laughter. As her family increased she devoted more time to them and it was John who continued the preaching work throughout the locality, walking thousands of miles to preach at small chapels scattered along the Welsh Border.

Their main aim was to establish a Methodist community in Eardisley village and to this end they began holding services in their house, which became known as Chapel House, which name it still carries today. Together with a Mr and Mrs John Jay they collected money until there was enough to build a chapel. John Saveker gave the land out of his own garden and on 28th September 1866 he laid one of the corner stones of the new chapel.

John Saveker lived until 1933, retaining a lively interest in the chapel and Methodist affairs and a remarkably retentive memory for passages of Scripture. His remarks made to a newspaper reporter in 1932 when he was 94 make interesting reading still. When asked if life had changed for the better he said, "I must admit that there have been many changes which have made the world a better place, but there have also been changes which one is bound to deplore. The poverty of today cannot be compared with the poverty of days gone by. Even for the very poorest people nowadays, the standard of living is higher than it was for the poor of my boyhood days; education has brought enlightenment; modern transport has revolutionised the countryside and the outlook of the people has been changed. We have had some glorious times and it was often the case that the lead was taken by men who had to work hard for their living. There was no talk of seven hour days then – it was mostly work and very little leisure, but much of the leisure time was given up ungrudgingly in the service of Nonconformity." '

SUNDAY SCHOOL

'On Sunday we went to Sunday school, mostly Primitive Methodist as there was a "PM" chapel in every village; it was held in the afternoon so our parents could have a rest at home.

Each Sunday at Weobley our names were recorded and we were given a card an inch and a half square with a biblical text. For ten small cards we were given one large card, and ten of these were given up for a bible signed with your name and dated by the superintendent in charge.

Every year for a treat we were taken for a ride in a 20 seater open horse-drawn waggon for ten or twelve miles, then had a picnic tea and games.

Our school anniversary was a big occasion. Parents and friends were invited to chapel and we sang, recited poems and acted small biblical plays.'

'The annual Sunday school outing was an important occasion. I remember being woken at three in the morning so that I would not oversleep. We walked with the children into Newton St Margarets and caught a local bus to Pontrilas station about nine miles away. This kept breaking down, but we caught a train to Barry Island, having to change at Cardiff. Lunch and tea were provided at the Merrie Friars Cafe. Everyone was afraid to wander far because of getting lost.'

'Sunday school outings were the highlight of the year with as many as eight buses leaving Kington at eight in the morning. It seemed more like a town outing. One person on each bus was given paper and pen to make a list of everyone on the bus, also a packet of small bags to distribute to any suffering from travel sickness. Each child was given a small brown envelope containing half a crown to buy their tea.

One year the children were taken to Dudley Zoo and I well remember our Sunday school superintendent standing at the exit of the zoo at home time with his enormous list of everyone in our party, ticking off their names as they came out, making sure that no one had been left to the lions!'

GETTING ABOUT

In the early years of the century, if you wanted to go anywhere you walked or, if you were lucky, you went by horse power. The first buses were a real boon in bringing more freedom to the country dweller, and the first cars are remembered with real affection – they were so rare! Train services are also a part of our past, and before so many country lines were cut in the 1960s the trains and the men who worked on them were personal friends to many.

HORSE POWER

'In the old days transport was bad and roads were worse. People walked immense distances unless they were fortunate enough to possess either a draught animal, or a trap, or both. Often Mrs A possessed a donkey and Mrs B a trap or cart – they would combine the two and both families had an outing. There was much borrowing of animals and carts, and everybody appeared to be most accommodating in the matter of lending. The railway improved matters considerably, and there were plenty of shortcuts by footpaths across the fields.'

'At the turn of the century, visits to the Kemble Theatre at Hereford were by horse and trap, and the horses were left at a pub, The Mitre, opposite, where a man was employed to look after them. The trap had a red oil lamp at the back and two candle-lamps at the front.'

'One day in the 1930s at Leominster I watched the. haulier Mr Jack Morgan delivering goods off his horse-drawn delivery station waggon, when suddenly the very large horse bolted in the High Street. It ended up with the front part of its body in the window of Ross's shoe shop and its back legs down the grating of the same shop. The cart was very high sided and was on its side across the road. What a sorrowful sight it was. The vet came and put the horse out of its misery; it had broken two legs and had great gashes down its side. I shall never forget this sad scene as Mr Morgan stood over the horse. He was too upset to move as they had been true working companions for many years.'

THE FERRY

'Bridge Sollars bridge was built around 1890. Until then, Preston-on-Wye had both a ferry and a ford. The ford was used, river height permitting, by horse-drawn vehicles and riders to cross to Byford and the main road to Hereford. Though this ford is no longer used, when the river is low I have seen canoeists in the middle having to get out and push!

A mile away upstream, the ferry took people across, who could then walk to catch the train on the Brecon line at Kinnersley. The ferry fare was a penny and when the last ferryman died in about 1920 the service ended. The next occupant of the cottage was sometimes asked by a regular passenger to be taken across. He also had a boat and would row the man across, and was always offered his penny.'

THE MAN WITH THE RED FLAG

'For most people going to town from Fownhope was a great event. In about 1910 my mother would go to Hereford once a year to fit the children out for the year. It was as though Mother were going to the North Pole, all the preparations she made for our comfort while she was away, for it took the whole day to go to Hereford and back.

Travel was indeed slow. There was no need for 30 mph signs in those days; in fact, when Mr Townsend went on the road with his new-fangled contraption, the traction engine, Bill Lewis was employed to go in front with a red flag. Thirty miles an hour would have seemed like lightning speed to him!'

THE FIRST CARS

'My grandmother was born in 1900. When she was 16 her father wanted her to drive his delivery van which he had purchased when his horses were sent to the war. She applied for a licence but, due to her youth, the authorities sent a man out to give her a test. There was no other traffic. There were only two cars in Bishopswood, one owned by the doctor and one by my great grandfather.

My grandmother was ordered to drive down the road, and after she had gone a few yards the examiner said, "Right, you'll do." For many years she answered critics of her driving with, "I passed a test!" '

'I remember a very early car owned by my father. We had gone for a trip to the Black Mountains and the radiator boiled over. It was refilled by scooping up water from a stream in my father's "baccy" tin.'

'I cannot remember any cars in the district at all in the 1920s; even the vicar had no car and had to walk everywhere over a very large parish. When I was in my first job in the early 1930s I asked, "Who's James?" when I heard that name used. The gardener explained that James was the name of the master's treasured car, a Morris Cowley with a dicky seat.'

'In December 1920 a car brought my mother and new baby sister home from Ledbury to our farm at Woolhope. That was my first encounter with a car, and the noise it made together with the cries of the new baby made the familiar farmyard noises seem insignificant.

In the summer of 1926 the same car and driver brought my grandfather up the Cockshute, Woolhope to inspect our recently acquired mixed farm. The only way they could ascend the steepest part was by reversing with my grandfather walking and giving directions. That way the petrol flowed from the tank to feed the engine. It was some time after that we heard someone had driven to the Top Cockshute, which was much steeper.'

'When my father acquired his first little car, he went to the police station to ask about obtaining a licence – this was in the early 1920s. The police asked, "How did you get here?" "I drove the car," he said. They gave him his licence without further ado.

I remember the treat it was to be driven in my father's small car. My sister and I used to stand up with our heads out of the sunshine roof, waving to everyone we passed. They nearly always

Cars were still few and far between when Frank Watson's Leominster Motor Works started their enterprising 'for hire' service.

waved back. The AA men on their motorcycles (with sidecar) used to salute my father as he displayed his AA badge on the bonnet, but if there was a police trap ahead they would not salute, thus warning us, and my father would drive very carefully for a while. This did not happen very often – and I don't suppose we went much faster than 30 mph in those days.'

'Picnics in the 1920s were a great treat. My father inherited his father's car in 1926 and not many people had cars then. There were always two or three punctures on our trips, and Dad got out and rolled his sleeves up. The next motorist along, maybe five or ten minutes later, would stop and help, and we of course did the same for others.

Much later, when there was more traffic, bottlenecks would form at, say, a narrow bridge, and then the engine would boil and you had to get out of the queue to let it cool. This was always happening to other people too – it made journeys interesting!

There would be an AA man at bad crossings; there were no traffic lights then.

Winter journeys were *freezing*, especially if you sat at the back. The sidescreens were made of mica and not designed to keep the wind out. Plenty of rugs and scarves were needed, and hot water bottles too.'

CATCHING THE BUS

'If people were unable to obtain the materials for their trades locally at Bodenham they would go to Leominster or Hereford, either on foot or bicycle, or later on by carrier's cart. This method of transport was at first somewhat erratic, as there was no fixed time for the trips, which depended on the whim of the carrier. In 1928 Mr Alf Burgoyne started taking people to Hereford in his Model T Ford, the first motorised public transport vehicle, and it had a canvas top and seats down each side. Two years later the Nell Gwynne bus service started, followed by the Midland Red.'

'I remember the first bus that came through Hampton Bishop. There were no cushions on the seats – just wooden slats. I don't think the bus went more than 15 miles per hour at top speed. How excited we were to be able to travel to Fownhope for one penny. It was as though we were visiting a foreign country. Prior to the arrival of the bus, one used the carrier's cart, a waggon-like contraption with benches on either side.'

'A bus travelled every Friday from Pudleston to Leominster. This was quite a social event; it was the only day most of the people were able to leave the parish.

The ladies made sure they were waiting at the gate in plenty of time, with their arm baskets filled with eggs, dressed fowls and bunches of herbs from the garden to sell at the Friday market.'

'Before the advent of anything like a regular bus service from Peterchurch to Hereford, Reg Hallard decided money could be made transporting people as well as goods and livestock. He was injured at the end of the First World War, came back to Peterchurch and bought a large van (probably a Model T Ford) which he converted to carry people and in 1920 charged three shillings and sixpence return to Hereford every Wednesday, a huge sum in those days.

The first proper bus started in the late 1920s and ran from Bob's Shop (the crossroads at the top of Slough Bank) every Thursday via Turnastone, Vowchurch, Peterchurch and Dorstone to Hay, starting at 8 am and arriving at 9.30 am. Schoolchildren who normally had to walk to school used to cadge lifts on it. On Wednesdays the bus went to Hereford (market day), Tuesdays to Abergavenny. It was an Albion bus painted green and yellow, driven by George Holt with Ernie Jenkins as the conductor.

About 1935 another private bus started running, owned and driven by Wilfred Pritchard. This ran from Longtown to Hay, Hereford and Abergavenny on market days, but using different routes. Yet another service started in the 1930s belonging to Bill Morgan, who owned garages in Hereford and Pontrilas. His bus used to pick up passengers on all the back roads, eg he came down from Urishay, left at Fairfield, and anyone from Peterchurch who wished to travel with him had to walk to Hinton Forge. The bus then went via Snodhill, Dorstone village and so to Hay. Bill Morgan also used to hire charabancs for trips to the seaside and to agricultural shows, etc.

At the end of the 1930s the Red & White Bus Company started a regular daily service along the main road between Hereford and Hay, which not only caused the downfall of the railway but virtually put an end to the private carriers.'

OUR TRAIN SERVICE

'In the first part of the century, ordinary people did not have the means to own cars, or even horse-drawn carriages, but Withington had a railway service. The trains pulled in at Whitestone, and took the villagers into Hereford Town for ninepence return, half price for children. It was a very busy little station, the housewives travelling into town for their shopping, the farmers in to market, the children in to school. When the reorganisation of the railways occurred in the 1960s, the station of Withington was closed, though the station house still stands.'

'One of my earliest memories is of moving into Station Cottage at Ashperton, on the Ledbury-Hereford line, at the beginning of the First World War. My father was head of the "gang" who kept the railway in good repair, so we really were "Railway Children".

The small station at Ashperton was very busy, because all goods were sent by train in those days (no lorries). This included farm livestock; the stockmen walked the huge bulls down to the station, but our favourites were Rimell's racehorses which had been put out to grass on one of the farms and were being returned and there was always one who refused to go in the van and had to be blindfolded and pushed and shoved.'

'On 17th July 1933 a new halt was opened by the Great Western Railway at Backney to pick up passengers, which previously had only been a goods station. There were six trains a day; the fare to Ross was fourpence single third class, and to Hereford one shilling and threepence. Before the halt, when we visited my grandparents at Sellack Marsh post office, my grandfather would meet us at Ross station with his pony and trap. About 1960 the Hereford to Gloucester line was closed.'

'The GWR stopped at Kingsland and Pembridge. To catch the train from Shobdon, the postmistress rang the stationmaster at Pembridge, and he held the train up until you arrived by bicycle. The post office had the first telephone in the village.'

'The railway was the lifeline for travel; the country children used to come to school by train, and the local trains (known as "stopping trains") were always full on market days. Travel was easy, and there were always porters, able to give information and to put you, plus luggage, into the right train. When a train pulled up at a station there was a porter to help you alight, collect any extra luggage that might be in the luggage van, and put the whole lot into the next train. There was also a wonderful service called "luggage in advance" – a trunk would be collected, usually some days before one was to travel, and delivered at its destination, be it school, hotel or private house. As children, my sister and I went to stay with relatives in Cheshire. We were put on the train in charge of the guard, and he would keep an eye on us until we were met at the other end.'

'The railway came to Peterchurch in 1878, and had a somewhat mixed success, but from the turn of the century until 1939 there were three trains daily plus the early Dorstone train. In 1939 when the ever-increasing number of buses poached passengers, the service was reduced to a morning and afternoon train between Hay and Pontrilas with a midday trip between Pontrilas and Dorstone. It was a leisurely affair with the train often running late after having to shunt back and forth at various stations to collect and deliver freight wagons, and for the driver to stop and shoot rabbits on the edge of the track.

During a particularly hard winter the road from Dorstone to Hay was blocked with snow. Tom Palmer living at The Bage was running desperately short of supplies, so he struggled down to the railway line which had been kept open and hailed the train which stopped to take him into Hay. Tom gave the driver some silver to get a drink while he went shopping for the provisions. He had been quite a long time, and on the way back to the station (which was where F J Williams & Sons, Builders Merchants is now) he heard the train tooting. Apparently the train from Brecon was due, and Tom's train had to move. He clambered aboard with his goods, and they dropped him off at the same spot on the return journey.

Jack Reece worked on the railway as a platelayer and general maintenance engineer from the end of the Second World War to the closing of the line altogether in 1951. When he was a child, back in 1914, the return fare to Hay from Peterchurch was one shilling and sixpence. GWR used to run excursions from Dorstone and Peterchurch to the seaside, but Jack had never been. He saved up the money he earned from ferreting, told his father he was going for a bike ride, then rode to the station in Peterchurch where he hid the cycle and caught the train to Barry Island. Total cost of the trip was four shillings and sixpence, but he considered it well worth it!

Jack remembered one day at Wilmaston when two farmhands were taking a large chicken-house across the line; it was on wheels and pulled by a horse. They went through the first gate, stopped on the line to close it and open the second gate, when they heard a train coming. They shouted at it to stop but the driver did not hear them until the last minute when it was too late. Crash – into the chicken-house it went, unfortunately killing the horse and spreading bits of the building together with chickens and feathers all over the place.

One day whilst working on the line they had reports of flooding at Abbeydore so Jack and his mates climbed aboard the gangers' trolley which was known as a "whickham", comprising a four-wheeled contraption powered by an eight hp JAP engine, the men sitting at 90° to the track. They arrived at the flooded area and started to clear the obstruction in the river causing the flooding, when they heard a train coming. Through the water it ploughed, seeming to lurch dangerously halfway through, but it continued on its way. When eventually the water was drained away, the men saw that all the ballast had been washed away from under the sleepers and the rails had been bent downwards permanently, so they had to set about replacing the rails and re-ballasting.

One of the best-known characters to travel on the railway was a Mrs Mainwaring who lived at Brynmawr on the Heads of the Valleys road. She used to travel on the main line up to Pontrilas, then change onto the Golden Valley line and go to Hay. She then started to purchase all the eggs and poultry at Hay and every station on the way back including Peterchurch. Folk who wished to sell their surplus eggs etc would take them down to the station and wait for Mrs Mainwaring to buy them. This happened regularly every week; she returned home via Pontrilas to sell the produce to the mining communities of Brynmawr, Ebbw Vale and Tredegar – no doubt at a handsome profit.

The passenger service stopped in the early war years, on 15th December 1941, and the line continued carrying just freight, also war materials to and from the Ministry of Supply depot at Elm Park. The branch line of the Golden Valley became part of British Railways in 1948, and then in 1950 the Dorstone-Hay line was closed as it was too expensive to maintain. The last passenger train to run in the Golden Valley was the annual outing for 300 schoolchildren from Dorstone and other villages to Porthcawl on 23rd August 1951. On 2nd February 1953 the line north of Abbeydore to Dorstone was closed, and the remainder of the line closed on 3rd June 1957. All that remains is the section to Elm Bridge which serves the Ministry of Defence depot. There are still a few crossing-keepers' cottages remaining and a couple of stations – and a lot of memories.'

'It was a sad day for Pembridge when the trains ceased to run. Pembridge and the surrounding areas were well served by the railway. There were four passenger and three goods trains every day from Kington to Leominster (Pembridge is about halfway). Until the advent of war in 1939, farmers used the railway for moving their stock – pedigree bulls to the Hereford Bull Sales, and sheep and cattle to markets at Leominster, Kington and Craven Arms. Local hop growers used the railway too, and trucks loaded with sugar beet for the Kidderminster factory were a common sight.

The Leominster to Kington railway was officially opened on Monday 27th July 1857; the last passenger train ran on 5th February 1955, and the last goods train on 24th September 1964. The New Radnor and Forge Crossings closed in 1952. The Beeching Report was finally published in 1965, so he was not responsible for the closures here. The reason given was lack of support and revenue. The last stationmaster at Pembridge was John Vaughan, whose brother still lives in the old station house today.

The Kington-Eardisley Railway was officially opened in 1874; the line ran via Titley, Lyonshall and Almeley. The rails were taken up in 1916 to go to France during that war – they never arrived, because the ship was sunk in the Channel by a U-boat. The rails were replaced in 1922. The branch was taken over by the Great Western Railway in 1923, and finally closed on 1st July 1940. Prior to 1923, GWR supplied and ran locomotives and rolling stock to both these local companies.

The last passenger train, in 1955, left Leominster at 8.25 pm, carrying over 50 passengers who were joined by others at Kingsland, Pembridge, Marston Halt and Titley, and there were about 70 people aboard when they arrived at Kington. Many stayed in the coach, and others joined them for the return trip, leaving Kington at 9.25 pm. Among the passengers was Mr Montague Young of Leominster who in a sense, represented the early days of the railways. His "topper" was a hat worn by a railway policeman of long ago. The following is an extract from a letter written by a passenger who took the round trip that night:

"Saturday evening was, mildly, a riot, though compared with some recent closures elsewhere, it was quiet . . . nothing much happened at Pembridge. More people joined the train here (Pembridge) on the outward trip and left on the return than at any other station on the line except Kington. We arrived and departed amidst a perfect barrage of exploding detonators. On the final trip we arrived amidst an even longer barrage plus an accompanying blast on the engine's whistle. Ten people left the train, the guard solemnly shook hands with the porter and flashed his green lamp. With a two-minute blast on the whistle and amidst cheering and more exploding detonators we puffed sadly on to Leominster." '

EARTHQUAKE, FIRE
AND FLOOD

Natural disasters are no stranger to Herefordshire, and many villages came to regard flooding in particular as part of the regular cycle of events. Fire, of course, was greatly to be feared in the days of thatch and wooden buildings, when fire fighting was often an amateur affair.

EARTH TREMORS

'There have been several earth tremors at Fownhope and even recently there were people who could still remember the great Herefordshire earthquake of 17th December 1896, when much damage was done in the village. The walls of some houses were cracked, slates shaken off the roofs and many chimneys fell. It is thought that it was caused by a slip along a fault running parallel to the Woolhope Dome.

The greatest calamity of this century was the destruction by fire of the 15th century tithe barn in 1937. This barn stood in the vicarage grounds and contained three original crutch trusses with later ties. In 1936 the Council for the Preservation of Rural England came to inspect the building to possibly take it over as an ancient monument. However, shortly afterwards it was destroyed by fire and the remains were demolished in 1938.'

FIRE!

'The fire at Ashley Moor Hall in the late 1920s made headline news in the daily papers and also on the wireless.

On the day of the fire my father had gone to Leominster in the horse and trap leaving us playing in our garden at Ashley Moor Farm. Suddenly someone spotted smoke coming through the slates of the "Big House" across the road. Mum was told and she ran over to tell Mr Johnson, the estate agent. He had a long white beard and was a very precise man so had to come back with Mum to confirm what we had seen. However, he soon realised that we were not imagining things and rushed back.

Sometime later a lorry came up the bank towing the Leominster fire-fighting appliance. This was quickly followed by Dad galloping home in record time thinking that our house was on fire.

The water in the brook, meanwhile, had been dammed but the fire engine was very ancient and was powered by a team of strong men standing either side of a contraption mounted on four wheels, lifting and lowering a pump-like machine. I would imagine similar machines were used in the Great Fire of London!

Unfortunately the house was completely gutted but the elderly lady owner, Mrs O'Connor, was safely evacuated from the house to a cottage on the estate.

Afterwards refreshments in the form of home-made cider were taken by the firemen and I can remember sitting with them in our cellar and trying on their helmets.

All the debris from the fire was hauled by horse and cart to fill a hole in our rickyard. We spent hours digging in the ashes looking for treasure!

When the Hall was restored the following year the top floor was removed and it is now a lovely two storeyed mansion.'

'My parents, with my sister and I, moved to Leominster in 1934 to start their own bakery business. In 1939 the bakery caught fire and because of walls of sandbags either side of the entrance to the old fire station in Broad Street, by the time the fire engine arrived it was too late to save the building.

My sister and I were being bathed in front of the fire in the adjoining house and were scooped up in large towels and taken to a neighbour's house where we stayed the night. I can clearly remember going to see the bakehouse next morning. There were tumps of flour eight ft high drenched in water, one big gluey brown and black mess everywhere. My parents stood at the side of it all in tears. However, the baker on the opposite side of the street very generously offered my father the use of his bakery in the evenings and early night, while he used it the rest of the time for his own business. Our new bakery was rebuilt in two months.'

'In the autumn of 1943 the appearance of Weobley was completely changed when a fire destroyed a block of black and white buildings. They were in the centre of the village, where the rose garden is now.

I lived in the corner house opposite. Hop picking had finished and Mother had been to town that day to buy material to make our winter clothes. We carefully drew the blackout curtains and went to bed for we were very tired. We were woken in the early hours by Mr Trumper who lived down the road. He had gone to let his dog out and seen the fire. We hastily gathered up our clothes and what Mother had just bought and went to Mr Fred Lewis's house.

Mrs Johnson who lived next door, and was an invalid, was carried on her chaise longue to The Throne (a 16th century house where Charles I stayed on 5th September 1645 after the battle of Naseby). She was holding her tin box with her valuables in. Mrs Purcell's furniture had been put outside Miss Hope's and I remember sitting on one of her chairs watching all the excitement.

When we had gone to bed it had been quite windy, but fortunately the wind had dropped. If it had not, more of Weobley would have been destroyed. It was also fortunate that there were no enemy bombers in the vicinity – we would have been a perfect target.'

FLOOD

'Preston-on-Wye church, the churchyard and Preston Court, the adjacent farm, are raised up areas with the road and surrounding ground being much lower and below the level of the river in flood, which causes the brook there to bank up and cut them off. This happens regularly, but about once in a hundred years there is a very high flood. My father told me that during one such flood at the end of the last century, the church and house were both flooded, as were all the farm buildings which were at a lower level. The cowman took the bull into the church, where he stood in the pulpit to keep his feet dry and held onto the bull's halter.

The next such high flood was in the 1960s, when the house was flooded to a depth of 18 inches but the church escaped. Then a hundred day-old chicks which had just arrived had to be kept in a bedroom for a day until the waters went down.'

'One day in the spring of 1929 Granny had gone to Hereford early to get something for baby Anne. Grandpop had driven her in from Hampton Bishop, but when they returned and got to The Bunch of Carrots the water was right across the road and they could go no further. Grandpop drove up to Court Farm intending to walk across the fields to get home. Meanwhile, whilst Granny was waiting she heard "plonk, plonk, plonk". Harold Wilks had driven in the horse and cart to find her as they knew at home that she was expected back at 2 pm to feed Anne. A kitchen chair had been set up on the cart for Granny to sit on. The flood was right up over the lawn at home, and all the mats had been cleared from the church as the water was almost in there. That was the year the river reached 18 ft six inches.

Floods were regular every year – the worst were after the war

Flooding was a regular hazard for many Herefordshire villages. During the 1960 floods at Hampton Bishop residents had to be rescued by helicopter when the stank (medieval bank) broke.

when the stank was breached in several places and we sat in the bedrooms watching gates and barrels float by.'

'Cradley Brook is really quite a small brook which rises in the Malvern Hills, runs into the Teme at Bransford, and is joined by several small tributaries, notably a most innocuous little trickle that runs past the post office, under the main road and down to Pound Bridge.

One year the brook came up 30 ft in half an hour, flooding one of the cottages at Pound Bridge. A young mother living there managed to get her baby upstairs and she was helped by willing passers by who managed to save most of her possessions. The water came up over the parapet of the bridge at Stiffords Bridge and poured into the cellars of The Red Lion. The little stream by the post office also flooded, and as on many another occasion, the poor shopkeeper had to put on his wellingtons and clear the grating to let the water back under the road. The streams still rise very quickly but these days the drainage is better so the results are not so drastic.

One hard winter an elderly lady was snowed-in in a near-derelict cottage over several fields with no track down to it. The village nurse rang up the farmer to see if he would go on his tractor. He had just emptied all the diesel out of his tractors, but nothing daunted he filled one up again, got dry firewood, hot soup and food to eat, candles and a spade. When they arrived they found the door of the cottage half open as she couldn't close it, a few wet sticks smouldering on the fire and no food in the house. So that mission really was a mercy mission, and she was kept warm and dry till the snow melted. One of our members who went with the farmer has the clearest memory of the cold and the silence, lit by a clear moon. They saw any number of animals hunting and were fascinated to see all the cows in a circle, huddled together but all facing outwards.'

'Everyone at Colwall remembers the village being cut off during the winter snows of 1947. Bread came in by train and milk in churns to the local pub. Afterwards there were floods. A coach party returning from a pantomime visit in Birmingham found the water up to bedroom windows in Powick. Water came into the coach and hedgerows were invisible. They later learned that the roadside verges had been washed away and they could all have ended up in the river.'

'In August 1957 the most awful tragedy happened at Clifford. A terrible thunderstorm broke out over Little Mountain when 4.12 inches of rain fell, the highest ever recorded in the Wye Valley. The cloudburst resulted in the cowshed door being burst off at Sidcombe Baige, the water was over the top of folks' wellingtons, and up to the bellies of the cattle. Worse was to come, when later that night Denzil Richards was returning from a motorbike scramble. He tried to cross the swollen brook at Clock Mill on his motorbike and was swept off his machine and drowned.'

'During the night of 12th May 1959 a violent thunderstorm caused flooding in Eardisley and other villages. There had been flooding before but this was the worst in living memory. Water came down the Woodseaves Road, the Almeley Road and the Kington Road, lifting two parked cars and carrying them 300 yards. Water swept three ft high into the grocery shop owned by Mr Godfrey Davies, causing hundreds of pounds worth of damage, and into most houses in the main village street. The bridge over the brook on the Almeley Road collapsed and an MEB van had a narrow escape when their van fell into the crater, which was by that time swirling eight ft deep. Fortunately the next day was bright and sunny so people were able to put furniture and carpets out to dry and set about the task of clearing the mud and slime from floors, furniture and walls. During the morning roads were impassable and school children were unable to get to Kington. Traffic on the Hereford Road was also restricted. The post office was flooded and a temporary sorting office was set up in the Curzon Herrick Hall.

A Flood Distress Fund was formed to compensate people for damage and it was agreed that first consideration be given to old age pensioners. After this considerable work was done to clear ditches and brooks and never since then has there been a flood of that proportion.'

CHARACTERS, TALES AND SUPERSTITIONS

Country life would not be complete without its odd characters and sayings, its ghost stories and its superstitions.

BOB COLE, THE RUNNER

'When I turned over my English exam paper in 1941 one of the titles I had to choose from was "A Local Character" and I had no hesitation in choosing that one. I knew immediately who I would write about . . . Bob Cole. At that time he was a most familiar figure in the Vowchurch area of Herefordshire, either riding his bicycle or carrying it. If there was the slightest bit of mud on the road or any hedge trimmings he would hoist it up on his shoulder and carry it. Or he was on foot, sprinting along with his most unusual manner, a lean upright figure with those bright blue staring eyes, his black bowler hat and long hair down to his shoulders. I don't think he would have looked out of place these days but then when everybody had their "short back and sides" it was most outstanding. One story is that he thought it "enhanced his appearance". The other is that he vowed that if he lost a certain race he would let his hair grow. He must have lost the race.

Robert Edward Cole was a professional long distance runner who became a legend in his own lifetime. His fame had spread far beyond the Herefordshire borders, but to us children he was a somewhat terrifying figure who would stop and stare at us, fixing us with those glaring blue eyes and grumble about something we were doing, or not doing. One day my friend and I were waiting for the bus to school at Vowchurch Turn when he came along on his bicycle. He rode across to us and stopped, fixed us with one of his glares for a few minutes, then in his deep gruff voice said, "Local schools not good enough for you, got to go to the High School you have." We were more wary of him after that, we always went the other way if we saw him in the street in Hereford, and we were careful about going to Woolworths where he had the name of worrying the girls on the counters. It was not so easy to dodge him on the country roads. We would often see him standing at the bottom of his lane when he was getting his buckets of water from the well. Especially if it was raining, he would be standing there with the rain dripping off his bowler hat, a bucket of water each side of him and grumbling about the weather.

Bob was born at a cottage belonging to Stowe Farm at Whitney. The family were very poor and Mrs Jones from Stowe Farm was visiting his mother one day and she found the little boy was very ill, and starving. She befriended them, sending him milk and soup every day until he was stronger. When he was old enough to work he became her houseboy at the farm. He later moved to White House at The Bage where he was a farm worker for Mr J O Davies. It was while he was at The Bage that his running career really started. My husband often spoke about his running track which was on "Bricklays", a field that now belongs to my family, where he practised every day. We are not sure if it was the running that took him to Scotland or his army service in the First World War. He served with the Royal Scots Guards during the last three years of the war. He spent some time at Edinburgh University where he studied German. It was there that he won the Powderhall New Year Marathon on 3rd January 1922. He had two gold medals for this, the scratch medal and the handicap medal. Bob was the World Professional Ten Mile Champion 1922 to 1929. He was also the undefeated British Marathon Champion title holder, so despite his unusual behaviour in those later years he had had a very brilliant running career.

He was a familiar sight at the sports at Dorstone Flower Show, dressed all in black with his white arms and legs which seemed to move like clockwork. His hair would be tucked up under his black skullcap and a Union Jack was emblazoned on the front of his running vest. He usually wore his gold medals on a black shoelace round his neck. He really looked quite normal when he was running. We think his last sports was at Knighton in 1951 when he was 60 years old. There was a young runner called Lionel Preece who had just returned from the forces in the Second World War. He had raced against MacDonald Bailey, the Commonwealth record holder and come a very close second. Preece was the favourite to win the Powderhall in Scotland that year but he had missed the train so he went to Knighton. He entered the 400 yards and was started from scratch. Colin Davies who had won the previous year was given 40 yards. Bob was there, and when the race was about to start he walked up the track and as he passed each of the competitors he stopped and told them that when Preece came up they were to move out of the way and let him pass. We are not sure if Bob actually ran himself that day. He certainly ran in the mile race at Bank Farm, Michaelchurch Escley at the "Welcome Home" sports in 1946. Even though it was only a little local village sports to raise money which would be presented to those young men from the parish who were returning from the forces and for the parents of those who did not return, he sent in an official entry form to the secretary signed R E Cole, "old veteran runner". I was very impressed, that day, with the local boys who had been winning the local sports that year. I'm sure they let him win, but the look on his face when he realised that he could still win made it all worthwhile. He ran straight from the finishing tape to the secretary's tent, without even stopping for a breather, for his prize. I think that was the only time I remember seeing him smile. He must have been in his late fifties by then and I'm sure any of those boys could easily have beaten him if they had tried, or should I have said dared.

Bob was not very impressed with the motor car. There is a story that one of the first cars to come to the Hay area belonged to the Webb family. Mr Jack Webb was driving down by The Moor when he saw Bob sprinting along the road. Thinking he was doing him a favour he stopped and offered Bob a lift. The answer came back very promptly, "No thank you. I'm in a hurry."

Bob eventually inherited his grandfather's smallholding at St Margaret's. The smallholding is now called The Corner but in Bob's notebook it is spelt "Cornell".

All the years he lived at St Margaret's he had a training track in the field near his cottage where he still practised every day. Neighbours still recall hearing him shouting and cheering as he ran, reliving his past moments of glory.

He was careful about security and every night he kept a loaded gun at the side of his bed. On the table the other side he had his bible. After he had finished his work and carried his buckets of water from the well about a mile away he would make sure that his garden gate was padlocked. This is what drew the attention of his neighbour, Mrs Pritchard and her son Graham to the fact that there must be something wrong, when they thought he must have gone to bed without locking his gate. They went to look and found him unconscious on his living room floor. They called the doctor and he was taken to hospital. He had lived alone so long that nobody knew who was his next of kin and my family were the only ones in the area with the same surname. We discovered that his grandfather was actually a brother to my great grandfather. The hospital sent for my brother. He and his wife went to visit but Bob was still unconscious, but he did seem to recognise them and smiled. They were surprised to see that the nurses had cut his hair. He died on 5th September 1960.

When my sister and I heard about the funeral there was only our father who was able to go from the family and thinking that he would probably be the only mourner we decided to go with him. Not expecting to see many people there we were a bit late getting to St Margaret's church, to find the farmyard adjoining the churchyard absolutely full of cars. The churchyard was full of men. When they saw us they divided out and ushered us through into the church which appeared to be full of men; thinking back now there were probably some ladies there but the general impression was of a church full of men. We were guided up into the front pew where our father was sitting alone, that was the only empty pew in the church. The coffin had been in church overnight. The main thing that I remember about the service was the singing. It was like listening to a male voice choir, and I remember thinking how strange it was that after all those years trying to avoid him, my sister and I ended up as chief mourners at his funeral.'

THINGS THEY SAID

'Nicknames were common at Huntington. A pleasant smiling old gentleman was known as "Pudding Puss". A very small man – a postman – was known as "Davey Dib Dab". Some were perhaps a little unkind. One very large gentleman met up with a very small man in a blacksmith's shop – "Get out of my way, you great big awkward beggar," said the small man. The other, after a moment's thought, looked down and grunted, "The little niscol sucked the back tit." As if to affirm this statement he would repeat, "sucked the back tit".

The same gentleman had a fierce row with a neighbour about a right of way. With him was a strong young workman, to whom he said, "Hit him, Twm, I'll pay." The outcome of this was that the man's wife was slightly hurt trying to defend her husband, and I think they really had to pay.

Another very good friend, proud of his bull always said to visitors when leaving, "Well thee'st better see the bull afore thee'st go." My husband, knowing this, told the vicar's wife on her way to visit. To her amusement it happened as he said – but it *was* a very fine animal.

One remark by a nice old lady amused the locals. Her husband bought a bike. "He got on his bike, and hadn't gone far when he had a function," (her name for a puncture).

Two very religious elderly farmers reached home and were told by the wife of one of them that a cow was stuck in a bog. One said, "Shall we say a little prayer?" "Never mind about Him," said the other, "let's go to the old cow".'

'My brother-in-law was in Hereford market sometime before the last war when he saw an old friend, Charlie Hiles with a new stock lorry. "Hello Charlie," he said, "what a lovely new lorry you have, but I thought your name was Hiles". "Yes," replied Charlie, "it is, but everyone calls me Iles so I thought I would have Iles put on the lorry."

During the 1920s apples were loaded at various railway stations in the county and sent to the Herefordshire cider makers. One day an old friend of mine met Mr Murrell of Almeley who had a coal business and ran a little old Ford lorry capable of carrying about 15 cwt. His lorry was fully laden with about a dozen bags of cider apples. Thinking Mr Murrell was taking the load to either Kinnersley or Almeley railway stations, my friend asked where he was taking them. The reply was:- "Straight through, yes straight through to Bulmers."

My parents many years ago used to keep the Sun Inn, Winforton. There was with The Sun, a few acres and various buildings running alongside the main road and close to Winforton village hall. In the buildings battery hens were kept. One evening during the winter months a Miss Leek from Eardisley came into the bar saying she had cycled over to attend the whist drive in the hall, but could anyone tell her how to get in, as she had been to the door, the lights were on and she could hear them talking inside, but the door was locked and no one came when she knocked. My father went outside with her and it transpired that Miss Leek had been trying to get into the shed containing the cackling hens.'

'Lizzie had been in service with a doctor in her younger days, but whether it was this or the book of potions she inherited from her father, which earned her high regard as a herbalist and folk doctor around Dorstone, one wonders. Children collected herbs for her, but some were afraid of her. For toothache she would rub some ointment on your cheek and "say some words". It left a dirty mark, but the ache would go. Warts she could charm away on man or beast, even without seeing them!

Another old lady who lived a mile out of the village was believed to be a witch and was well versed in magic charms. She had been born with only three fingers on each hand, had a sharp tongue and a head full of folklore. "I knowed you were comin'," she said to the rector's sister who had come to visit her, "because the cock crowed after dinner, which do always mean a visitor comin'." "How did you know it was me?" asked Miss Powell. "Nobody else ever comes," said Liza.

Tom Bowen was a sexton who took his bellringing very seriously, never missing a service on Sundays. When anyone died, he would toll the bell for them, and "Pull-down Bow-en" the children would chant to his four slow strokes. Neighbours came out to ask who had gone, and Sarah Davies would set off to see to the laying out. On arrival she would give the deceased's ear a vigorous tweaking and pronounce him dead. Then, firmly but kindly, would organise the distraught relatives. "Come on, get hold of him. You know what's to be done."'

'Percy the Poacher was a local character at Hampton Bishop. My mother always took his part because he had a very sad beginning to his life and she would often cook him a breakfast and his Christmas dinner, but it didn't stop him pinching her eggs. He would wait for cider apples to be picked before pinching a couple of bags. He once told a reporter that his cider was made from selected fruit; yes, we said, from every orchard in the village!'

THE HOLY THORN

'It is uncertain if this flowering thorn still exists, but it used to grow on the boundaries of the parishes of Orcop and Llanwarne, beside what was once an old inn called The Seven Stars. A ceremony was held there annually on the night of Christmas Eve.

During the winter of 1950 much publicity was given to this occasion in both local and national press. Crowds of people, many from far afield, came to see the Holy Thorn bloom. The road from Orcop to Pontrilas right through to the Hereford-Monmouth road was packed with buses and cars, making it difficult for people to walk from the main road. Some bus drivers left both doors of their vehicles open to enable people to walk through and continue their journey. Tradesmen set up stalls selling cups of tea, sandwiches and even fish and chips.

The meadow in which the Thorn grew was well lit by lanterns, torches, camera flashes and one or two small searchlights, which were directed onto the Thorn. The BBC sent a television recording unit to make a film of the event; however, the owner of the land objected to this, not wanting to commercialise the Thorn.

The last known visit to the Holy Thorn was on Christmas Eve 1955. It was very bleak with thick snow on the ground and a freezing wind. The party of people, which included some Llanwarne residents, were rewarded for their efforts by the sight of some buds bursting into bloom, although it must be said that they were not of the quality reported from previous years.'

WHO KILLED THE BEARS?

'If you live in the Forest of Dean this heading is one you should never use anywhere near Cinderford. Many years ago – before radio and TV, when people amused themselves in their own villages, once in a while travelling people came through to entertain the folks in the village. Mummers came at Christmas time – even since I was married (in 1931) we had a party of young people to our house, uninvited, to perform St George and the Dragon. It was very entertaining, their Forest speech somehow adding to the charm of it all.

But I digress. A party of four men came to Cinderford with two bears to perform for the Cinderfordians. If you know that area you will remember that the main street runs down a long incline towards Steam Mills where, opposite the school, is a piece of forestry woodland, where the bears and their owners stayed for shelter for the night. Some mischief-maker started a rumour that one of the bears had injured a child – that was just what the local firebrands needed: they collected a crowd and hurried down to the wood where the bears and their owners were sleeping, and killed the bears. The rumour was false, of course, and the bears had been killed for nothing. Cinderford will never live it down!

Another ridiculous saying in the Forest, in the Ruardean area, has been repeated over the years. Apparently a smallholder who kept pigs became very fond of one particular pig, and when the Ruardean Brass Band put on a show he lifted up his pig and put it on the wall to watch the band go by!

Now that is a very dangerous thing to say in any inn – "Who put the pig on the wall, to watch the band go by?" So be careful!'

DUCKING AND PLUCKING

'Legends are always a cause for reticence but some people believe that a lady who lived in a low-lying cottage near the bridge in Eardisland used to open her doors to allow the floodwaters to rush through because she believed that this kept the Devil on the move. It was also believed by some that this constituted her annual spring-clean!

Other rumours tell of earlier times when suspected witches were ducked in the river Arrow to see whether they floated (guilty) or drowned: some wives who nagged their husbands were also treated to the punishment of the ducking stool, such as may be seen in the Priory church at Leominster. This ducking stool records the last known occasion upon which a woman named Jenny was humiliated by this method.

Stranger yet is the statement that a cottage in Broome Lane, known as Penny Pluck, received its name because geese, who wore leather shoes to protect their feet, were driven for many miles to the markets at Leominster or Kington and were allowed to graze (or "pluck the grass") in the fields adjoining the cottage for the cost of one penny.'

GHOSTS AND SUPERSTITIONS

'It was considered bad luck at Kingsland to take snowdrops into the house. My mother once took a bunch of snowdrops to a neighbour to enquire after an ailing baby. The baby died.'

'My mother was born in Colwall. She had a saying which could be exasperating to us as children when we asked after the whereabouts of any particular person – "Oh, they've gone to Bosbury to see the tide come up!" During a thunderstorm, which usually started over the Herefordshire Beacon end of the Malvern Hills, she said, "It will go to Cowleigh and come back foully." True, we generally had thunderstorms in twos!

She used to tell us tales of the ghost said to haunt Barton Holloway at midnight. Apparently, a young woman thwarted in love had been locked in her room and had eventually died. When my mother was a young girl at school, the rector told the children that as a boy he had witnessed the exorcising of this ghost by the then rector – this had been done at midnight with bell, book and candle, the rector walking from Barton Holloway to the church.

51

One day my grandfather was visiting his mother who lived at Chances Pitch and was returning home about midnight, when near Barton Holloway he saw an apparition approaching him. Being a tall, fearless man he went ahead and grabbed the "ghost". It was a local woman wrapped in a sheet. She begged Grandfather not to tell anyone and the ghost was never seen again.'

'A lady living in a stone cottage in Withington tells of an elderly gentleman who enters her lounge from time to time, coming in through the door and crossing the room to leave by walking through the wall! He has been seen by the lady herself and by her grown up daughter. On enquiring of native residents in the village, she was told that there had been a door in that wall, leading to other rooms, which had burned down in a fire, taking the old man's life as he ran to and fro with buckets of water from the kitchen pump trying to extinguish the flames.'

'An elderly lady who lived in the King's Caple area was working in her garden at dusk, her dog beside her. Suddenly the dog began to growl and bristle. The lady looked where the dog was "pointing", and saw a woman in an old fashioned lilac coloured dress with a bonnet, who appeared to be floating several inches above the ground and was moving silently towards the corner of the lady's bungalow. The apparition moved round the corner, but when the lady rushed over to see where she had gone, the Lilac Lady had completely vanished.

A farmer saw a woman in a white dress, carrying a basket. She too faded from view. Later that day he took some friends to see the place where his ghost had vanished – and there she was again, still carrying her basket! All the men saw her. When the farmer went towards her, she disappeared at exactly the same place as before.'

'At Little Hereford, horses were never worked on Good Friday, which was reserved for gardening, planting parsley and the cutting of lambs' tails. It is said that cattle will go down on their knees at midnight on Twelfth Night, and it is considered bad luck if a woman is the first to come to your door on New Year's Day.

Our home was reckoned to be haunted, and although nothing was ever seen there would be the sound of heavy boots on the flagged floor in the back hall, and anyone sleeping in one of the front bedrooms would be woken up in the early hours by the sound of someone walking in the room. August seemed to be the most likely time for these phenomena, and because they were accepted by successive generations of the family, there was no sense of fear attached to them.'

'At Shobdon, if you walk backwards round the Arches three times, saying the Lord's Prayer backwards three times, the ghostly carriage of the Bateman family will appear driving up Bury Lane, and someone will fall out of it and go under the wheels. This supposedly echoes a fatal accident to one of the Bateman family in the 18th century.

There is also the Lady in Grey who walks the churchyard, looking for her lover who went off to war and never returned. She is said to have died of a broken heart.'

'Fownhope had its share of sayings and omens:

A windy winter, a good crop of apples.

Fine Friday, fine Sunday.

Rain on Good Friday or Easter Day, a good crop of hops but a poor one of hay.

If you want a parsnip good and sweet, sow it when you sow the wheat.

If the wind's in the east on Candlemas Day, there it will stay till the end of May.

If the train from Stoke Edith is heard on Common Hill it's going to be fine, but if heard from Holme Lacy it will be wet.

Death omens included a circle of dark green grass, and a sheet folded with the middle doubled up so that the crease resembles the shape of a coffin when opened.

He has washed his hands in the Tan House Brook. (Anyone who has washed their hands in the brook will never leave Fownhope or if they do, will always return.)

When Noah lived in Bullingham. (Speaking of an event which happened a long time ago.)

I'm not one to hang my head out for a saint. (When speaking of anyone who had committed a misdemeanour.)

Aye, aye, there be worse folk than him but you mun go a long way to find them.

Sharp as a needle with two points.

Go to Ross to be sharpened.

Cut in June come again soon, cut in July surely die. (Thistles)'

A WANDER THROUGH YESTERDAY

'The biggest change one has seen this century is in the attitudes of people. In the early part of the period the most obvious thing would be knowing one's place. This meant that a certain job or position was yours and that you were trusted to do it and it was your job to do it to the best of your ability, and if you did this you earned the respect of your fellows and the community at large.

If one was a gardener or cowman, therefore, one could be as highly respected by one's fellows as was the gentleman at the big house. Of course, one did not ride to the hunt, because one did not want to, did not have the time, and would be shunned by one's fellows, that is those with whom one had to live and work, for "nob running" and may even be "annunted" for it, especially if they suspected certain knowledge of poaching and drinking and other tittle-tattle was finding its way to the big house and hence the landlord. One must remember that almost all property was on estates and rented with one month's notice to quit, with no appeal.

Today everybody expects to be able to give their opinion on everything, but this would not have been so before the First World War.

Professional men were expected to be utterly truthful, and anybody of position rejoiced that "their word was their bond"; to lie, or the betrayal of trust, led to disgrace and ostracism. For an ordinary man the biggest social sin was to be "independent"; for to be independent one showed no respect to the one who was good enough to give you employment and perhaps also to supply you with a house to live in.

At the beginning of this era many of the working class were illiterate or possessed only very basic elementary education, and for great numbers a Sunday school trip to a local beauty spot was an event to be remembered. It would be recalled at every available occasion with descriptions of the number and colour of every beast and sheep in all the fields passed, who had met who, and who had subsequently got or had to get married as the result of that outing!

For the more adventurous there was a trip to Penarth to catch the paddle steamer to Ilfracombe, a four hour trip, pleasant on a fine day with the sun shining and a calm sea, very different on a dull windy day with a choppy sea. The paddle steamer had a flat bottom and would pitch and roll, with the result that by the time Ilfracombe was reached a number of the passengers would be quite sick and ill, wanting only to sit on the shore until the ordeal of the journey back to Penarth.

If one was fortunate enough to have an employer who would allow a few days off (without pay of course) then it was possible to catch the train to Aberystwyth, enjoy the beach, go up the cliff railway, live on fish and six pennyworth of chips and spend the night in the public shelter (free) and have a bath at the public baths (sixpence with hot water), plus a couple of boat trips round the bay, not to mention seeing Charlie Chaplin and either Roy Rogers or Hopalong Cassidy at the local picture houses, all for £10 to £15, and be able to enjoy a few pints of beer if one wanted it!

An excursion to Swansea cannot be omitted, for at Swansea there were trams. Many towns had trams and trolley buses (trolley buses were like trams, electric-driven from overhead cables, but did not run on rails like trams), but Swansea's trams ran to Mumbles and if you had not been to Mumbles on the tram you were nobody.

Otherwise on days off you stayed at home and did something in the garden, oiled your bike and got up late, because you had no spare money to do anything else, with the odd occasion of taking the bus to town to buy new boots or clothes.

The clothes worn by men have changed little over the period, except in the earlier part nearly all men wore a hat or cap, very few went without for fear of catching a "chill", a condition brought on by getting one's head wet, washing hair and going out, not changing wet clothes or sitting in a draught, or taking off one's clothes too soon in the spring. If one went out at night without hat and coat a chill was sure to result; many deaths were attributed to catching chills.

Professionals and men of position always wore black bowler hats, salesmen and horse dealers wore brown bowler hats, Jewish businessmen and bookmakers wore Homburg hats, while working class men and "navigators" were always to be seen in cloth caps, often with the "yorks" below the knee of their corduroy trousers. These consisted of leather straps, the purpose of which was (if enquiry were made) "to keep the dust from my eyes, of course". The real purpose of the "york" was to compensate for the pouch which developed with the bending down, picking and shovelling, causing the knee to burst out and making a hole in the trousers.

Bowler hats had another purpose in bygone days, it being believed that if the husband went to the marriage bed wearing his black bowler hat straight on his head there would be a baby boy, but a brown bowler hat was a sure harbinger of baby girls. If the above failed, then one had to resort to strong medicine and go to bed with one's boots and bowler hat on, as well as borrowing a neighbour's baby and cot to sleep in the same room as yourself (preferably of the same sex as the baby desired). There is no written record of this failing!

An article of attire which has also become much less popular is the scarf, which everyone wore in the winter and which everyone learned to knit in school, boys included. Romany men and horse dealers wore their scarves in a peculiar fashion, round their neck then crossed back round behind their back under the arms, then finally tying in front at the waist.

Scarves were worn as an aid to good health rather than a fashion, it being considered important to protect the "gully" which is the small hollow at the base of the neck. Failing to do so could result in a chill or bronchitis, asthma attack or even pneumonia, certainly a cold or the 'flu especially if one got in a crowd or draught.

Another area of the body to protect in earlier days was the "loins", a region from just below the top of the hips to just above the lower ribs; draught or getting the "loins" wet would certainly result in a chill or lumbago or other back trouble.

In the farming community breeches and leggings are no longer seen, whereas in earlier times at livestock markets farmers of note and respected in the agricultural scene would wear shiny black boots and leggings with a black bowler hat, livestock dealers would wear brown boots and leggings with a brown bowler hat, while the auctioneer always wore a black bowler hat and everybody wore a waistcoat summer and winter, with a gold watch chain if you were anybody.

Social activities from the male point of view consisted of gardening, often with local rivalry over a certain flower or vegetable, which could sometimes get quite serious with people refusing to speak to other members of the village for some breach of ethics observed by "decent people". Rabbiting with ferrets and nets was looked on both as a pastime and a means of supplementing one's food supply, while surplus rabbits could be sold and the skins of the rabbits which had been eaten also commanded a market from threepence to sixpence each, which was not to be dismissed when a farm labourer's wage for a six-day week and having to feed animals on Sunday was 35 shillings.

Bell ringing was practised with both church and handbells, with trips to other local churches and belfries, with often a barrel of beer from a rich farmer or gentleman for extra effort when their oldest son came of age, sometimes causing ringing till ten or eleven o'clock at night.

The local barber's house was often a place of not only haircutting and shaving with the old open razor but also a place of discussion of everything from the time to plant shallots according to Rafael's or Old Moore's almanac, to the Yellow Peril. General Franco and Mussolini, not to mention those in Germany, were sure to cause the barber's kitchen to be filled with smoke from pipes filled with Franklin's Best and Navy Twist, with quite heated arguments to ensue. Old Moore's and Rafael's did not always foretell the same future!

Once a year the local sports would be held which besides the athletics held today, also had such things as catching the greased pig and climbing the greasy pole to get the pound note nailed to the top. There was also the block test, which consisted of driving a six inch nail into an oak post with four blows of the hammer and dropping pennies into a bath of water to cover sixpences in the bottom (not as easy as it may sound!). Finally there was the bowling alley with the prize of a pig, which was very popular as most people kept a pig in a cot for bacon.

At the sports, besides the activities, one met and talked and had a drink with relations and acquaintances that there had neither been the time nor opportunity to spend time with since the last sports; it must be remembered that most people had little money to spare other than for utilitarian purposes and most had no motor car.

Perhaps another of the things which has gone, through the motor car's ability to bring far too many people for it to be any longer practical, is the effects sale held in the house. In times past when someone had died or gone to live with relatives when old or infirm, their effects were often sold at the house by public auction "in situ"; this brings memories of people carrying armchairs on their backs and neighbours and friends sharing the burden of a settee, putting it down from time to time to sit on for a few minute's blow and conversation before taking up their burden again and proceeding towards home.

Often owing to the crowded conditions in a small room, arguments would arise as to who did or did not bid on this or that, worse still two members of the same family who had got separated in the melée would bid on the same article; this certainly caused a row followed by a period of not speaking to one another.

If some one in a house auction came forward and played "Roll out the barrel" on the piano, this would raise the price from £1 to £2; and feather beds were felt to see if the late owner had used them as a deposit for any savings that he may have had. Yes, auctions of house effects were quite an event.

Memories come back of Grandma with her hair in a bun and of aunts with their hair in "earphones" on their ears, held with many hairpins, and sisters with "Alice" plaits which went all the way down their backs, all of which had to be brushed at least 100 times every morning and evening, and which must not be cut except for medical reasons, and certainly must not be washed when one is "not well".

There could well be a reduction of attacks on women if there was a return to the habit of Grandma's day of using two or three pins of six to eight inches long with an ornamental knob to secure their hats, quite a formidable weapon, as was the rolled umbrella with a duck's head or silver knob handle; many a would-be suitor or other miscreant was the recipient of one or more blows from this implement of retribution.

Looking at the toys of today, the mind goes back over the years to the "berry guns" made from the steel strips taken from old "stays", or to give them their proper name corsets, which every woman of any pride wore with hooks to fasten the front and laces to adjust the back; gone too are the numerous cotton reels which most homes had. These cotton reels were turned into knitting machines which knitted belts and, when wound round and sewn, the belts made teapot stands; the reels could also be turned into toy tractors with the help of a piece of candle, a length of elastic and a short piece of wood.

In shops and mail order catalogues of today we see the briefs and scanty underwear currently in vogue, a far cry from the old "Directoire" safety model knickers which reached to just above the knee, pink and elasticated at the waist and knee, with two or three safety pins at the waist for extra security, or even closer to the beginning of the era under examination the pair of trousers which were two white cotton legs with a piece of tape an inch or so wide tied round the waist. The legs would be plain for everyday wear and ruched in the Little Bo Peep manner for weddings, Sundays and other high days and holidays.

Young women of quality certainly did not ride horses in the brazen manner of one leg on either side, but in the decorous manner of both legs the same side (side-saddle). Any young woman that had been well brought up fainted at the sight of blood and smelling salts was an essential part of every woman's bag, to help to revive those who had fainted; ordinary people who fainted were liable to have a bucket of water thrown over them so were not so liable to have a touch of the vapours.

When we see pictures of the turn of the century, the better class ladies invariably wore evening dresses that were sleeveless and backless. To our thinking this would be to make them more attractive to the male members of the party, but nothing could be farther from the truth. This manner of dressing was to show respect to their host, recognising in him a man of discipline and desires well worthy of the adage, "Be not as ass and mule, who has continually to be held by the bit and bridle", and who would not wrongly behave himself nor indeed invite anyone to his house who he thought would be likely to misbehave or fail to control themselves in an acceptable manner. The wearing of jewelry was to show affluence of family and husband.

Owing to the foregoing reasons the relationships between the nobility and servant girls, gipsy maidens etc, much vaunted on television, stage and in books, were in truth extremely rare; a servant entering service should on leaving service be no worse off, even if no better. The noble man on leaving this life should leave what he was entrusted with no worse than when his trust began.

At the early part of the century an officer in the army or navy was recognised as such when he accepted the sovereign's commission to act as an officer and gentleman; an officer to accept the orders of those properly set in authority over him, to be a leader and example to his men and protect them from the worst enemy they would be likely to meet, themselves, through lack of personal discipline and personal control; secondly, to be able to control himself in a manner to bring respect to himself, his family, his sovereign and his country. If he felt he could not do this, he should resign his commission. The better-off families were convinced that the British Empire was all-enduring and supreme in the world in quality of value. In this vanished world, was not the Englishman's word his bond?'

HOUSE & HOME

THE WAY WE LIVED THEN

Cold, draughty cottages, primitive and overcrowded conditions and certainly no 'mod cons' – that was the way we lived until fairly recently. Hard to imagine when we look at those picturesque cottages that we admire so much today!

COTTAGES AT ASTON INGHAM

'Most of the cottages at Aston Ingham were of the two-up, two-down variety except for the larger farmhouses and of course the rectory and Aston Court. The loo was always at the end of the garden and usually only a one-seater, although it was rumoured that the rectory had a three-seater! Landing bedrooms were almost always to be found.

Water was drawn either from one's own well or from one of the five village wells. Every cottage had its iron copper which was built into a stone wall and heated by a fire lit underneath.

Gipsies called regularly selling pegs, heather and lucky charms, elastic, tape, ribbons etc. They were kindly people, not pushy. Indians called selling blouses and knitwear. There were also tramps, real "gentlemen of the road", doing odd jobs, who were always paid in kind with cider, bread and cheese. The postman walked great distances and delivered twice a day. He would blow a whistle to let you know he was coming, even if he hadn't a letter for you, in case you had something for him to take.

The rent collector, Sam Jackson, was a familiar figure with his black bag. People also remember their fathers paying tithes to the rector from the farms, sometimes in kind not money. There is one very vivid memory, some 70 years on, of a family being put out on the road for non-payment of rent. Those who saw it still remember the furniture piled up and the hopeless family.'

THE POST OFFICE AT BACKNEY

'In 1937 we stayed at my grandparents' home at Sellacks Marsh post office, Backney. This was a thatched cottage with a large vegetable and flower garden and orchard. Drinking water came from a spring in the field opposite and was piped under the road into the orchard where it was collected in buckets. The front door opened into the post office and living room, separated only by a screen. The post office itself consisted only of a large chest of drawers on top of which stood a small letter scales and a larger parcel scales. The floors were flagstones covered with home-made rugs. Grandma made wine of every description, which was kept in barrels in one of the pantile sheds. Instead of coffee at mid morning we had a glass of wine and a piece of cake.'

THE STONE HOUSE AT WITHINGTON

'Abutting the church burial ground at Withington stands one of the original stone-built houses, now the home of a doctor and his family. Much has been done to the house in the way of sympathetic improvement in latter years, but I recall living in Church House as a young woman. The front door was very thick and heavy and hadn't been locked for years when I moved into the house with my mother. Once inside the house, there was a large room to the left and a small one to the right. In the room on the left beside the fireplace there was a small wine cellar. Perhaps it had originally been a bread oven, or some such. In the kitchen there was a huge salting stone, presumably where many a pig carcase was summarily dealt with. There were hooks in the rafters where the smoked bacon flitches were hung. The staircase to the upper rooms was exposed by opening a stout wooden door at its foot, and the stairs spiralled away to the first floor.

Sitting beside the fire in the small room, one was never alone, as the graves in the churchyard came right up to the wall of the house. Peaceful company indeed! Once, when the fire was blazing away in the hearth, clouds of smoke blew through the chinks and crevices in the chimney into the churchyard, so I mixed some mortar and filled the cracks and holes. Those repairs still hold good to this day! There was one enormous room at the back of the house, underneath which was a cellar, and there were various outhouses, plus a pigsty at the end of the small paddock. All the household water came from a pump at the back of the house. Some people said that they would not care to drink the water which drained from the churchyard, but one wonders how it would compare with our present-day water supply for purity. This house was quite large and roomy, and occupied an important position in the village centre. An even larger stone house stands close by, on the other side of the church, which was once a public house, but not within living memory.'

PRIMITIVE CONDITIONS AT COLWALL

'Colwall is unique in that it has two distinct areas: the village down below centred round the railway, and Upper Colwall where the hill people live. A distinguishing feature of the original hill people was said to be their loud voices. A lad standing in the playground of the Wyche School was remembered at break time shouting what he wanted for dinner down to his mother standing in the garden below.

People remember squatters' cottages built almost overnight on the common-land on the hill, and terraced houses built for quarry workers. Primitive conditions existed, earth closets, no running water, gas or electricity. One particular row of poor cottages adjacent to a villa was known as the "Barracks" and the villa as the "Officers Quarters". After the war many of the terraced houses were modernised or knocked down as they were considered an eyesore in this area of outstanding beauty. Consequently there was less housing and one of the village schools had to be closed. All the land was privately owned and there were several larger houses built by the wealthier families.

Each cottage had a cooking range, a pig was kept and a few chickens. Home-made wine and fruit preserving was an annual chore. A piano and even an organ was invaluable for home entertainment, along with reading and sewing. The front sitting room was only used on Sundays. The lady's best hat might be seen on the chenille tablecloth during the week.'

ALMSHOUSES AND THE PUB AT PEMBRIDGE

'There are two sets of almshouses in Pembridge, both founded in the 17th century. In 1953 they were described as having "a door at the back of the living room which leads out to the gardens. There is a "ladies" at the corner of the back garden and a "gents" at the other side of the plots. The occupiers of the six houses have to carry their water from the nearest village pump; each house has a rainwater tank outside the back door. They are lighted by electricity, the occupiers paying for current used. Each house has a tiny coal range and gets £1 per annum towards fuel and two shillings and sixpence per week towards general expenses."

Typical of many old houses in the village in the 1950s was the New Inn. When new owners took it over in about 1950, "it was in a pitiable state of delapidation, daylight showing through the walls in many places, cracks filled with paint, hideous layer upon layer of wallpaper, cheap and ugly small high fire-grates which had

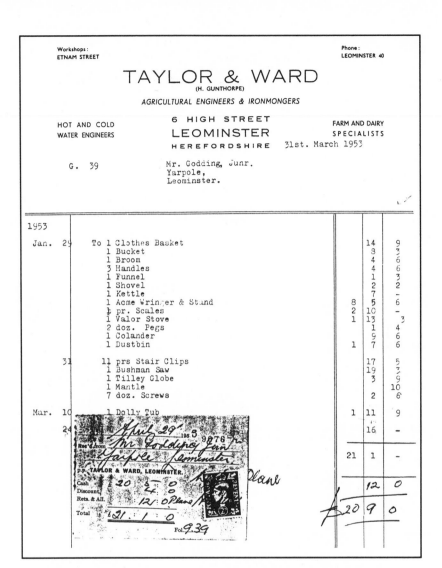

A quarterly bill for household goods purchased from Taylor & Ward of Leominster in 1953. The most expensive item for the new home was the Acme wringer and stand – essential for washday and probably guaranteed to last a lifetime!

been fixed in front of the old stone ones and filled in. Mine host and hostess picked and poked about, finding beauty behind the rubble and rubbish, and set to work to uncover treasures in the shape of old stone fireplaces with great oak mantels, secret rooms and so on." All the old houses are now in a good state of repair and are a great draw for the tourist trade.'

FARMER'S DAUGHTER/FARMER'S WIFE

The farmer's daughter often became a farmer's wife, and she was expected not only to run the farmhouse and the family, but also take a full part in the life of the farm. 'No wonder,' this lady thought, 'that my arms and legs are worn out!'

'When I was ten we moved to Herefordshire; it took a week to move. We only had horses and carts and all the farm animals had to be walked (it was about 25 miles). The sheepdog went back several times, he didn't seem to like his new home.

I started school in Titley in 1930 – that was about two and a half miles to walk but I had company by then. From the time I was twelve I was expected to loose out and feed two lots of hens (which were in two fields in the opposite direction from school) or milk a cow. I mostly milked the cow. I left school when I was 14 and worked at home. I went to Sunday school about a mile down the road at Noke Lane Head chapel at 11 am then I walked with Dad to Lyonshall Baptist chapel for 2.30 pm, once a month, and the 6 pm service as well. We mostly got asked to tea somewhere near chapel on those days – that was a three mile walk.

We washed on Monday, and ironed if it was dry. We had two water tanks in the yard which we had to carry from to fill the furnace and swill the clothes. When they went dry in the summer we took the clothes to the river to wash, where we had a brick-built fireplace and a big tin boiler to heat the water; you had to wring them as dry as possible because it was about a quarter of a mile to carry them up to the clothes line to dry.

Tuesday was churning day, when we made twelve to 20 pounds of butter. We always carried the drinking water, two buckets mostly did for the day, but on churning days we used up to ten buckets – it was about 400 yards to carry that, all up-hill. We milked five or six cows twice a day to get the cream, and put the milk through the separator. The skim milk was fed to the pigs.

Wednesday was baking day – we made our own bread, cakes, tarts and a big milk pudding on that day, so there were extra sticks to collect to heat the big baking oven.

On Thursdays we feathered and dressed ten or twelve chickens (I always hated that day). They were weighed up and priced ready to go to Leominster on Friday, and ranged from two shillings and sixpence to three shillings and sixpence.

On Friday morning I had to catch the 7.30 train from Marston Halt which was two miles. Mum used to come to help me carry the baskets part of the way. Mr Rawlings, station-master at Pembridge, used to be looking out for me and would bring my ticket out to the window of the train for me. When I got to Leominster I called at the houses nearest to the station first; I mostly had two or three ordered from the week before. If I couldn't sell them I had to put them in the auction and take what they made – sometimes more and often less than we had priced them at home. They would weigh from four lbs to six lbs each. I was allowed sixpence to buy a cup of tea and a cake. There was an old gentleman who worked for the auctioneers who often called at my home to see Dad, so if I could meet up with him he always treated me to tea and cakes, so I could save my sixpence. His name was Mr Knott and he used to shake a lot – people called him "Shaky Knott". When I had saved enough sixpences I bought a box camera for twelve shillings and sixpence, which I still have.

My home was a big house with stone floors which we got down on our knees and scrubbed out on Saturdays. Big black range to blacklead, and steel fender and fire-irons which we cleaned with Wellington Knife Powder until you could see your face in them. There was a boiler on one side of the grate which held four buckets of water, with a brass tap on the front. You had to keep that full, woe betide you if you slopped water on the grate when you were filling that with a bucket. There was lino and mats in bedrooms and on landing and stairs, until grandmother (who lived with us) fell down the stairs; then we had carpet on the stairs after that, and brass rods to clean. We got on our knees to polish all that. Oak boards on the landing, the front hall and two front rooms were also lino and mats, and were polished out every week.

If there was stock to go to market I used to go to help to drive them. When we had pork pigs ready to go we used to drive them to Titley station to go on the train about two miles; there would be about 20 ready to go at a time.

We had a truck of coal once a year, about eight tons. The men lugged that with horse and cart from the station.

A farmer's wife never had money out of the farm for housekeeping or clothes for herself or children, so she had to make money on poultry, butter and eggs. Butter was two shillings a pound, eggs from sevenpence in spring and summer up to a shilling a dozen in winter. I never had wages. I was allowed a fowl house and a dozen hens. I could have what corn they ate from the granary – that was my pocket money. Mum would buy me a coat and dress, a couple of jumpers and a skirt; Dad bought me a pair of wellingtons for lambing time each year. When I was 17 he bought me a new bike which cost £4 15 0d. Up until then if my friend and I wanted to go anywhere we shared her bike; one of us would ride about half a mile and put the bike against the bank and walk on, and when the other got to the bike she had a ride.

We joined Lyonshall WI for twelve months, then we joined the dairy students and used to cycle to Kington to the old National School up on the square. We were given some cream and had to churn that and make the butter up – our teacher was Miss Jenkins. That would be for about eight weeks in the summer. Then we were supposed to compete at Kington Show. I had first prize and a cup once.

At haymaking time we turned all the hay with rakes, and put it up in cocks ready to pitch on the wagon. I loaded all the loads, Dad and Martin pitched it up to me, then we took it all home to unload over the cowhouses and stables. They were tin roofs, and was it hot up there when the sun was shining. Martin worked for us for years – he lived in and was hired for twelve months from Knighton Fair each year. The corn was cut with the binder, we had to stick it up in stooks of six or eight sheaves, and that was left out two or three weeks; if it was a wet season we would have to take them apart and stick them up again several times. Then it was lugged home into bays in the barn and thrashed during the winter. It would take ten men on thrashing days, so the neighbours came to help. We went back to help them. It would take about three days in November and three or four in February or March. The men came in to "bait" at 10.30, dinner at one o'clock, tea 5.30, so there was plenty of cooking and washing up, but it was great fun to listen to the jokes at mealtimes.

We looked forward to May Fair time, that and the Sunday school outing to Aberystwyth were about all the outings we had in the year. When I was 18 Dad bought a Ford 8 car. It had been the pony and trap if we went out before, and we walked to chapel on Sundays, when the pony was not allowed to be used. When the car came we went in the car. When my brother left school when I was 20 Dad bought a tractor, and it was a bit easier on me after that.

I was married when I was 23; the war was on then and we were not supposed to use cars for pleasure – Dad risked it and took us to my aunt's in Llandrindod Wells for a week's honeymoon. We came back by train from Llandrindod to Knighton, walked up to the bus and came to Presteigne, by train from there to Forge Halt, and walked up to my home. Dad was going to market at Kington so we had a cup of coffee, my husband rode my bike, and I came in the car with Dad to our turn and started to walk with our cases about a mile to Downfield. That was how we arrived home!

My husband's parents were both in their seventies, and the man that worked there was retired off the railway, so as far as I was concerned it was out of the frying pan into the fire. Labour was very hard to find; we had German and Italian prisoners to work, who started at nine and left off at five o'clock – as the clock was on two hours there was a lot to do after they went home.

When I read through this I am not surprised that my arms and legs are worn out!

The worst patch of my life was March 1940. Dad went to Hereford market and bought some sheep which a lorry delivered home. The sheep were all right but the cattle walked across where the lorry had turned on the yard, and by Saturday it was confirmed we had foot and mouth disease. A man had taken pigs to market when he knew he had it at home (I think he got six months for doing it). I remember Stan McCartney coming on the Sunday to value everything; we were not allowed to go from home, and there was a policeman at the gate to see no one called. Fourteen butchers from Birmingham came on Monday morning to slaughter everything – anything not affected went for human consumption, and everything else went into a huge hole and was buried in hot lime. It was lambing time, all the little lambs were thrown in. We were milking six cows who were personal friends, and I shall never forget the last morning I milked them. The sheep were registered Kerry Hill flock. I can still see Dad sat with his head in his hands when they were being slaughtered. We were not allowed to loose the hens out, and we had to let them out and clean the fowl houses out about an hour before dark; a gang moved in and scrubbed all the buildings with hot soda water. We were not allowed to restock for three months.'

THE DAILY ROUTINE

In the past we seemed to have a job for every day, whether it was washing on a Monday or cleaning on a Wednesday. In those days, of course, household tasks could indeed take all day, without any of the modern conveniences we now take so much for granted.

SOMETHING EVERY DAY

'At Shobdon we lived in small cottages, usually belonging to the large estates. They had small rooms with earthen floors, and were lit by paraffin lamps. Cooking was done either over a large coal fire with a side range, or on an oil stove. Water was carried from the local taps and wells until 1957, when the mains came in.

The week was segregated into specific household duties: Monday washing, Tuesday ironing, Wednesday cleaning, Thursday baking, Friday shopping, Saturday bath and pub night, and Sunday church!'

WASHDAY MONDAY

'I suppose those were the good old days, but life was harder. The kitchen fire had to be lit before there was any hot water; a coal fire heated only part of the room, fine for those who sat at table with their backs to the fire, but chilly for the ones who sat opposite. Then the weekly wash day, always a Monday: the boiler was lit early, the wash had been sorted the day before, the washerwoman arrived, and it was all hands to the pumps!

First the whites were washed and boiled, and while that was going on everything else had its turn. Each colour had to be washed and rinsed separately, as in those days most dyes were not fast, and colours ran with disastrous results. Then things had to be mangled, but of course they were folded first; a great many things were starched, and whites had an extra rinse with Reckitts Blue – a small square tablet put in a muslin bag and swished around in a bowl of cold water. When the water was the right shade of blue, the articles were rinsed in it, resulting in a "whiter than white" (unless the blue was too blue, in which case the garment had to be rewashed, or put up with until next time!)

After that it was hanging out to dry, and then ironing. Ribbons had to be removed from underclothes and babies' dresses, ironed, and then run in again with the help of a bodkin. Then the mending, always a few buttons and tears – and the stockings! Big toes out, and heels, either with a "potato", or a large thin place needing reinforcing. With a large family (we were eventually seven children) there was always plenty of mending. Washing-up was not so easy (no Fairy Liquid); old bits of soap were put in a little wire box with a long handle, and swished around the water to make a lather. It helped, but did not dissolve the grease, and before long the washing-up water was disgusting.

The old days are lovely to remember, but not many people would choose to go back to them.'

'Our house at Cross Farm, Kington was old and had a large kitchen with a stone flagged floor which was scrubbed once a week. We had two farm workmen living in (during the First World War, only one), a maid, and a woman who came in twice a week to do the washing and ironing. Her wages were one shilling per day, but Mother said she usually gave her one shilling and sixpence or occasionally two shillings if she felt after a hard day's work that a shilling was not sufficient. There was no electric or mod cons, of course.'

BEFORE ELECTRICITY

'Electricity did not come to the hamlet where my grandparents lived until after the Second World War, and what a difference it made.

When I was a child all the cooking and heating of water was done on the range or open fire, even in the summer with windows and doors open there was always a fire with the kettle on the hob or on the swing over the flames. Ironing was another very warm job; my grandmother did washing and ironing for the lady of the manor, delicate silks etc, also the parlourmaid's caps and aprons, starched just right and the frills goffered. Of course, before the ironing was the big wash, which took all day. First, lighting the copper fire, then boiling the sheets etc, rinsing and wringing with the old iron-and-wooden mangle. If fine, the clothes were hung out, if not lines were put up indoors and the fire stoked to warm the room. To help with the ironing the sheets and towels were folded before they were bone dry and put carefully through the mangle again. In those days the men wore stiffly starched collars which were glazed with a special iron. All the irons were heated on the range, then rubbed with soap to make them glide over the clothes.

There were no mixers to make cakes easily, it was all done with a wooden spoon or a whisk, and to cook them was a work of art.

71

The times I heard my grandmother say, "The fire is just right, please don't touch it until the cake is cooked".

After the midday meal on cold winter days, fire bricks were put into the grate oven; a little time before retiring they were wrapped in flannel and put into the beds – beautifully warm, but hard on the toes!

Friday was cleaning day. The mats were taken up and put on the clothes-line to be beaten, but if there was a carpet on the sitting room floor we saved the damp tea leaves from breakfast to sprinkle on the carpet to help stop the dust rising when sweeping.

There was no fridge or deep-freezer. Food was either salted, pickled, dried or bottled to preserve it. The marble or slate slab in the pantry and cellar helped keep food cool. On Saturday mornings all the lamps were trimmed and candlesticks cleaned. I can remember us having a new Aladdin lamp; the mantle was very fragile and smashed at the least touch.'

'Many homes in Orleton were wattle and daub with flagstone floors. Many had open slate roofs or corrugated iron, some were thatched. Larger houses were brick, but all were cold. My family home was brick and beams with a lean-to open slated kitchen which contained a sink, a furnace and a bread oven. Mother sterilised feathers in this oven for use in pillows or a feather bed. The living room had a red quarry tiled floor which had to be scrubbed with milky water. A black range was used for cooking and heating water. The kettle was hung on a sway over the fire. A large scrub-topped table was always covered with a cloth. On it stood an oil lamp for lighting. Candles were used at bedtime.

Patchwork quilts, usually lined with men's old pants and vests, were made for beds. Strips of old garments were made into rag mats. Lace doyleys were crocheted for cake plates. Embroidery of all kinds was popular as was knitting and sewing. Most of these handicrafts were essential to make ends meet.

When we were small we listened to a crystal set with a pair of headphones. Then we advanced to a wireless run off an accumulator which needed recharging regularly.

To keep draughts out of the living room we had a high backed settle. Mother brought the zinc bath in front of the range for our weekly scrub.

Water was saved in tanks from roofs or carried from a spring at the bottom of our fields. This spring also served a neighbouring farm. Father used a yoke to carry buckets of water home.

Soft water was used for our daily washing and for the clothes wash. All whites were boiled in a furnace continually stoked with wood. These whites were blue-rinsed and if appropriate starched. Colours and woollens were hand washed. The old wooden roller mangle squeezed out excess water. Really dirty garments were put in the dolly tub and dollied or put on the scrubbing board, soaped well and scrubbed clean.

Time to iron and the old range was used to heat the flat irons. These had to be rubbed on a cloth or maybe across a piece of soap to get them clean before using on garments. Larger articles like unbleached calico sheets and towels were put through the mangle to be smoothed.

Iron pots and pans were used for cooking, baking and preserving. They became very black from smoke and were horrible to wash.

Because money was short, families made good use of vegetables which were grown in their gardens and fertilised with farmyard manure. Most cottages kept a pig for bacon and a few hens for fresh eggs. These were life savers during rationing in war time. The local pig killer was renowned for chopping off the tail and chewing it while he jointed the animal.

Our sofas, armchairs and some mattresses were stuffed with horsehair which caused irritation if it poked through the cover. Other mattresses were flock which tended to go lumpy, or lovely soft feathers. Many of our bedsteads were iron framed, some with lovely brass knobs.

Heating in our homes was from open fireplaces burning wood from the farmer's woodland or old fruit trees mainly. Coal came from Bayton Colliery near Mamble or the Clee Hills. Even bedrooms had a tiny fireplace which was only used when someone was really ill.

In the 1950s electricity for heating and lighting was brought to the area, making life easier.'

CLEANING AND SCRUBBING

'Blackleading grates took a lot of time and it was a very dirty job – no rubber gloves then. There was a certain satisfaction when you could see your face in the reflection, however.

I never got that satisfaction from scrubbing floors, or understood why people scrubbed not only their steps but the pavement right to the edge of the kerb. As a result, streets looked striped cream and grey, where people had or had not done this scrubbing and stoning. These blocks of sand-coloured stone were given away by the rag and bone man – presumably in exchange for old rags and bones.

Knives were mostly made of steel and needed constant cleaning. Unless you had a fancy machine, this was done with a cork and Vim after every washing up.

Fetching water was a time consuming task which had to be undertaken every day. At this farm at Orleton, water was carried by yoke and buckets from the spring across the fields.

Irons were heated by the fire, and to be sure they were hot enough you spat on them, and the spit had to bounce! Then they were rubbed with soap, and then rubbed on the doormat before putting them on the clothes to be ironed.'

FETCHING THE WATER

'I grew up in the country on the borders of Herefordshire and Radnorshire. In the late 1920s drinking water had to be carried from a well which was half a mile away. My father made a wooden frame for carrying water. Two buckets were carried, not on a yoke but on a U-shaped frame which was carried across one's front, the buckets hanging at one's sides and held away from the person, so that the body was not knocked and the precious water not spilled.'

'When we visited my grandparents at Linton in the 1930s, one of the things we did when we arrived was to get more water from Talbot's Well, to which there were several small paths down the steep hill. When I first remember it, it was just a hole in the wall surrounded by stone and a little door. About 1931 they were getting worried that the supply was going to dry up in the summer, so they built a reservoir tank for an overflow, with a big lid that you lifted up. That in fact was cleaner water because sometimes before there were tadpoles. The rest of our water was from a big tank in the garden. We washed using ewers and basins in the bedrooms and the slops were carried down the garden.'

'At Woolhope every home had a water butt to collect rain from the roof. Drinking water was carried from a wooden pump in the Crown orchard. Households away from the village had, if they were lucky, their own well, otherwise they obtained water from streams.'

'Our cottage at Linton in the late 1940s was on the lane at the foot of Linton Ridge and had no water or electricity. Luckily we were near the well, but if it was a dry summer and the well went dry I had to walk up the Green Lane to the top road to fetch water from the tank that was filled by the Fire Brigade from Ross on Wye.'

'Until the 1950s most houses at Bodenham had their own water supply from their own wells, but in the village there was, and still is, "The Well", which always had a constant supply of pure water by gravitation from Dinmore Hill. However, in the 1950s this supply began to fail, and for this the gravel workings got the blame. About this time piped water was introduced, although at the present time there are still some cottages without it. Electricity was also introduced in 1950, though it was a long time before outlying parts of the village got it.'

LIGHTING UP

'Houses were generally lit by candles in the early part of the century, and lamps filled with paraffin. These had to be trimmed and refilled every day and the glasses washed. Sometimes the lamps flared up in a draught and the whole room was filled with black cobwebs!'

'Candle lanterns were still being used until quite late, even when hand torches were available. Acetylene lamps were sometimes used, like those on bicycles, which smelt horrendous. Batteries were sacred objects and hard to come by.'

'Our home in the 1930s at Pudleston was a large rambling farmhouse without electricity or piped water. Oil lamps were used for reading and sewing, with a candle to light us to bed.'

'All the cooking in the house was done on the range and on a Valor Perfection cooking stove. Lighting was by paraffin oil lamps and Aladdin hanging lamps, while out of doors the main lighting was by hurricane lantern, often in danger of being blown out in a high wind. The price of two gallons of paraffin in the 1920s was one shilling and tenpence. If a fox was about at lambing time a lantern would be hung in a tree to scare him off, because a light was rare at night.'

AT THE BOTTOM OF THE GARDEN

'The toilet was usually at the end of the garden path, often hidden from view by a huge laurel or some other evergreen shrub. It had a wooden seat with holes in and a bucket into which was put some chemical which dissolved the contents, which had to be emptied into a hole dug in the garden.'

'There was one journey my sister and I hated to make at night. It was around the house, down the garden to the earth toilet. It did have a "little and large" hole so that we could go together and then run back carrying the torch. If the family needed the toilet during the night there was always the chamber pot in the bedroom. We also had a washstand with basin for our daily washing.'

'No newspapers, magazines or telephone directories were ever thrown away – I remember, as a child in the 1930s, that one of my household tasks was to tear up the paper into suitably sized squares. These were piled into neat blocks, an inch or so thick, and a hole was punched in one corner, usually with the point of a pair of scissors. A string was threaded through the hole, and the whole thing was then hung on a nail in the loo at the bottom of the garden to serve as toilet paper.

Even when we graduated to having an indoor loo, the use of this economical loo-paper continued until well after the end of the war in 1945. Paper had been very scarce anyway, and every scrap was saved – brown paper for parcels, and string, was always re-used.

I had an aunt who owned a town house with all mod cons, *and* "Bronco" toilet paper. I thought she was very grand!'

'I must have been about six years old – living in the country. At that time nearly 50 years ago, the house had an outside loo, in other words an earth closet at the bottom of the garden.

My mother and I were in the back garden and as my mother was on her way to make a visit to you know where, she said to me, "Don't walk through the rhubarb because it is wet and you will get your socks soaked".

As she disappeared inside I looked longingly at the lush rhubarb leaves so tall and invitingly cool on this hot day in summer.

Knowing mother was occupied for a few minutes, I thought I would risk a walk in the rhubarb. It was cool, walking through the leaves and I heard mother coming so got back to the path before she caught me.

I stood there looking innocent and then she opened the door and came out and stood looking at me for a second, and pointed to my leg. Thinking my socks were wet I looked down and saw crawling on my leg, a large black slug.

I never walked in the rhubarb again.'

FOOD AND DRINK

Fresh butter wrapped in dock leaves to keep it cool, free range eggs from our own chickens, well hung game, home-made wine – just some of the memories of days when food and drink may have been plainer, but it was fresh and wholesome. And of course, there was the home-made cider, produced in practically every farmhouse in Herefordshire and an everyday drink for young and old alike.

MILK, BUTTER AND CHEESE

'Butter making was a day's work with the cream that had been separated from the milk every morning and night. I had to turn the handle of the separator which sent the skimmed milk through one pipe and the cream through another. The separator was made up of cups that had to be washed every day in hot water and fitted back together. The cream was put into the churn and fastened down. There was a bung at the bottom that let the air out after you had been turning the handle for some time.

There was a knack in doing this job. If you turned too fast the butter would come out soft and lumpy and if you turned it too slow it would "go to sleep". My mother would then put some hot water into it to wake it up.

When the butter had been formed it was put into a stean. You then had to use your hands to get the buttermilk out. It was then salted and made into half pound pats with wooden butter mitts ready for market.'

'We lived on a small farm and my mother sold milk, butter, eggs etc. Most customers came to the back door for their produce, but, for the privileged few, it was my job to deliver their milk before going to school. I could be seen, early in the morning, pedalling away on my old sit-up-and-beg bike with cans of milk swaying from the handlebars. Full cream milk was twopence a pint and skimmed milk was one penny a quart. My mother also made and sold butter. The half pound pats were beautifully decorated and wrapped in dock leaves to keep the butter cool, the leaves having been swilled under the pump. Butter was two shillings and sixpence a pound and eggs were one penny each. My mother also sold and dressed poultry, especially at Christmas.'

'There were often geese on farms to be killed for the Christmas trade, and ducks and poultry. Eggs would be put under a sitting hen to produce chicks, and these were reared for food. There were plenty of rabbits in the fields, also pheasants, woodcocks, partridges and pigeons. Wild field mushrooms were picked in autumn and, apart from the soft fruit in the gardens, there were blackberries, cherries, walnuts, hazel nuts and apples and pears from the orchards.

Butter was made, the buttermilk being very good for baking. Cheese was also made on the farm, the curd being put into cheese vats and the liquid squeezed out with a machine. Cheese from ewes' milk was even nicer, and after the spring lambing some of the ewes were milked, a fiddly job, and cheese made. Some people also had goats.'

PULLETS ON THE STUBBLE

'Most people know only of deep litter or battery hens to provide them with their eggs. Occasionally one sees "free range" ones for sale but it is not the norm as it was when I was a child, living on a farm in pre-war days.

We used to hatch our own chicks from our own eggs under broody hens. The procedure took three weeks from the day we placed the sitting of eggs under the hen until little sharp beaks cracked open the shells and lovely yellow balls of fluff appeared.

An empty fowl house, away from the rest of the poultry, was used, nest boxes being made from used orange containers and after the broody hens were placed on the clutches of eggs, they were covered with lids and sacking.

Turkeys were hatched in the same way. Twice a day the hens were taken off the nest for food and water and they were always anxious to get back on their warm eggs. They seemed to know that they must not get cold.

I must have learned the art of putting hens "to sit" at a very early age, and before being old enough to go to school. One evening my mother went along to collect the eggs and the nests were empty and the hens were in full lay. Had the dogs eaten them, or had someone stolen them? When I was questioned, I happily confessed to having taken them to "put the hens to sit". The nest boxes were covered over just as I had seen it done by my mother.

Sometimes we bought a special "sitting" of eggs from someone who kept "Well Somers" or "Barny Veldors" which produced rich brown eggs and I remember walking over from Canon Pyon (Nupton Farm) one evening to Cox's Park at Wormsley for a sitting of these eggs. It was a long walk up Nupton Hill and through the woods to get them. The moon was shining through the trees on our return journey. I don't recall being nervous for we had Bonny the sheepdog and the light of the hurricane lamp to guide us.

The chicks grew and were ready to lay at the same time as the corn was cut in the autumn, and a fowl house on wheels would be taken out to the stubble and there the pullets would have the freedom of the field to scratch for wheat from dawn to dusk. They would remain there until the ground was ploughed for next season's crops and no grain was wasted.

The pullets were a lovely sight on the stubble with their shiny feathers and red combs glowing in the autumnal sunshine – a sure sign that they would soon be laying.

To see the first small eggs in the nest boxes was quite exciting and made the hard, non-paying work of the last six months all worthwhile. Nowadays the corn is combined, the straw baled and ploughing started the same evening. I have not seen fowls on the stubble for a long time.'

HOME-MADE ICE CREAM

'In the 1930s, salt was bought in big blocks, maybe 26 inches by eight inches by eight inches, and you had to rub it with a grater to make it usable. A rotten job for sore hands.

Home-made ice cream was a tremendous treat. Dad used to go down to the ice works (presumably they produced it for fishmongers) and take an old sack in the car. He bought a big block so we had to chip it and put layers of ice and salt in the freezer round the ice cream container. Then you turned it with the handle, rather like a small butter churn. Parents had to be persuaded that it *must* be nearly ready so you could have a taste.

Weighing of foodstuffs was of course done with weights on a scale, or maybe a bag of sugar on one side and the stuff to be weighed on the other. Many people had no scales and measured by cupsful.'

HOT BUTTERED TOAST

'I only have to smell hot buttered toast and my mind goes back to the time when I was a small child and my mother made toast in front of the kitchen range. She would pull out the damper – which I always thought was magic – and in a few minutes there would be a hot red glow coming through the bars. She would then get a long-handled toasting fork, and patiently hold a slice of bread in front of the glowing coals until the required degree of brownness was reached. Then she would turn the bread and toast the other side. When cooked, it would be spread lavishly with home-made butter. This would be continued until there would be a delicious pile of toast keeping warm on the hob, until the tea was brewed and we were seated at the table. My mother sat at the head of the table, and I always wondered why her cheeks were red and glowing! A far cry from modern automatic toasters, but so much nicer. Can you smell the toast?'

GAME

'This is a mid 19th century recipe which was still used in my family in this century – but possibly in smaller quantities!

Game Pie for a Hunting Breakfast: A goose, a turkey, a grouse, two woodcocks, a pheasant, two partridges, one and a half bullock's tongues, half the meat from a hare, a pint of good gravy, a pound of grated ham, seven pounds of flour, one and a quarter pounds of suet, and two pounds of butter. Make an ornamental crust with the flour, suet and butter into a fancy shape, with top to fit, and bake.

Cut all meat into small pieces (gosh, that would take *ages*) and stew gently. Put into the crust with the gravy, cooked grated ham and seasoning. Cover with the paste top and warm well in a slow oven (it would need to be a jolly big oven too!). Time: three hours.'

'Pheasants, and other birds, and hares were hung till maggots were in them before people cooked them.'

CHICKWEED

'Chickweed was used as a vegetable – and very good it was when cooked with nutmeg.'

WATER AND WINE

'When I came to Lyonshall in 1952 many cottages had no water laid on so there were "country toilets" at the bottom of the garden and standpipes for water shared between the cottages; the best drinking water was from a standpipe by the Royal George Inn (there were three pumps in Lyonshall then). The water was, I understand, spring water. It was certainly very cool and clear, and because of that we thought it would be good to make kitchen wine once more, so we made marigold, parsley and lemon, red clover, gorse, gooseberry champagne and many others, the recipes being from my grandmother's cook books – only I made them in smaller quantities! I can't help wondering what sort of container she made her wine in, with such vast amounts.

Here is one of her recipes. "Fetch ten gallons of pure river water and boil for half an hour. Add 45 pounds of ripe apricots, stoned and sliced, and add 25 pounds of loaf sugar. Boil, and stir in eight eggs well beaten. Take off scum as it rises. When clear, press and strain through a fine sieve. Add broken stones. Spread yeast on both sides of a piece of toast. Leave for two days, strain into cask, and then add two quarts of best French brandy. Put in bag and ferment for twelve months."

When I joined the WI they heard I made wine so the first talk I gave to WIs was about wine. Anyway, I went up to the village hall with a selection of wines that were ready for drinking and showed them how I made it. Then of course they all wanted to try some, and a very happy evening was had by all!'

MAKING THE CIDER

'In the orchard at Yew Tree House there were several cider apple trees (some of them are probably still there). We kids just loved the

The cider mill at Dorstone. Cider making, and drinking, was a great social occasion – though the results could be extremely potent for the unwary.

taste of them, especially when they were bruised against the tree trunk, small and sweet, they tasted of cider and as we were not allowed to drink the real stuff it was the next best thing! However, the time would come in October when these apples were ready to harvest, then were made into cider. Dad would use Mum's clothes prop to shake them and, of course, got into trouble if he broke it! (No modern clothes line prop for our Mum, it was made from a tree branch with a fork at the end.) We would then have to pick the apples up out of the long wet grass and nettles (long, because animals were never allowed to graze where there were apple trees as if they ate too many they would get "blown", or sometimes an apple would get stuck in the throat; either way it would be a hefty vet's bill).

Having picked up the apples we would put them in sacks (real sacks, none of your plastic or paper), then on to the next tree, and so on. We had to pick one tree behind where Dad was shaking or we would most likely get a "lump on the bonce" from falling apples.

When the picking was finished, the sacks of apples were transported into the yard – mostly by Kit (our mare) and cart; then into the cider mill. Kit was harnessed to the mill stone and the poor dear would have to walk round and round, usually led by one of us kids, to crush the apples. Dad would have added some "pot fruit", cookers or eaters, to add to the flavour of the finished product.

When the apples were crushed and the fruit drained off, the pulp was spread onto coconut matting, made into layers (matting, then pulp, and so forth) and placed on the cider press, which had a huge screw on the top. This screw was gradually tightened to squeeze out all the remaining juice – and there you have it, the real scrumpy! A bit cloudy maybe, but ready to put into barrels to mature for many weeks (mostly by pig-killing time in January). By that time it was really potent.

Dad used to say, "It will make you talk about friends you never even had!" New cider would never be drunk – if anyone was foolish enough to do so, it was with dire consequences.'

'My grandfather A E (Bert) Herbert was licensee of The Major's Arms at Bishops Frome from 1906 to his death in 1947 and he used to make and sell his own cider and perry for a penny ha'penny a pint. He used to boast that his perry was so strong that no one could drink more than three pints of it. Many tried and some succeeded but Bert would say, "Ah, but you haven't walked home yet!" As they went outside, the fresh air hit them and they went down as if pole-axed. The comment would then be made, "See, Herbert's dog has bitten you."'

'Most of the farms around Cradley had cider apple orchards, but only a few had a press. This consisted of a circular well built of stone, with a trough at the bottom for the juice to run out. The press was a heavy wooden lid, attached on either side by a heavy screw. The apples were put into the well, each layer covered by a hessian sheet. When the well was full up the presses were screwed down until the juice started to run. Gradually more layers of apple and hessian were added until all the juice was extracted. Water was then added to the apple juice and it was left until it finished fermenting. Sugar was then added and after another wait, the cider was ready to be drunk. It was incredibly potent, but very popular in the local pubs, or it was taken by van into Worcester.

After the main crop was finished, anyone who had a small orchard could bring their apples and use the press.'

'Cider production at Aston Ingham was a major industry. Nearly everyone had their own cider mill and a horse to work it. In some areas a travelling mill would come round. The local mills do not sound too hygienic as fowls generally roosted in them at night, regardless of whether cider was in the process of being made, and traditionally a rat was always put in the brew. The men all had either a cider horn or a small barrel in which to take their cider to work.'

'At Fownhope at the turn of the century it was common for children to be "reared up on toast and cider". In winter the cider was warmed, powdered ginger added and then some toasted bread. They slept like tops! Children used to take small casks of cider to school for elevenses!'

'I was brought up on a smallholding at Bishopswood. Cider making was done on cold dark nights when you couldn't work outside. Grandfather came with his horse during the day to grind a mill full of fruit. In the evening my sister and I had to help my father put up the "cheese" – this was the name for the horsehair mats which were filled with the apple pulp, and placed on the press, one on top of the other, to have the apple juice squeezed out. I hated the job, working by candlelight, fingers growing numb with cold. To this day I still dislike the smell of cider.'

BAKING DAY

'I always liked it when baking day was on a Saturday. Our farmhouse kitchen had a range, a large black stove with two ovens and an open fire in the middle. My father lit this every morning early before he went out to do the milking, so that by the time we came down for breakfast there was a cheerful warmth. Saturday was blackleading day, so the fire was not lit until the whole range had been polished to a clean, shiny black. This took several hours and in winter the house was very cold with no other heat. The next room was the large back-kitchen where the sink, the pump for drinking water and the bread oven were. Baking day meant that this oven had to be lit.

The oven was a cavity in a solid brick wall. It was about three feet wide, six feet back and perhaps two feet high with an iron door and a flue at the back. A fire was lit in it and long sticks were put on and allowed to burn for several hours till the bricks were heated through. Meanwhile we had all been busy preparing things to be cooked. Flour was bought by the sack – several at the time – and stored in a large galvanised chest with a lid. This flour was used for everything, with yeast or baking powder added when necessary. A large tin bath full of bread made 20 loaves, enough to last a week. There were pies and tarts, buns and cakes to feed our family of seven. These were lined up on the large, well scrubbed wooden table which filled the middle of the room, waiting to be cooked. We could stand in front of the open door and feel the warmth.

When the sticks were all burnt, the remains of the fire were raked out of the oven and the ashes removed with a long-handled mop made out of strips of material and dipped in water. My mother would put her arm inside the oven to test the heat – she didn't need a thermometer – and cooking began. The pastry and buns went in first when the oven was hottest, then the cakes and finally the bread, and oh! the taste of a warm crust from one of those loaves with some home-made butter.'

'Baking day always meant an early start for my mother. She had to start the fire in the brick bread oven to get it red hot. This was heated with wood and when it was hot enough she would bake all the bread, cakes, milk puddings and meat for the week. The aroma of fresh bread and cakes remains with me to this day.'

'The special bread oven had to be prepared by putting in dry sticks of wood to make a good fire. When the sides and top of the oven turned white and the wood was burned the ashes were cleared out. A besom was used for this – a besom was a strip of wood with a handful of small branches tied round it.'

'Baking day was quite an occasion. Each Friday at Dorstone Mrs Goodwin of Great House Farm would use a 140 lb bag of flour. Her large brick oven was heated with wood, ash for preference, to make it white hot. She used a pitchfork to refuel, and added gorse, which gave a sweet taste to the crust of the bread. When the bread was out of the oven she would put thick layers of brown paper down, making an excellent place to air clothes.'

'When I was about eight years old, living on a farm in the shadow of the Black Mountains, I remember setting off early on Friday mornings across fields and a footbridge to the local shop. This was kept by a portly lady in her front room, and I had to buy three pennyworth of fresh yeast. By the time I returned my aunt had started the fire in the baking oven and put the flour from the sack in the huge flat bowl. The yeast and sugar were added and the dough put to prove by the big open fire. Huge loaves were made and lastly a couple of small "baches" for tea. Whilst these were cooking, fruit tarts were made. The loaves were pulled out with a very long handled spade and put to cool, then the tarts were cooked. The bread never went mouldy and stayed fresh until the next Tuesday.'

'I vividly remember blackleading the kitchen range in the 1930s. Every Friday it was necessary to "do the flues" or it would be impossible to cook the joint on Sunday. The cooking pots and pans were all of heavy iron and I developed a painful swelling of my wrist from all the lifting I had to do.'

'In the 1950s our Triplex grate served as a heater for the sitting room and an oven for baking cakes, pastry or roasting meat. Extra cooking facilities came in the form of paraffin stoves, which could take a square oven on top if needed. It was possible to bake an excellent Christmas cake in this way, by simply leaving it for hours on a low light in the square oven. One had to watch for flaring up, which would leave a black film of burnt paraffin on everything, especially the ceiling.'

KILLING THE PIG

It was once common for a pig to be kept in a sty at the bottom of the garden, fattening up to be the family's main supply of meat for the year. Everything, it was said, could be used except the squeak!

KILLING AT THE VILLAGE PUB

'In 1916, the war had been on for some two years, and we were allowed to kill our pigs for our own consumption, giving up some of our meat coupons.

My mother called out to my father, "When are we going to kill that sow, Fred, we are getting short of bacon? Look at the rack in the kitchen." "Next week," said Fred. I took a note, too.

Mr Williams, the pig killer (Piggy Williams – not to be confused with Shoey Williams, his brother) agreed to be at the "Wye" at 6 am sharp the following Tuesday.

The piggeries at the "Wye" were well hidden with rustic wood frame covered with loganberries clinging all over, together with a few marrow plants. Unfortunately the wind was not always westerly!

Saturday evening, Dad went to the piggeries with Charlie Baugham (head waggoner for W G Andrews of the Manor Farm, "Billy" Andrews out of hearing) and Fred Gilbert, second waggoner. I followed, aged nine, to listen. Charlie said, "I be dankered, she must nigh on 18 score she be." Fred Gilbert thought she was more like 20 score. I am almost sure he licked his lips under a huge moustache. They went away and brought some straw for burning the hair off the sow (with Billy's permission) and had some beer.

On Monday came the pig bench – a huge affair six ft long and 24 inches wide, of two and a half inch thick elm, legs well apart to prevent overturning, pulley blocks, rope, two props to strengthen the washhouse beam, a galvanised washing bath and three buckets. The copper was filled with water, and the fire laid underneath.

At 5 am on Tuesday, the fire was lit, the bench and straw made up in the yard. Charlie and Fred arrived, and with my father started to get the sow quietly down from its sty to the yard, using a hemp sash cord tied to her rear leg to prevent her going astray.

Piggy Williams arrived on his bicycle and helped to get the pig on to the bench and tied down with hemp cords. Mr Williams, with a quick movement sharpened his knife on a steel and nodded to me with my bucket. Now I did not like this moment very much, but when you are promised liver for breakfast and, later on in the week, the brains done in breadcrumbs, you stifle your feelings. When the bucket was full, and the sow was dead, the straw was laid out on the yard close to the bench and the pig lowered gently on to it. The bench was taken away, more straw laid over the pig and lit. Afterwards the other side of the pig would be burnt to remove the remaining hairs. Great care was taken to see the skin was not burnt or marked.

The pig would then be thoroughly scrubbed with hot water from the copper to remove the hairs. Finally the pig would be placed on a short ladder and taken into the washhouse and hung upside down with legs hooked up to a chain on the beam. Charlie and Fred would go off to work with a, "See you tonight, Boss", to my dad.

Seeing the pig hung up like that gave me a certain amount of pleasure. She was so large and awkward when we had to take her to the boar – a three mile walk to Twyford and again to bring her back some days later. She was a large white and always had too many piglets. My sister (seven years older than me) and I would have to feed some of the "nestlings" with the bottle because they were pushed out by their larger brothers and sisters when trying to feed from their mother.

Mr Williams now split the pig down the centre and removed the bladder, stomach fat, small intestines, stomach, liver, lungs, heart, windpipe and tongue. The carcase was washed down and dried and left for two or three days. We would have our breakfast of the liver! After breakfast the small intestines would be taken down to the brook, washed out, rodded and washed several times, then brought back and cleaned with clean pump water. They would then be soaked in salt water, using a large clay vessel, and later boiled. The "chitlings" were now ready for when required.

Chitterlings in a Dutch oven in front of the bright kitchen range fire (with mustard, vinegar, sugar and sauce) – beautiful! Mother would make black puddings and faggots. Even the bladder, when cleaned and dried would be useful for inside a football case.

Three days later, the butcher would come back and cut the pig into joints. Two front legs and shoulders; two back legs (ham), and two sides for salting down. Loins and belly would be butchered and the head split for making brawn. The pig's brains were now ready for me! The pig's trotters were nice but messy. "Don't use so much salt, and be careful with saltpetre, Fred," said Mother to Father when the salting down was being done. "No, Minnie," Dad would reply, rubbing it in a little bit harder.'

A PIG FOR THE HOUSE

'Up till the Second World War, most farms and many farm workers at Preston-on-Wye kept at least one pig for the house. This was fed on all the scraps from the house and garden, supplemented by meal.

When pig killing day came, always in the cold, winter months, the village pig killer would come down at eight o'clock in the morning and the pig would be led squealing to the place of slaughter. I hated this to be a Saturday because I liked to go to school out of sight, sound and smell. After killing, a fire of straw was lit round the carcase to singe off the bristles, and then the pig was cleaned inside and out and hung up by the snout from a strong beam overnight. I would come home to find this clean, pink thing hanging in the back-kitchen.

Next day, the pig killer came back to cut up the carcass into two flitches, two hams, head, bath chaps, trotters and chines. The flitches, hams and chines were dry cured with salt and saltpetre on a salting stone – a large table of stone with a groove round the outside to drain off any liquid. The bacon was much fatter then, but the fat was lovely and different and tasted so good, as did the hams; there is nothing like it now.

Odd bits and pieces were made into sausages, pork pies, faggots, black puddings and the fat rendered down for lard to last the whole year. There were scratchings, brawn, pigs fry, liver and kidneys, and best of all, pigmeat, the spare ribs with white meat attached.

The hams and flitches eventually hung from the kitchen ceiling in linen bags or on racks, the so-called farmhouse pictures.

There were no freezers in those days so some of the fresh meat was given to neighbours, who returned a piece when they in turn killed their pig.'

'Mr Bevan, a pig killer, lived in Madley. He was a big, stout man with a high-wheeled gig and a little pony. On the day he was sent for, a bench was set up; he cut the pig's throat and there was much blood and squealing. As a special treat a child might be allowed to hold the pig's tail. Then straw was lit and the bristles were burnt and scrubbed off. The farm kept its own lard, of course, and then there were the lovely scratchings. Brains in batter was a treat to look forward to.'

'In the winter two pigs were fattened to enormous size for killing. Our pig killer in the 1920s was Charlie Morgan who had once been the estate stonemason on the Snead-Cox estate and had lived in a small black and white cottage near our farm at Broxwood, but who now lived at the Post House at Moorcroft. As children we always watched the bloody slaughter when the poor pigs were dragged resentfully to the pig bench with much squealing.

At cutting up time we were always given the pigs' bladders which, when dried and inflated, made good footballs. Then we were sent round the village to deliver joints of meat to our neighbours who returned the compliment when they killed their pigs. This was a sensible arrangement as the meat could not be kept long without fridges and freezers.

Then we helped Mother to cut up the fat into cubes for her to melt down in a large jam kettle over the fire. The melted fat was strained and put into large earthenware vessels called steans where it cooled and set. Thereafter it was called lard. The two pigs provided enough lard for cooking purposes until the next pig-killing time. The crunchy bits that were left after the cubes had melted down were called scratchings and were very popular to eat sprinkled with salt.

Pig killing was a busy time, what with pork pies, faggots and brawn to be made, and I recall that Father always had the pigs' brains for his breakfast.'

SHOPPING AND CALLERS
TO THE DOOR

Going to market, or to the nearest town for shopping, was quite an occasion when travel was still a difficult business and depended on real horse power or Shanks's pony. The village shop was a lifeline, and most traders delivered to the door on a regular basis – the delivery men were almost part of the family! There were other callers to the door too, less regular but still welcome.

GOING TO MARKET

'Twice a week, Wednesday and Saturday, was market and shopping day. At nine o'clock in the morning the local carrier left Weobley, driving a long two-horse open waggon with ten seats each side, taking fowl, ducks (both dressed and alive), eggs, butter and other home-made goods to be sold. Several people had a stall in the open market and the money made was a bit on the man's wages. We returned from market about four o'clock. The fare was two shillings return for a ten mile ride to Hereford. A friendly chat with friends and relatives who travelled the same way to town made our day.'

'Hicks' van used to take us into Ross from Linton in the 1930s, three or four people sitting each side at the back and all the chickens and things. In those days we used to take surplus flowers and vegetables and eggs to a large covered market in Ross. It disappeared before the war. Just outside the Market Hall, going down the hill there were small square pens of poultry – geese, ducks and turkeys.'

'Most marketing from Newton St Margarets was done in Abergavenny, the "Great Market" at Christmas being the highlight of the year. Poultry were dressed and taken there by pony and trap. It was necessary to be there by 4 am.'

THE CARRIER

'Old Townsend lived at The Old Shop with his old horse and waggonette. Twice a week, Wednesdays and Saturdays, he went into Hereford and would take fare-paying passengers and do errands for people. The village of Preston on Wye is nine miles from Hereford and this was the only public transport for the majority of people when there were few cars. He continued into the 1930s after which a carrier from Bredwardine came through the village with his small lorry equipped with seats in the back. This he did on Wednesdays and Saturdays, taking passengers and doing errands, but on Thursday he came to this and other villages collecting rabbits, eggs and other local produce. Then on Fridays he went down to the Welsh Valleys to sell everything.'

THE LOCAL SHOPS

'The red letter day in the week was when Mother went to Kington to do the shopping. Often she would drive the pony and trap herself. Thinking back, there must have been many cold and wet drives for the six miles into town. We had a very large trap umbrella, and a trap rug which was warm plaid on the inside and waterproof outside. A long switchy whip was lodged in a pocket beside the driver – it had a leather-bound end for easy handling. The trap carried the driver and one passenger in front, and two in the back facing outwards.'

'For dry goods and other items not produced on the farms there was one village shop at Madley, run by Mr and Mrs Enoch Christopher. You opened the gate and walked up a cobbled path. Children were not keen to do this, as they lived in fear of Mrs Christopher: she wore a crochet shawl and was inclined to shake a finger at children, to whom she seemed very old. The shop was crowded and mysterious, with flagged floor and rag mats. On the scrubbed wooden counter stood the wooden till with a drawer that went "ping". Whatever else might be in short supply, Mrs Christopher always had plenty of plum jam. If you went in for damsons or potatoes you would as like as not be handed a container and told to go out in the back garden and pick what you wanted for yourself.

In this shop Mrs Christopher also ran the telephone exchange, a wooden structure with plugs and wires, and the village believed she must "know everybody's business". Her husband ran the village taxi, and at a time when no one else had a car, he was thought to be well informed too!'

'For clothes and larger items, people from Colwall shopped in Ledbury or Malvern. Market day in Ledbury was Tuesday. The village had quite a good selection of food shops, and people living on the hill shopped for groceries at Grundy's at the

Wyche Cutting. Bread was baked daily at the shop and delivered in a horse-drawn van. Everything from snuff to duck eggs was sold there. One lady brought a cup with her every Tuesday when she made her order. She sat in the shop chair, broke a duck egg into the cup and swallowed it. Another woman came from Worcester to buy snuff (weighed on the accurate beam scale) and immediately took a pinch and sniffed. Tea and coffee were also weighed on the beam scale. Once a birthday cake for a cat was requested, inscribed "Congratulations to HRH Prince Solly on his birthday".

The enterprising shopkeeper once decided to offer teas for daytrippers. Tables were laid in the front room and a sign displayed outside, "Teas for sale". After getting no response from walkers on the hills on a lovely day, the sign was being removed when it was noticed that the wind had turned the board round and it read "House for sale".'

'On Saturdays I would go to Ross with Mother to do our shopping. We walked to Kerne Bridge station with the baby in the pram to catch the ten o'clock train. The pram was left at the station, and when we arrived at Ross, Mother would carry the baby and I the shopping that could not be left for the shop boys to bring to the station. They would walk the platform calling your name, and they collected a few pennies too.

On our return to Kerne Bridge, our parcels were taken out of the train onto the platform, and our pram was then loaded with baby and goods for the three miles walk home. My brother would be waiting to carry things up to the back of the house.'

THE VILLAGE BUTCHER

'Our business started with a small shop, a bicycle and a horse and cart in 1925.

On Monday, animals were purchased either from the market or local farms. If cattle were bought in Leominster market, they were walked home (about five miles). Sheep and pigs were carried in the cart. These animals were killed and hung in the slaughterhouse, which was across the farmyard and behind the shop.

On Tuesday, a bicycle ride was taken to obtain orders for midweek and weekend delivery.

The joints of meat were delivered on the bicycle, which had a basket carrier on the front. The large basket was covered with a white linen tea towel.

Fridays and Saturdays were busy days when joints were cut and delivered. Any meat left over on Saturday evening was given to less fortunate families, as there was no refrigerator.

The business gradually progressed until in the late 1930s there were four men, two vans and two bicycles, and meat was delivered to many villages over a wide area.'

THE VILLAGE POST OFFICE

'In the early 1900s post for Bodenham was collected from Dinmore station and taken to the post office which was near the school. It was kept by Mr and Mrs Harford. From here mail was delivered to the Moor, Pool Head and Maund Common and the postman would cover up to 16 miles a day, either walking or cycling. In 1955 the two postmen were presented each with a silver watch and chain in recognition of their long service. About this time, motorised transport took over.'

'The Foy postman would cycle from Ross, deliver and collect post, then return to Ross. He then came back to Foy where he would stay in the postman's hut, which was situated in a field opposite Carthage Farm, until the next collection at four o'clock when he cycled back to Ross. Later motorcycles and sidecars were used.'

'The postmen were all well received, especially in the outlying areas around Dorstone. They were a link between neighbours, bringing news of any births, marriages or deaths. At Christmas it took nearly all day by foot and/or bicycle to get the mail round. One particular year it was six o'clock when Postie made his wobbly way to the last farm, but he was not too drunk to chase the two daughters round the table with a piece of mistletoe. However, that was his last fling. By the farm stood a rick of fern, gathered in the summer for use as winter bedding, and under this the postman collapsed and slept the night.'

'I remember the very early telephones, on a tall stand, and how you had to place all calls through the operator, who was often the village postmistress and consequently the best informed person in the village! These phones were superseded by standard black ones, which seem to have been standard issue until after the war when white and coloured sets started creeping in.

Pembridge's old postmaster used to say that a letter to Manchester, posted early in the morning, would catch the 7 am train from Pembridge station. If the recipient was quick off the mark, the writer might well receive a reply the same day.'

'We had no telephones at Hampton Bishop, but we managed by riding to Mordiford and sending a telegram from the post office there. If we received one, the Mordiford postmaster biked here waving the orange envelope and shouting, "Nothing to worry about!", especially during the war.'

MAKING DELIVERIES

'At Orleton very few people had their own cars but tradespeople called regularly. The postman on a bike delivered letters in the morning and collected mail in the late afternoon. He would affix stamps on envelopes if the money was dropped into the box. He also took shoes for repair and returned them later.

The baker delivered by horse and trap at first, then later in a van. Mr George Millichip, a local grocery store owner and great champion of the village, delivered weekly. Gaius Smith of Ludlow came monthly, to take an order one week and deliver the next. Papers were delivered daily. Customers fetched milk in their cans from farmers or it was brought round in a milk bucket and measured with a pint measure into the customers' jugs. Poultry, rabbits, eggs

and fruit were collected weekly from farmers by Peacheys of Ludlow. An oil man came in a car and Goldings in a van selling the usual household requirements. A fishmonger also travelled round.

Ned Gazy came at regular intervals selling clothes from a suitcase. We also had visits from a long-nailed mole catcher, tramps wanting a crust or warm clothing, and gipsies with their baskets containing elastic, ribbons, hair clips, buttons and pegs. If we purchased from the latter we received a "blessing". Jack and Jim Lock, the gipsies who lived in a caravan near our home, played their fiddles for a drink of cider every Sunday morning.'

Mr Pound, baker, delivering bread to Mrs Allen at Kingsland in 1936. Before the war, tradesmen called regularly at most homes.

'Everything was delivered in those days and everyone who came to the house for whatever reason had a cup of tea and a slice of cake. Our butcher delivered the Sunday joint on Saturday afternoon for many years. The meat was unwrapped; each joint was labelled with name and price. The roundsman picked up your joint from the wooden rack in the van, put it into the basket that had held raw meat all day, opened your gate, brought it in and placed it on the waiting plate. The environmental health people would have a field day if they saw such a thing happening today, but we thought nothing of it and certainly took no harm from it.'

'The post office at Titley was also a local shop where most goods could be obtained – this included five toffees for a penny, or liquorice pipes and bootlaces! Bread, meat and groceries were delivered by horse-drawn vans from Kington, the order man on his bicycle from one grocery store coming every two weeks and the other the following two weeks. Some kind order men brought a few free sweets – usually liquorice allsorts – for the children of the household. One bus came from Presteigne to Kington on market day and trains which took you out into the big wide world ran from Titley Junction and had to be caught by walking two and a half to three miles or hiring the pony and trap from the post office.'

'We had a shop in the village at Stoke Lacy which had a notice: "Please do not ask for Trust, as refusals often offend." For a long time I thought Trust was a tobacco, like Biggs.

There was a baker's cart delivery twice a week and if you were lucky you could hold on going up the hill. The butcher had a speedy horse and a high trap. He used to drag the whip along the spokes to make the horse go faster. You gave next week's order as you accepted this week's joint. Groceries and poultry food came once a fortnight from Bromyard.'

'One of the grocery stores in Hay on Wye had an arrangement that on delivery of your weekly goods, a blank postcard was given to you to write down next week's order. No one could have extra provisions, or visitors requiring more than the usual amount, without the whole village knowing.'

A FEW PRICES

'How our money has changed this century! I can remember the huge, crisp white £5 notes with the printing in black (though I seldom saw one and certainly never possessed one!). I don't remember guinea coins, or even sovereigns, but the guinea was in common usage for pricing. It was equal to 21 shillings.

We counted our money in pounds, shillings and pence – lsd. Green pound notes, orange ten shilling notes, half crowns (two shillings and sixpence), and florins (two shillings). We had shillings, sixpences (tanners), and silver threepenny bits known as joeys; these were later replaced by heavy alloy coins with a picture of the thrift flower. Our copper coins consisted of pennies, halfpennies and farthings. It was even possible to *buy* things for a farthing.

I remember my aunt smoking Craven A cigarettes during the 1930s, at ten for sixpence or 20 for a shilling.'

'A grocery order dated 1954 from the village shop at Eardisley included these items:

1 lb butter	4s	3d
1 lb bacon	3s	8d
¼ lb Hornimans tea	1s	6d
Pkt Shredded Wheat	1s	0d
Pkt Cornflakes	1s	4½d
1 lb icing sugar	1s	1d
1 lb jam	1s	4½d
½ lb biscuits	0s	11d
4 bottles Corona	1s	10d
3 lb McDougall's flour	1s	8½d
Pkt Tide	1s	0d
2 small Breeze soap	1s	2d
1 jelly	0s	9d
Large tin pears	2s	9d
½ lb tomatoes	1s	7½d.'

'A list of the ingredients for making lemon curd, comparing prices from 1928 with those of 1955, is interesting:

	1928		1955	
1 lb best farm butter	1s	0d	6s	0d
12 lemons	0s	10d	4s	6d
4 lb sugar	0s	8d	2s	6d
24 eggs	2s	0d	7s	0d
Total	4s	6d	£1 0s	0d

Today the same quantities would cost about £8 50p!'

OTHER CALLERS

'About once a month the pedlar called at Longtown. He came off the train at Pandy and walked with a large basket on his head. He was a tall, big man and used to say, "Cups and saucers, plates and dishes, here is the man with the calico britches!" He also sold small items of clothing and hard brushes, and would say, "Please buy something off me to relieve the load."

'Every two weeks a Mr Richardson travelled from Hereford seven miles by train to deliver fresh fish and bananas. He must have walked about six miles during his round, and carried a large flat basket on his head.'

'Mr George Cook was a well known hawker who lived in Newton St Margarets. Mostly he sold rock salt to the farmers. His wife travelled with him in his pony and cart, buying feathers and rags. Twice yearly they went to the Potteries, buying china to sell.'

CLOTHES AND HANDICRAFTS

Most clothes were made at home, and make do and mend was the order of the day for many families. Rag rugs, home-made, were common as floor covering in those days of cold linoleum or bare wooden floors.

PRACTICAL CRAFTS

'Before the Second World War, handicrafts were practical ones as not many people had money or time to do things for pleasure.

Patchwork quilts were made for use in the home – thick woollen ones for winter and cotton ones for summer. They were made of scraps left over from dressmaking or work clothes, with the best bits cut out and washed and then cut into squares or oblongs. They were sewn together with the sewing machine to form a pattern in the centre, with the rest of it just how the pieces fitted. It was lined with a blanket or a cotton sheet, whichever sort was on the making, and quilted by hand. It was quite a long process with many weeks of work to complete it, but well worth the time.

The hessian sacks that feeding stuff was bought in were very useful when washed, to make aprons for doing the rough work in the house. They were also used for the backing for making rag mats. The pieces left over from making quilts were cut in lengths of about five inches long and one and a half inches wide and pushed through the hessian with a home-made wooden peg. Sometimes a pattern was formed, but usually they were pushed through as they came. When finished it was lined with hessian and quilted. They made very warm and useful rugs.

Dressmaking and patching were an essential part of life during these years. Very few country dwellers bought ready made clothes. The sewing machine was always in use. My mother made most all our clothes, even our overcoats and my brothers' trousers out of old ones. The collars of the shirts were turned when worn thin.

Sheets were turned sides to the centre, to give extra wear.

The men's socks in the families were hand knitted with a thick wool and done very long to reach up to their knees.'

FASHIONS DIDN'T CHANGE SO MUCH

'Fashions didn't change so much in those days. Fur coats were "in", and tweed coats, and men's suits with plus-four trousers; some men used to wear britches and leggings, or moleskin trousers, or corduroy ones. Denim clothes were working clothes in those days, and cheaper than today. Little boys' trousers were worn to calf length, and girls wore three-quarter length skirts. Hats were always worn in church, and you weren't a lady if you didn't wear gloves! Lace collars were used a lot in those days.

We were a bit late following the fashions in the country. My mother was from the town and I was about the first in Hampton Bishop to have a sleeveless frock – which I hated! The dress materials then (apart from cotton) were voile, Macclesfield silk, shantung, georgette, serge and of course tweed.'

'As the youngest daughter, I nearly always had my sister's outgrown clothes (and they were often from older relatives), so fashion passed me by. It has ever since!

At primary school we usually wore jumpers knitted by an aunt – my mother did not knit, and we often had knitted skirts to match attached to a bodice. They must have been most difficult to wash as wool tended to shrink and matt in those days. My mother very occasionally made me a summer dress out of a remnant bought from the local market, costing two or three shillings. I remember one especially, when I was about seven or eight, made from green cotton with white spots – I was IT!

My father used to wear shirts with detachable collars – we were always searching for the studs. The boys wore jerseys with knee length shorts until they were 13 or 14.'

'We didn't have many clothes, one on and one in the wash, one for best and one pair of shoes at a time. A pair of wellingtons was handed down as a rule and slippers were knitted, the soles being made out of cardboard and replaced as they wore out. Mum made most of our clothes from others she bought at jumble sales.'

'Before her marriage, my mother was apprenticed as a tailoress. The thing that fascinated me was that after making a skirt, costume or overcoat, it was brought back a few years later when it was showing signs of wear, for the garment to be turned so that the worn side of the material was on the inside, to enable it to last a few more years.'

FROM BIRTH TO DEATH

We were much more likely in the past to be born, to suffer our illnesses and to die in our own homes. Calling the doctor in was for emergencies only, and most families relied on tried and trusted home remedies, passed down from generation to generation – though some of them sound worse than the ailment they were meant to ease! The District Nurse was a well respected figure in the community, always ready to call in for help or advice.

NO FORMAL TRAINING

'My father's mother was the midwife at Ruardean. She had no formal training. Doors were never locked, and people would walk in and shout from the foot of the stairs that the midwife was needed.

Babies were bound and we went to watch the babies being washed. Linen bandages were sterilised by being held in front of the fire until they scorched.'

'Villagers at Holmer seemed to have superstitions handed down. My mother considered it bad luck to enter anyone's house after having a baby before being "churched". Cutting a small baby's nails would make them grow up to be "light fingered".'

HOME REMEDIES

'At six years old I was very ill with whooping cough. The doctor said the illness would have to take its course but my mother, fearing I would choke, resorted to an old remedy, just an old wives' tale. She gave me mare's milk. I recovered, but for a long while wondered what effect it would have on me. I knew that young colts were very strong. It was a vain hope.'

'At Orleton several men came from Ludlow annually to pick foxglove leaves to be used by herbalists. Herbs were used as cures for all kinds of ailments. Mother bought herbs to make cough mixture.

Rock sulphur was burnt in rooms to kill germs after illness. Thick black cobwebs were used to stem the flow of blood when a finger end was chopped off.'

'At Fownhope, mouse pie was used as a cure for bed wetting. For swollen glands in the neck, take the patient to a dead body, place the dead hands on the glands and the disease would be transmitted to the dead body (there is no alternative treatment should a body be unavailable!).

Other remedies included goose grease for croup; hot blackcurrant juice for a cold on the chest; a long black stocking filled with hot salt and wrapped round the face for toothache; a hot onion in the ear for earache; a pillow case filled with hops for insomnia; boiled worms as a cure for styes. To cure chilblains, rub them with snow or beat them with holly.'

'In my grandfather's time at Hampton Bishop, calves lungs were used to poultice chests for pneumonia. A raw onion eaten just before going to bed was good for a cold, with camphorated oil rubbed on the chest and Vick put up the nose to help one breathe. For an upset stomach, equal quantities of port wine and brandy, about three tablespoonfuls each; also parsley tea.'

'A cough mixture recommended in the Leominster Cookery Book of 1915 is as follows:

> 2 pennyworth of oil of aniseed
> 2 pennyworth of oil of peppermint
> 2 pennyworth of paregoric
> 1 pennyworth of liquorice
> ½ lb golden syrup
> 1 pint of boiling water.

A 1920s recipe book of the area recommends a Quick Cure for Earache. Take a small piece of cotton wool, make a depression in the centre and fill it with as much ground pepper as will stand on a threepenny piece. Then gather it into a ball and tie up. Dip the ball into sweet oil and insert it into the ear, covering with cotton wool.'

'Home cures for colds were dried elder flowers made into tea taken on going to bed, and blackcurrant jam made into a drink. Children were given cod liver oil and malt each morning for good teeth, eyes and bones, and flowers of sulphur for keeping bowels in order. In Hereford there was a dispensary run by local doctors where you could pay threepence a month to get treatment and medicine for each child when ill.'

'At Aston Ingham, cuts were treated by laying part of a cow pat on them. Poultices were commonly made from either comfrey leaves or arum lily leaves. Our mothers would gather all sorts of hedgerow plants with which to make herbal remedies. There was also a secret recipe from the Forest of Dean which was known as "Blue-it" or "Blewitt", which was a marvellous cure-all for both humans and animals.'

'As a result of living in damp and badly ventilated cottages, chesty colds in the winter prevailed. At the very first sign of a cough, out came the thermogene wadding. This piece of monstrosity, with a very pungent smell, was pinned to the inside of your flannel vest, back and front, and must never be left off until it dropped off.

Festering abrasions and suchlike were given the poultice treatment, both linseed and bread, piping hot and slapped onto the afflicted sore spot (usually to the accompaniment of the agonised screams of the sufferer!). A whitlow would have a lily of the valley leaf wrapped round the finger, and as chilblains were rife, out would come the Snowfire. A more drastic remedy – put your foot into the chamber pot first thing in the morning!'

'At Weobley in the 1930s people still used old remedies. One was using stinging nettles as a relief for neuritis. They had to be picked before they flowered and applied directly to the painful area. The lady I worked for used them for her back and said they were the only way she could get relief.'

ILLNESS AND OPERATIONS

'My father had the middle finger of his left hand hurt under a waggon wheel – in time a tumour formed on it. At this time his parents had a pony and trap for hire which he drove. Dr Avery Jones of Fownhope hired him to go to Hereford to bring out Dr Turner, who was to operate on the finger. On the way out Dr Turner said to my father, "I'm going to take some poor chap's finger off." "Yes," my father replied, "and I'm the poor chap." The finger was taken off at the second knuckle and for years stood in a jar of spirits in Dr Jones's surgery.'

'I remember having my tonsils out in the 1930s. They promised me that I was going to blow up a balloon, and I was really looking forward to it. When I found that what they meant was the rubber mask over my face, I was furious – my first experience of duplicity! I got pneumonia a few days later, after returning to my aunt's house, and was nursed there. This was long before the days of antibiotics and penicillin – I had poultices of boiling hot antiphlogistine slapped on my back and chest, held on and kept warm with a sort of jacket made from something like lint and cotton wool. I had a day nurse and a night nurse. The day nurse, Miss Brown, was kind, but I hated the night nurse with a passion that I don't think has ever been equalled.'

'Some of my happiest childhood memories appear to be when I was ill. Not any serious illnesses but just the usual measles and chickenpox variety. The thrill of a coal fire being lighted in the bedroom fireplace and the wonderful feeling of warmth upstairs for once. And lying back and watching the shadows on the ceiling and imagining all sorts of things. And those trays of grapes wrapped in coloured tissue paper and the jars of calves-foot jelly on the bedside table, which were all for me. I think the jelly was bought from the butcher's shop but I don't recall seeing any since the war. And I can still feel that lovely glowing warmth generated by the wodges of pink thermogene which were invariably slapped across my chest and joy of joys, the gorgeous smell of Friars Balsam as I sat inhaling it with a towel over my head whilst balancing a bowl of steaming liquid on my knee. Bread poultice – which smelt horrible – and those vile tonics when convalescing were not much fun but I quite enjoyed the iron tonics which were sucked through a glass straw in a vain attempt to protect our teeth.

Last but not least, my family of paper dolls which was added to every time I was ill by a kind aunt and which kept me busy for hours on end, dressing and undressing them and which I treasured always. No expensive toys in those days, just a simple drawing on a bit of cartridge paper, with clothes that fitted with tabs that wore out and the clothes fell off.'

THE DISTRICT NURSE

'When I had finished my general nurse, midwifery and district nurse training and gained some experience in all these fields, I wanted to gain my District Visitor's certificate. At that time Herefordshire County Council were offering sponsorship to do this training and I applied for one of these and was accepted. I had to promise to work as a District Nurse Midwife/Health Visitor in any part of the County of Hereford for two years after I had completed the training – I took this training at the Royal College of Nursing in London. In July 1945 I had completed my training and was ready for work in Herefordshire.

I travelled to Hereford by train on a July day having no idea of my destination. I was taken by car to a remote part of the county on the Welsh border and told roughly how far my area would extend. I had three widely separated villages and rural farms and cottages, part of my district extending to the lower slopes of the Black Mountains. I lived for a month in a pleasant farmhouse and during this time got to know something of the lie of the land. I had a 13 year old car which was not very reliable but generally got me there. Whilst I was staying at this farm I got to know the family quite well and one day the farmer came to me whilst I was having my lunch and asked me to have a look at a cow that was calving. I knew nothing about cows but was willing to go and see, and with the use of a rope and a lot of pulling I managed to deliver a calf. To the farmer I had proved myself a good midwife before I delivered a baby.

At the end of the month I moved to another small farm about a mile away. My landlady here was a retired nurse and made me very welcome and we became good friends. The house was pleasant but had no electricity or gas, and hot water only in the kitchen; there was no bathroom and no indoor WC. My bedroom had a four-poster bed which was very comfortable. The only thing I lacked was a telephone and an application for one was made immediately. This was at first refused so an appeal was made to the local MP. It was refused a second time and finally another appeal was made to Dr Charles Hill, the Postmaster General and it was then agreed that I should have the phone. Then the fun started. The nearest telephone was more than a mile away and it took 40 poles and nine months to install my telephone. Every time I drove up the road it was to see another pole hoisted into a hole. As my area was very scattered and public telephones very few and far between, in many cases it was still easier for families to contact me on foot, by bicycle, or to saddle a horse. Even if they could get to a phone few people knew how to use one – if I was wanted by night they came to the house and threw up a handful of gravel to my bedroom window and that method worked as it always had done before.

Work in the area was plentiful and varied – all babies were born at home and most were straightforward deliveries and I got a great deal of pleasure from this work. There was the usual amount of chronic sick nursing and I had three schools in my area. Health visiting took up a great deal of my time, this included tuberculosis visiting, a disease very prevalent at that time.

The winter of 1947 was one that I shall never forget; the snow came during January and it was still there at the end of March. It was impossible to get my car on the road due to the depth of snow. One patient was due to have her baby at this time and the only way to take care of her was to move my place of abode until conditions improved. Transport consisted of a trailor behind a tractor and I stayed in a neighbouring cottage until the mother was delivered.

The contract of two years soon passed but I stayed on in Herefordshire for another year on relief duties. The climax of my stay in Herefordshire was delivering twins at Christmas 1947. I did not see this patient until she was actually in labour but fortunately for us both everything proceeded normally and a healthy girl and boy were born. The twins were a complete surprise to both parents.'

'Up to the 1940s there was always a resident doctor in Bodenham, making his rounds first by horse and trap and then by car. After that for a time people had to go to Hereford or Leominster if they needed a doctor. A dentist would call once a week.

In 1918 Bodenham got its first certified midwife, and in 1925 a large meeting took place in order to find out whether people were willing to support a Nursing Scheme to be run by subscription. The next year Nurse Speir started her duties. Charges for the nurse varied: widows and single men paid two shillings, labourers' families four shillings, farmers ten shillings to £1. Maternity charges varied from £1 to £1 10s 0d. Non subscribers paid double. This scheme lasted until 1948 and the coming of the National Health Service.'

'A Nursing Association was formed at Clifford before the last war. Miss N Edwards (schoolmistress at Whitney on Wye) was Secretary, Miss Sharples was Treasurer, Captain Hope of Whitney Court was Chairman and a Miss Wilkinson was employed as a District Nurse.

Mr Edwards of Wyeside went to Clifford station to collect the monthly baby foods and tablets for pregnant mothers, in a wheelbarrow, and then they were distributed by the District Nurse. As soon as funds allowed, a car was purchased for her.

A family clinic was started at Whitney school in 1959. The mothers and children arrived on the first day, Clifford all sitting one side and Whitney arranged on the other side – and neither side spoke. Several mothers have cause to remember Sister Tracy, District Nurse, a very large lady, reputed to have worn size 14 shoes!'

'The winter of 1940 is remembered in Bishops Frome for its icy conditions. There was freezing rain for three days. People sitting in The Major's Arms at the time, on one of the steep hills called Snails Bank, remember how they could hear trees falling one after another as the ice built up. The only way they could use the road was on all fours with socks over their boots. It was a difficult time for the District Nurse. Called to a confinement on the other side of the village, the daughter of the house accompanied her, walking on top of the snow.

But the deepest snow came in 1947 when the village was completely cut off for several days till they managed to dig a way through for a tractor to get supplies from Bromyard. It was in this snowstorm that the nurse's car was buried and quite lost for a time.

Marion Daniel had arrived in the village in 1935 as a 22 year old nurse. She was put up at the Firlands for a month while she looked for other accommodation – but in the end she did not bother to look and stayed with the family through her 42 years nursing service and with the daughter of the house during her retirement until her death. Affectionately known as Danny, she has been one of the best known and best loved characters of the village.'

THE WORKHOUSE

'Every town had a workhouse, so that they were about eight to ten miles apart, a day's walk for tramps. It was a building with accommodation for aged men and women and some unmarried mothers, with a hospital section. There was a master in charge, a nurse, a porter and the master's wife. People were recommended there by the local doctor or Relieving Officer – mainly the aged and infirm or those not suitable for mental institutions. The men tended the garden of two to three acres, dug by hand and planted with vegetables. A bell rang to start work, again for dinner at one o'clock, to start work again at two, and lastly at five o'clock to stop, six days a week.

Tramps walked from one workhouse to another. They were frisked by the porter, and if they had ninepence they were sent to the common lodging house. Some were wise to this and put their money in a marked place in a stone wall. The men were bathed and their chiropody done by the porter. When they arrived they were given a pint of tea, two large slices of bread and cheese. They were put in a cubicle with a slung hammock. After breakfast, two cwt of blockstone had to be broken to pass through a two inch grid, for use in road mending, to "pay" for their keep.'

'When I was eight or nine, I saw an elderly man come down the lane at Bishopswood and wait. Mother called him in for a cup of tea. He was waiting to be taken to the Union Poor Law Institute as he had no family to care for him. He was crying.

My aunt and uncle were in charge of a workhouse. The men were in cubicles and had to chop wood until they had chopped a shillingsworth. They could then stay for the night. There were also some young women who had had babies out of wedlock, and who were permanent residents.'

'It was from Weobley we used to have an annual visitor, a "gentleman of the road" named Morris! He spent the winters in the workhouse, where he had warmth and food, but come the spring he would take to the open road, spending a few days or weeks at various farms in the neighbourhood, including ours at Tillington.

He was as welcome as the cuckoo, telling us that spring was here. On the first warm days with longer evenings, my mother would remark, "It's been a nice warm day. I expect we will soon be seeing Morris again." Sure enough he would arrive, coming down through the fold and up to the back door. He usually went to a farm at Norton Canon first, before coming to us, to do such seasonal jobs as mangold hoeing or potato planting. Others like him did hop tying in the Ledbury area.

He slept in the warm hay in the French barn and had his meals of good wholesome farmhouse fare, sitting in the sunshine on the oak pig-killing bench which stood against the back-kitchen south-facing wall. A large mug of tea completed his meal.

We heard vague stories of his youth spent in the army in India and he spoke a little Hindustani. My mother, always kind to the under-dog, would buy Morris a new pair of boots or perhaps a nearly new tweed jacket, but after being with us for a week or two the open road beckoned and he went to visit and help my aunts who had a dairy farm at Tupsley. He set off down the hill and we would not see him for another year.

One year he did not come; I have no idea what happened to him or where his final resting place is, but I well remember him, this "gentleman of the road", with happy blue eyes, a healthy complexion and a love of the open countryside, who appeared with the cuckoo, not from South Africa, but just over the hill from the workhouse in Weobley.'

GETTING MARRIED

'After a wedding at Dorstone in 1906 the church bells rang at frequent intervals and salutes were fired on the anvil. This "firing of the anvil" involved packing a hole in its base with gunpowder and setting it off with a fuse – a village version of the 15 gun salute. Apparently there was some competition to make the anvil jump. It sounds a highly dangerous affair but there are no reports of casualties. It was also a custom in the village to place fog warning crackers on the railway lines to be fired off by the train taking couples on honeymoon.'

'At Holmer it was customary for a rope to be put across the road so that the newlyweds' car could be stopped as they left church. This was called "roping", and the groom would throw money to the rope holders so that they would release it and the car would proceed. Everyone in the village attended a wedding.'

'Before the Second World War not many brides wore white, just "Sunday best". Blue was considered lucky – "Married in blue, you'll always be true". However, "Married in black, you'll wish yourself back", and "Married in green, ashamed to be seen"!

During the war white became fashionable, but wedding receptions were a small affair because of rationing, and also the bridegrooms often had only a few days leave from the services. The cake was often fruitless, and lacking in icing.'

'If local gentry were married in Hampton Bishop church, a red carpet

107

was put down from the church to the gate, and the church was smartly decorated.'

FUNERALS

'Funerals in the 1930s were very sombre and dignified – most people died in their own homes, not in a hospital, and they were taken from their home for burial. In the 1930s a hearse was used, before that a horse and wagon would take the coffin to the church; if near, the bearers would carry it.

Four bearers, or six, would be asked, usually friends or relatives. They would be at the house in plenty of time to help. Sometimes, a service would be held at the home before they started out.

The family mourners and bearers would be dressed in deep black, the men wearing black bowler hats and the ladies hats with a veil. They would be in deep mourning for three months and then reduce it for another three months.

Most people walked to the service – a representative from most of the homes in the parish was in attendance. The curtains would be drawn at the windows of the homes on the route of the funeral procession, as a mark of respect. The flowers were usually sheaves of lilies from the family.

On arrival at the church gate, the bearers carried the coffin shoulder high to the church door. It would then be placed on the wooden funeral bier and, led by the rector and choir, would proceed up the aisle to the altar, followed by all the mourners and the service would begin. At the graveside, the sexton scattered the soil on the coffin.

After the service, all the family went back to the house for a high tea of home produced ham, bread and cheese, pickles, apple tarts and farmhouse cake, washed down with home-made cider and cups of tea.'

'At funerals at Aston Ingham it was the custom to always walk to the church, carrying the coffin all the way. There were two-day funerals sometimes because of the distance to be walked. There were no funeral parlours and the body was kept at home, generally in the parlour.

One villager remembers the funeral in which a leg only was buried after it had been amputated. The disposal of it had caused some concern and burial seemed the best solution. The amputation had been carried out on the farmhouse kitchen table.'

'I can remember seeing a funeral when the coffin was pushed on a wooden bier which still stands in St Weonards church. It travelled up a cobbled lane, then two and a half miles on the main road and part of the way up a steep hill to the church.'

'Before the Second World War, coffins at Shobdon were carried on a hand-pulled bier the half mile from the church to the cemetery down Bury Lane. As mourners often got wet, it was decided to raise the money to build a small chapel of rest at the cemetery. The stone for this came from Nash Court. To raise the necessary £500 to erect the chapel, the women of the village used to hold whist drives every week in their homes for one shilling entry fee. Before the total could be raised, however, war broke out. The stone was used to build the convent at Presteigne after the war, as the advance of the motor car had led to the use of motorised hearses and removed the need for a chapel of rest!'

'In the 1950s when my mother-in-law had a severe stroke, she had to stay at home in bed in the living room, where she had collapsed. Here she died a few days later in the small hours. After being laid out by the family she remained in the bed in the living room while the undertaker made her coffin. Fortunately we had a screen to place round the bed, otherwise life had to carry on as usual.'

'I don't ever remember seeing women attending funerals. In a family where there had been a bereavement, the women used to wear black, often for months afterwards, and the men would wear black armbands on their jacket sleeves.'

'I have seen coffins taken by boat up the river Wye; this was customary when a fisherman or boatman died. The church bell was rung on the morning following a death, known as the "passing bell".'

'Most people at Clifford died at home, compared with the majority of hospital deaths today. A typical funeral would begin with the arrival of Mr Humphrey Webb the undertaker, in morning suit and top hat. It was customary to offer a glass of whisky. Next to arrive were the bearers, wearing black ties, bowlers and black gloves. They too were given a tot of whisky as they viewed the open coffin – the last drink with the corpse. After the lid was closed, the body was carried downstairs, where all the family and neighbours were gathered, then began the long journey to church. The bearers carried the coffin from house to house en route, and when the first bearers were fatigued, a second four took over.'

CHILDHOOD &
SCHOOLDAYS

GROWING UP

Whether we grew up in town or country, we seemed to have so much more freedom in the past – freedom to wander with our friends and enjoy talking to people we met. Times might be hard, but we felt secure and we knew so much about the countryside around us.

GROWING UP ON THE FARM

'My father and mother went to live at Court Farm when they married in 1915. They were both local people, my father from Lower Green Farm, Broxwood and my mother from Upper Dewell in Dilwyn parish. They were both from farming families originating in Radnorshire. Court Farm was part of the manor of Broxwood which had been in the hands of the Snead and Cox families for over 300 years.

Our home was a rambling farmhouse with half-timbered east and west wings connected by a stone-built structure. Father had great respect for old buildings and he pointed out the old carpenters' marks on the timbers and told us that clumps of nettles often indicated the site of a former dwelling house.

There was a time when Ethel and I were forbidden to go down the cellar steps, and later when we did venture down we found a huge iron stencil which had been used by Zachariah Watkins, a former occupant of the farm, to mark his hop pockets. It was resting in the old brew-house. We were also to discover trams for the barrels of cider, and in a corner there was a kind of pantry with shelves and a door. Father said it had been the wine cellar.

The west end of the house was always in a fairly dilapidated condition. The dairy was on the ground floor of this part and the large bedroom which was over it was very bad and was used for storing the wool after shearing. The bedroom which adjoined it, and which was over the back kitchen, was our playroom in bad weather.

The very first thing I can recall was being out in the fields with my father and losing my fur hat. I could have been no more than three years old. I remember the hat well. It was pill-box in shape and there was a muff to match. Mother sent us back to look for it, but we failed to find it and it did not turn up till a field of corn was cut the following summer.

When I was a small child in the 1920s Broxwood was very different from what it is today. It had a shop and post office, a Roman Catholic church and school, a Church of England school, a chapel, a village blacksmith, a carpenter and undertaker, a mason, and a public house, the Yew Tree Inn at Gorsty Common.

Alas, all these have gone, The RC school closed in 1920 and the C of E school in 1962. By 1945 all the village tradespeople had ceased to function, and soon the shop and post office closed. With the closing of the C of E school the village lost its communal meeting place for everything was held there, concerts, whist drives, dances, parties and Youth Club.

In the village lived a woman named Liza Miles, at a small black and white cottage near the school. She was the school cleaner and came to us on Mondays to do the washing and on Thursdays to clean the bedrooms. She worked from 9am to 4pm and was paid two shillings per day. My mother had a very high regard for her as she was so honest and trustworthy. Liza's hands were all crinkled, for she went to several houses to do washing. All her teeth had been extracted and

Children pose for the photographer in Pembridge high street in about 1900. The street was the playground for most children before the advent of the motor car. This road is now the busy A44 – and it would certainly not be safe to stand in the road today.

she did not wear dentures. She was a tiny woman with very thin fair hair swept up into a wee top-knot. She regularly scrubbed the school desk tops and wooden floors till they were quite white. Her little house was spotlessly clean. She had a lovely polished dresser and a grandfather clock and a brass warming pan. Every week my sister and I would take her some of mother's home-made butter. What a dear soul old Miley was! Once when my father and mother had gone to a funeral she was left in charge of us and my sister and I took our little brother Richard sliding on the pools. The ice broke and we fell in. It wasn't deep but Miley gave us a good dressing-down, especially as we had little Richard with us. He was the apple of her eye and to think of anything happening to him was the last straw. Her father had worked for my grandfather Richard Thomas at Luntly Court and was very fond of his clay pipe. One day, so my father recalled, my grandfather seeing Miles with a pipe in his mouth said, "Miles, I wish tobacco was a guinea an ounce". "Ay," replied Miles, "and every ounce as big as a haystack."

Miley would spend hours walking the fields picking up dead wood for firing. My father also employed her for stone picking on the meadows. Along she went with her bucket picking them up and piling them into heaps later to be picked up by horse and cart. These stones would have damaged the blades of the mowing machine and were very useful for road-making especially in muddy gateways.

I recall the happy games we played when we were often joined by other children from the village. One of our favourites was hide and seek. There were so many lovely places to hide in like the tallets, the lofts over the cowhouses and stables, and beams for clambering up and the straw in the French barn. Another game we enjoyed was sliding down the straw which was tied in bundles called boltings, for balers weren't around then. I remember how scratched our legs were and how the hot water made them smart on bath-night. Mother would dust them over with Robin starch. Bathing took place in a large tin bath in front of the kitchen fire, followed by the weekly dose of syrup of figs. Ethel always rebelled about it and on one occasion spat it out down her clean nightie. Mother was not pleased. After that Father was called in to hold her nose whilst Mother poured it down.

We all took an active part in the general run of household and farmwork. On Saturday mornings Ethel and I chopped enough morning-wood for the week and cleaned out the henhouses. In the afternoons we collected the eggs which the free range hens laid in all manner of places except the proper nestboxes provided, in the hedges, in the straw, in mangers and tallets etc. Sometimes a hen would "steal" her nest, that is lay in an out of the way place, and if the fox didn't get her would appear later with her new little family of chicks.

We all learned how to milk the cows at an early age and at busy harvest times we would take over, fetching the cows from the fields, chaining them in their stalls, foddering them and doing the milking. In winter there were roots to cut up, the swedes or mangolds were put into the hopper of a root-cutter, we turned the handle and out came long fingers about an inch square. These were mixed with chaff (cut straw) and ground corn, to provide a supplement to the hay-fodder. The swede fingers often found their way to our mouths.

Father always did the corn-grinding in the granary on winter nights, usually Mondays I think. The corn-mill was driven by a large paraffin oil engine. As children we were always fascinated by this engine with its governors and huge fly-wheel tearing round. To start it off Father soaked a small piece of rag in paraffin and set fire to it, but I never did understand how it worked.

The sheaves of corn at harvest time were stacked in the big French barn or in ricks to await the coming of the steam threshing machine during the winter months. Mr Simmonds from Hardwick, with his son, would arrive at about 6am to light the fire in the engine and get steam up. They came in for breakfast at 7.30am and at around 8.30 men would arrive from the neighbouring farms to augment our own labour force. In return our men would be sent along to help the neighbours with their threshing. Our job as children was to rake out the chaff from under the threshing box. Bait time was 10.30am, bread and cheese and cider, 1pm was dinner time, a huge joint of beef and vegetables followed by apple tart, and at 6pm a meat tea. The gentle humming of the threshing box was a familiar winter sound and you could always tell who was threshing by the direction of the wind. Mr Simmonds usually went to the Collier's Farm from our place and it took as many as eight shire horses to haul the engine down Green Lane and along the cart track to the farm. The engine was not designed to propel itself. It is lovely to remember those happy days when we all helped our neighbours and no money ever changed hands.

Spring was a lovely time with the coming of the lambs and the spring flowers. We knew exactly where to go to find them. The wood called Ashbed for bluebells, the Front Meadow for cowslips, Bolton for wild daffodils, Lower Green for sweet white violets, the Church Bank for primroses. What a shame that the great ploughing-up campaign of the last war destroyed the cowslips and the wild daffodils. As I remember my father saying when he had to plough the pasture of our Front Meadow, "It had never been ploughed *time*

115

out of mind". How sad that children will never have the joy of making a cowslip-ball.

On May Day we decorated an old trolley (I think we made it from an old sheep-cratch) with branches of may (hawthorn blossom) and draped ourselves with lace curtains, upholding in our small way an old tradition.

In summer we went up the Church Bank to pick wild strawberries which we took home to eat with cream from the dairy.

Autumn was nutting time. Armed with crooky-sticks to pull down the hazel boughs, we shook the brown nuts to the ground and took them home to store for the winter. We gathered chestnuts in the wood by the Court and walnuts from a tree in Kelley's paddock at Lower Green. We spent many happy hours playing among the leaves when they fell from the trees, especially from the big beech near the Court.

We had one penny on Monday mornings to spend at the village shop. We could get liquorice pipes and liquorice bootlaces, gobstoppers which kept changing colour, and sherbet fountains. To augment our meagre amount of pocket money, my sister and I caught moles in traps. One of our workmen would skin them and nail the skins on a door till they dried, then we posted the dried skins off to Augustus Edwards, the Furriers of the West, who paid us threepence per skin.

In the autumn we picked large baskets of blackberries which we sold to Mr Barrington from Leominster who came to collect our eggs on Thursdays. I think we had one penny a pound.

Spring was also bird nesting time and we were avid collectors of eggs. At one time we had over 50 different kinds which we kept protected by cotton wool in a box. We took only one egg from the nest and piercing two holes in the shell, carefully blew it to remove the contents. I well remember once finding a long-tailed tit's nest; it was quite one of the most wonderful things I've seen, a veritable dome of woven hair and moss and containing twelve of the tiniest white-speckled eggs you can imagine. I also remember going to the old sally (willow) tree at the bottom of the orchard to get an owl's egg, and of finding a yellow-hammer's nest in a gorse bush in the Roughs. This was the name given to the land which lies between Winney Wood and the Ashbed.

Autumn was apple picking time and around November Bob Morgan came with his portable cider mill to make the cider. We children always liked to taste the apple juice as it poured through a spout from the cider press into a tub. It was very sweet and not a bit like the end product. The neat juice was put into hogsheads (50 gallon barrels) and watered down with water fetched from the pond in the stable yard. It was maintained that the water from this source produced much better cider than clean drinking water would. I can't remember quite how many hogsheads of cider we made, but I do know that our cellar was lined with them. The men took cider into the fields with them, and it was also drunk in the house at mid-morning break and in the evenings. Sometimes, to take the chill off it, a red-hot poker was plunged into a jug of cider.

Often when we lay in bed in our room which was over the cellar, voices and laughter would drift up from below where father would be entertaining some of the local worthies to a horn or two of cider. The ones most likely to be there would be Bob Morgan, the local carpenter, undertaker and cider maker, "Dad" Preece, an estate woodman who was also an excellent hand-shearer and always came to help at shearing-time, and Lionel Thomas whose wife was the postmistress.

Tuesday was churning day and we gave a hand turning the handle of the churn, especially at times when the butter took a long time to "come". The cream had been saved in large steans and stirred daily. Mother would often make 30 pounds at a time and much of it was sold to Mr Manley the grocer from Weobley who came delivering the groceries in a high horse-drawn van, the groceries being wrapped in large brown paper parcels tied round with string. Sometimes in hot weather the butter was very soft and unmanageable and it was put in a bucket down the well to firm up before being patted into half pound blocks. Plenty of butter was kept for house consumption and margarine was unheard of.

We all helped at spring-cleaning time. Carpets were hauled out on to the lawn and after a thorough beating were dragged to and fro across the grass to bring up the pile and the colour. The furniture was all polished with home-made polish made with beeswax and turpentine. The beeswax was bought in a large lump which had to be finely shredded with a sharp knife and then allowed to dissolve in the turpentine.

On winter evenings Father sat by the kitchen fire making rabbit wires or snares which consisted of a noose of wire attached to a short pointed hazel stick. These he would set in rabbit runs, visible tracks where the rabbits had made a pathway through constant usage. Next morning he would go the rounds to see if he had been successful. This was in the days before myxamatosis decimated the rabbit population and at a time when they were doing untold damage to crops.

Boxing Day was a big rabbiting day. I remember a man named Ted York from Lower Green was asked on one occasion to bring along his ferrets and we accompanied them to the Roughs, which was a favourite haunt of rabbits. Imagine my horror when I was asked to hold one of the ferrets.

Another winter evening pastime was making paper spills for lighting candles and lamps. These were made with long narrow strips of newspaper tightly rolled into a long thin spiral shape. These were tied into bundles and placed in a spill-holder on the mantelpiece.

The hurricane or storm lanterns used for outside work in winter months had to be kept clean and filled with paraffin. My father cleaned the glass globe with crumpled newspaper after blowing into the glass to produce moisture from his breath. The house paraffin lamps had to be cleaned in a similar way though I remember mother having a kind of cloth mop which she bought off the Kleenezee man who sometimes called.

The hurricane lamps bring to mind another fond memory. Often when my sister and I lay in bed and my father or the workmen were going about their late night chores, the hurricane lamps cast window shapes across the ceiling of our bedroom. Talking about our bedroom window reminds me of the occasions when Father, if he was expecting a cow to calve in the night, would come into our room and stand by the window and listen for the lowing sound which would indicate that it was time for him to dress and attend the confinement. Our window was the nearest point from house to cowhouse.

From time to time the gipsies visited the village and pitched camp in the green lane. Apparently, green lanes were official highways and police had the right to remove gipsies if they caught them in the act of setting up camp. I never remember the police turning the gipsies out of our green lane. The gipsies would stay for several days making clothes pegs from the branches of the hazel and willow trees that grew beside the stream running through the lane. The men would cut and shave the sticks (remove the bark), split them up the middle and bind the tops with thin strips cut from an empty can. The women would then carry them in large baskets to sell to the houses in the village, at the same time begging for "just a bit of bacon for the children". I think they must have been true Romanies for they were always swarthy-skinned with very black hair which the women usually wore in plaits. As children we were rather frightened of them but they were never known to have caused any trouble. The horses they used to haul their caravans and carts were tethered to graze the roadside verges but the farmers, my father included, often suspected that late at night they were turned into the fields to graze there.

Tramps were quite common and I remember one very clearly called

Peg Leg. I think he was quite fond of children because he would sit in the hedge bank and take out his wooden leg to show us.

It must have been very cold in our bedroom which faced north-east. Mother heated bricks in the oven and wrapped them in pieces of old blanket to heat our beds and often on winter mornings the chamberpots under the beds were frozen solid and our face flannels as stiff as boards.

Corn cutting was an exciting time. Word soon went around the village and in the early evening young and old assembled as the field was nearing completion and placed themselves all round the ever-diminishing square of uncut corn. Rabbits in abundance had avoided the binder but were forced eventually to leave their refuge. Then the cry would go up "Stye-eye-eye-eye-eye" and in all directions the rabbits ran, dodging the fallen sheaves of corn, with everyone chasing with sticks and stones. My father would never allow guns in the field and when the last sheaf of corn fell from the binder the dead rabbits were piled in a corner of the field, as many as 60 to 100, and Father shared them out to all who had taken part in the chase. With wages at 30 shillings per week rabbits formed a cheap and valuable asset.

Next day the sheaves were stacked in groups of six to allow wind and sun to dry the grain. Winter oats were first to be cut and the saying was that it had to stand in the stooks for the church bells to ring on three Sundays.

On Sunday mornings we went to the chapel Sunday school, and in the afternoons we walked across the fields to Moorcourt church, negotiating three brooks via stepping-stones on the way.

In the evenings, weather permitting, we all walked round the fields, Father no doubt assessing the progress of the crops and planning the week ahead. Thus we all knew what was going on and learned the rotation of crops. Passing through a swede field Father would pull one up, peel it and sharpen it to a point and give us one each to eat. Many years later he was to do the same for his grandchildren. It never occurred to us that he was using the same knife with which he foot-rotted the sheep.'

GROWING UP IN HEREFORD 1920

'I can't recall events quite as far back as 1924, but I do know that I entered the world, and Hereford specifically, on 16th May of that year, becoming what was commonly known as a "white-faced'un", like one of the famous red and white cattle, born and bred in Herefordshire.

By the time I was five years old, my father had saved enough money to buy our house at Holmer and my earliest recollection is of the holiday we took to celebrate this. Not having a car, we went everywhere on "God's Wonderful Railway", because Dad worked for GWR and we all benefited from fare concessions including four free trips anywhere each year – no wonder my schoolfriends thought we were rich!

Life at 20 Holmer Road must have been much like living at Crewe station – always people coming and going on their way to somewhere else. Our door was always open, indeed it was never locked, even at night. With so many visitors I never knew where I'd be sleeping – in a bed, under a bed, in a chair or in the garden shed . . . I even remember one exciting summer night in a hammock in the garden! With my mother the eldest of twelve and Dad one of seven children, you could say ours was an extended family, and the house was filled with aunts, uncles and countless cousins "passing through" on their way to Scotland, on their way back from Egypt or between duties in India etc. I made an early resolution that when I grew up I'd never give up my bed for anyone again!

Behind the house was Hereford Racecourse, our own adventure playground on non-race days, with the steeplechase jumps and mountains of tanning bark which were later spread where the circuit crossed the main Hereford to Leominster road. On race day itself the horses ran right alongside the garden which would always get trampled as the world and his wife jostled for a better view of the runners. I remember the Three Counties Show held on the course and since the many stands took what seemed like months to build, these too became our climbing frames. I remember trying to follow a gang of boys and like them, climb the clock tower at the entrance. I was bribed with half a Woodbine cigarette to leave them alone: I was six!

Just beyond the strip of racecourse was the elementary school, yet despite being so close I was late every morning, waiting until I heard the bell ring before sprinting the 200 yards, but the cane was all too often waiting for me.

I was eleven when the country celebrated the King and Queen's Silver Jubilee – that is King George V and Queen Mary of course. There was a commemorative photograph at school, and a party. Three years later the Queen came to the city and I saw the great lady for myself from a vantage point in High Town as she visited The Old House. She was dressed from head to toe in pale mauve and carried what seemed to me to be the longest umbrella I had ever seen – in matching mauve of course!

Another excitement was the opening of the brand new Odeon Cinema, complete with electric organ which rose out of the floor

120

at the interval, like magic to us twelve year olds. There was the Kemble Cinema too, with its stylish glass-domed foyer plus shows at the Garrick Theatre. With market day on Wednesday, church socials or dances on Saturdays and of course, church itself on Sundays, the weeks were full and busy. Church played a big part in our family's life. I was in the choir for many years and later taught Sunday school, after first attending training at the Bishop's Palace. We girls always had a new hat for Easter Sunday.

My mother was not strong, crippled with arthritis and with a rheumatic heart, but still found time and energy to visit those unfortunate enough to be in Hereford's workhouse. One of my aunts was nursing sister there when it was run by Mr and Mrs Harding, whose son Gilbert became a household name in the 1950s. I was haunted by the gloomy wards whose windows were too high up to see out of and so many "patients" confined to beds in regulation calico nightgowns. Mother dragged me along behind her while she cheered up old ladies with presents of fruit and pretty hankies. We were all glad to see the workhouse close soon after the county hospital was built on the site.

Hereford's many shops were all so different then. Greenlands' arcade-style frontage made it the classiest shop in the city. Augustus Edwards specialised in fur coats and Gardiners in beautiful hats of every style. The best little dress shops were in Church Street – Madame Mountstephens was there for decades. Wakefield Knights in High Town stocked every item of clothing you could ever need, and my very sensible underwear and lisle stockings came from here! The Tudor Tea Rooms were a favourite meeting place and I will never forget the exciting smells of coffee and spices which wafted out of Marchant's the grocers, where everything was wrapped in individual brown paper packages. I'd often go into town on my bicycle, leave it (without a padlock) outside Greenlands and return home in a friend's car: when I returned the next day it would be just where I'd left it!

It was during this time that I first became acquainted with Withington. Three of my high school friends came from the village: Nancy was the daughter of the village school's headmaster; Dorothy, the daughter of an engineer working at Withington Court; and then there was Hazel whose father was, I think, a coal merchant. Dorothy's home was a real country cottage and I was amazed when she showed me how the table in the kitchen turned into the family's bath!

In those days the annual Withington Show was an event which drew crowds from across the county, and beyond. Apart from the awesome displays of vegetables, fruit and flowers lovingly grown in cottage gardens, there were sports and entertainments of every description. I remember "Cole the Runner", an athlete who raced a bicycle. He cut a strange figure which quite frightened us children. He dressed from head to foot in black, including a black skullcap beneath which his long hair streamed behind him as he raced around the circuit.

I was 16 when war was declared and I came to know Withington better. With the farmhands called to the forces or munitions factories, it was a question of "all hands on deck" for that autumn's hop picking. School children from all over the county forsook their classrooms for the hop-yards. I suspect we were more of a hindrance than a help, but we had a lot of fun "cribbing" with the boys from the High School – that is throwing each other into the great cribs into which the hops themselves were picked.

At home we were soon invaded by soldiers who were billeted on us. The Hereford Regiment mustered on the racecourse and several officers and NCOs stayed with us, turfing me out of my bed yet again! When the soldiers left for France we had the first of a steady stream of evacuees from London. These young mums and their children were complete strangers to "country" life and hated every minute of their stay, most soon opting to return to their homes, even at the risk of being bombed. In the meantime Hereford became a seething mass of servicemen, both British and American and it's fair to say the female population had the time of their lives! There were dances every night and on Saturdays, big bands like Billy Cotton, Harry Gold, Billy Turner and Joe Loss played at the Shirehall.'

HARD TIMES

'No electricity, no gas, nothing but oil lamps and candles. There were single burner oil lamps for ordinary folk, but if you were better off you could afford the double burner lamp. The oilman came round on Friday, but if there was no cash left from last week's wages you had to carry the bottle or can to town on the Saturday to get oil. I lived with my uncle and aunt, and my uncle earned 9s 6d a week. If he worked extra hours during the hay and harvest time, I think he had 12s 6d for his week's work.

I used to go to town occasionally. It was a four and a half mile walk on stony roads, no tarmac, no footpaths, and I was in hobnail or heavy sprigged boots. No wonder that when our age group grew up their feet were bad. I thank the good Lord that mine are good. The main shops where you could buy boots were Dicks who were in what is now Eign Gate, Briggs, who are still in business, and Cash & Co in High Town. If the boots were too tight, or hurt, they would change them the next week.

When we went to town I always wanted a penny doughnut from Rumsey's, who had a shop near where the Belmont Roundabout is now. Our next stop would be Spurways in Bridge Street for a cup of tea and a penny bun. (My doughnut was more important to me). When my family went to town they sometimes brought back a pennyworth of sweets from Haines in Eign Street.

Sometimes we had a jumble sale in our village. I remember once buying a freak outfit: a cap for a penny and a coat for threepence. Wasn't I a *toff*! I wonder if anybody recognised it when they saw me out?

In spite of all the ups and downs, those were the days! We were happy.'

FREEDOM TO GO WHERE WE LIKED

'Memories of my childhood are of freedom to go where we liked. Our parents did not have to worry about where we were; somebody would send us home if we were late.

After we had completed our chores we would walk miles around Pudleston looking for birds nests and wild flowers. There were always people around to talk to. A visit to the local shop was a must for a pennyworth of humbugs or gobstoppers out of the large glass jars displayed in the window. The shop opened at eight in the morning till ten at night, or later at harvest time as the farmworkers would call for cigarettes or tobacco.

We children enjoyed harvest time. We walked from farm to farm when the binder was cutting the corn to chase the rabbits as they came out of the corn. We never caught any as they were far too fast for us. Sometimes a fox would come out of the corn which would cause quite a noise everywhere with everyone shouting, "Tally ho!"

In winter when the snow was deep on the ground we used to toboggan down the banks on our home-made sledges. It got very slippery at the end of the day with many a tumble and bruised knees.

The winter evenings were spent around a roaring open fire either knitting or sewing. Sometimes we played games such as tiddlywinks or ludo or snakes and ladders. My father was a keen reader so there were always plenty of books to choose from. For a change we would wind up the gramophone and put records on, such as *After the ball was over* or *Two little girls in blue*.

In 1939 when war was declared, my childhood ended.'

SEEN AND NOT HEARD

'We were always taught to be seen and not heard as children, and were put to bed if naughty, which was not often. At school if naughty we had to write 100 lines after school had closed, which meant getting home late and then we were punished again.'

MY TWO GRANNIES

'My two Grannies were very different from each other; one very old-fashioned and the other very modern, but both played a large part in our childhood days.

When we went to Bullinghope school, we had to pass our Granny Davies's smallholding and we were always expected to call in and see her. She would give each of us a spoonful of brimstone and treacle, and made us blow our noses in paper. Every teatime my Grandad would put on an embroidered smock and make his way to get the two cows from the cowshed. Granny would follow, in her long dress, and wearing a hat. Then she would milk the cows, while Grandad held their tails.

Granny used to take my two sisters to Aberystwyth on holiday. They went on a Saturday by coach, and the girls longed to go on the beach on Sunday but they were not allowed to as they had to go to chapel – and the service was all in Welsh!

Granny died when she was 69 years old and was buried next to her eldest son, who had been drowned in the river Wye, aged 16, after bravely rescuing two boys who had got into difficulties. His schoolfriends subscribed to a brass cross as a memorial, which still hangs in Dinedor church. This must have been a great sorrow in her life, but she never lost her faith.

My Granny Bishop was a schoolteacher and took her headmistress's examination after she was married, taking my mother along, when a baby, so that she could breast-feed her during the breaks. She was headmistress at Dinedor, then at Bullinghope, until she retired in 1931. They then went to live in a cottage on Checkley Common and we used to visit her often on our bicycles, going to pick wild daffodils and lily of the valley in Checkley Woods. During the war my friend and I would stay with her in the summer holidays. She would take us hop picking, which we loved. We got very hungry in the fresh air so Granny always took lots of bread and dripping, or jam sandwiches, and apple pies. They all tasted lovely. We used to catch hop-cats (green furry caterpillars) which we kept in matchboxes.

In August 1945 Granny and Grandad celebrated their Golden Wedding. She asked all the village children to a party and we had tea in the orchard. We all queued up for ice cream with our dishes and spoons and we all had second helpings. It was the first ice cream I had ever tasted. We also had lemonade made from crystals which you bought from the grocer. After tea we had races and games, while the grown ups celebrated with Grandad's home-made cider and Granny's parsnip wine. All the children went home with home-made toffee.

Granny was a very industrious lady. She used all her scrap material to make toys and patchwork quilts. We had to collect all the sheeps wool from the hedges for her, which she washed and dried to stuff toys and make rugs. One of my last memories of her was when she was very old. She was putting feathers in her cushions because they had gone a bit flat.

Although she had a hard life and must have been sad at times, as she lost two sons in the war and two other children very young, she was always full of life, and taught us all so much. She and Grandad lived to celebrate their Diamond Wedding.'

THE CLOTHES WE WORE

'Why one, when an infant, was sent to school wearing a starched white pinny with frills over the shoulder and ribbon threaded through the yoke, I'll never know – but that is what I wore on my first day at school. My mother was a great believer in starch and one walked to Sunday school, arms stiffly held out and petticoats creaking. If one's shoes squeaked, that was bliss, because everyone would know you had on new shoes. I remember my sister, when in her late teens, having a "best" outfit consisting of a dress with a very low waist and a skirt ending in handkerchief points which revealed her knees when she walked – how shameless!'

'In the early 1920s wellingtons became the "in thing". I was treated to a pair, long, black and very shiny, and I was so proud of them that I wore them to go to the pictures one Saturday night.'

'We didn't often get the chance of a day by the sea, but I can remember when I was about five and my sister 13, our auntie knitted bathing suits for us. They were of fairly thick wool, like shorts reaching to mid thigh, with a bib top which had knitted straps over the shoulders and crossing behind. They were in two shades of green with an embroidered fish in yellow and orange on the bib piece. I thought they were rather smart, even though they did tend to stretch and sag when they got wet.'

GAMES AND CHORES

We all had our chores to do before or after school, but once they were out of the way we could be out and playing in the fields and woods, or on the streets, which in those days of little traffic were quite safe. The games we played went in seasons and all had their own intricate rules, well known to all the local children.

HELPING OUT

'My brothers worked on the farm – my eldest brother worked with a team of horses. We had no tractors in those days. My other brother looked after the milking, the cows and the sheep.

My sister and I had quite a lot of chores to do on the farm, which included feeding orphan lambs and calves, collecting morning-wood for starting the open fire, feeding the hens and collecting the eggs

Helping with the haymaking was part of growing up on the farm. Everyone, from youngest to oldest, was expected to do their bit.

126

and washing them ready for the dealer who came once a week. We used to pick the moon daisies that grew in the hay fields and the dealer gave us a penny a bunch for them.'

'Sometimes my brother and I would spend hours cutting strips of material from outgrown garments. These our parents would peg onto pieces of hessian to make warm rugs for the hearth.

In summer everyone had to help in the fields. At haymaking time the men would start to mow at 4.30 am, but first the horses had to be fed and watered before being harnessed to the mower. Haymaking and harvesting was a community effort, neighbour helping neighbour. Even children had to do their share after school. My brothers would help to shake up the hay and rake it into "wallies" ready to be loaded on the waggons and taken to the farm. My job was to carry huge baskets of food – bread, cheese, and huge lumps of fruit cake, together with cans of tea and home-made ginger beer – to the workers.'

'I was brought up on a smallholding at Bishopswood. My father was also a miner, so it was work from morning until night. My sister and I delivered milk before and after school, to three of the principal houses in the village – the vicarage, the Grange and Hazelhurst. Milk was delivered in tin cans, which were brought back home to be washed and scalded by our mother ready for the next delivery.'

PLAYTIME IN THE WOODS AND FIELDS

'In the field to the right of our house, Number 7 Firemans Quarters, Rotherwas, Hereford, there was a huge gun turret and soldiers' huts, surrounded by fields with the Hereford to Ross railway line running along behind. As youngsters we used to know the times of the trains. We knew all the drivers and used to stand on the adjoining fences, waving.

We used to spend most of our time, during the summer holidays, playing in the fields; we picked wild flowers and strawberries off the railway embankments, and walked for miles to Dinedor Camp and the tea gardens. We went fishing in the local streams and rivers, with our jamjars on pieces of string. Blackberry picking was another pastime, although we used to eat just as many as we picked. All the local families used to go potato picking for the local farmers. I can remember my brother getting one shilling for working all day potato picking on Dinedor Hill; he was so disgusted with the amount he had been given he threw it into the bushes. All the local families were great friends. We used to help one another, and the older children would look after the younger ones when our mothers were busy.

Cricket, football and rounders were played in the street or fields until dark. The boys would play marbles and conkers, the girls hopscotch and skipping. When it was too wet to play outdoors, we used to play hide and seek, card games, dominoes, "I spy", word games, draw and paint, and help Mother with the chores. Dinedor Sports was the attraction of the year and is still running today. If we were lucky we would have one trip a year to the seaside, nearly always Porthcawl, but we were always happy and had such fun.'

'Bishopswood school was in the wood, next to the church. In the summer, playtimes were spent in the wood. One of the favourite games played by the girls was "house". Three or four girls used leaves and twigs swept in lines for walls, sometimes adding rows of stones, and fern for beds etc. There was great competition between households. The boys' favourite game was to scoop out earth and cover the hole with sticks and leaves to make a "man trap" for other children to fall into. No one saw any danger in that in those days.'

'A favourite game at Clifford was to slide down the castle mound. Sometimes the boys would set fire to the briars that grew there, and send the girls down on pieces of corrugated sheets to see if they could put the fires out!'

SHEEP, SHEEP COME HOME

'I remember a playground game or two. One which springs to mind is "Sheep, sheep, come home". A caller would stand at one end of the playground; in the middle would stand the Wolf, with all the Sheep at the other end of the playground. The caller would say, "Sheep, sheep, come home," and the sheep would reply, "We're afraid". Next, caller said, "What of?" Whereupon the Sheep replied, "The Wolf". The caller then responded with, "The wolf has gone to Devonshire and won't be back for many a year, so sheep, sheep, come home." (Which was a blatant lie, of course!) So the poor ignorant sheep would try to run home to the caller and, inevitably, on the journey, whoever the Wolf caught would be "out". The caller would then switch to the other end of the playground, to call again. So it went on until the one Sheep remaining would be decided the winner.'

WELSH AND ENGLISH

'Fee, Fi, Fo, Fum,
I smell the blood of an Englishman;
Be he alive, or be he dead,
I'll break his bones to make my bread.
                    War-cry of the Welshman.

Taffy was a Welshman, Taffy was a thief,
Taffy came to my house and stole a leg of beef.
I went to Taffy's house, but Taffy was in bed,
So I picked up a hatchet and chopped off his head.
                    War-cry of the Englishman.

Have you ever played "French and English"? It is a grand game based on an earlier and still more exciting one called "Welsh and English". If you have lived in a border district (and Pembridge is only a few miles from the Welsh border) you will realise the enmity that existed at one time.

In or out of school a Welshman, usually the leader of a gang, had only to let out a blood-curdling cry of "Fee, Fi, Fo, Fum" to be joined from all quarters by his gang, and on hearing the reply "Taffy was a Welshman, Taffy was a thief", and the Englishman being joined by his gang, the scrap was on! If any boy came out of the skirmish in one piece he was lucky, but it was seldom that his clothes did so.'

TIGER TIM AND HIS FRIENDS

'We had a maiden aunt who lived in London and occasionally she would send us comics through the post. Luxury indeed! There was Tiger Tim and his friends, and Chicks Own, and Tiny Tots for the little ones. How we loved them.

We had the *Daily Express* through the post also, one penny for the paper and a halfpenny for postage – I always remember Rupert Bear. There used to be coupons in the paper; so many had to be collected and then books could be bought at a reduced rate. We had a complete set of Charles Dickens, I remember, and also Arthur Mee's Children's Books of Knowledge.

We had a few "uplifting" books as Sunday school prizes, and my mother had three or four huge tomes called "Sunday at Home". These, together with a nursery rhyme book and a few boys' and girls' annuals comprised our reading matter.

We played cards (whist, rummy, strip-jack-naked, sevens, old maid), ludo, snakes and ladders, draughts, dominoes, solitaire, and

129

a game we loved called Sorry. Does anyone remember this game? We played hopscotch, French cricket, skipping (with an old piece of rope) and numerous ball games – we had a large blank wall to throw the balls against.'

ASH WHISTLES

'My father taught me how to make corn dollies from rushes, similar to the ones made from straw. In the springtime he would make whistles out of an ash stick. This could only be done when the sap was rising in the trees and the sticks were easy to peel without splitting the bark.'

TISTY TOSTY AND ALLY O!

'Games we played at Fownhope included hopscotch, rounders, netball and football. Tisty Tosty was a game played with a ball tossed between girls who called out the names of actual or possible lovers, until at the right moment the ball fell to the ground! We also played shinty, a simple form of hockey.'

'At Shobdon we played many ball games involving a wall and repeated catching, whip and top, skipping, bowling a hoop, and sticks or bones, a version of Ker-Plunk. Ally-O involved a line of children who held hands, the first one with his hand against the wall. The end of the line passed under it to the tune of "The good ship sails through the ally-ally-o" three times, followed by "On the last day of September", until all the children were knotted up.'

THE BEST YEARS OF OUR LIVES?

Remember walking to school, often a mile or two over fields or along village lanes; the school outing and the school cane? Just for good measure, here are three reminders of how schools have changed over the last hundred or so years.

GETTING THERE

'I was a schoolgirl of the late 1920s and 1930s, and it really was a very happy period of my life. The village school was a good mile away, and from the age of five to ten-plus I walked with my brother and children from the nearby cottages, to and from school, wet or fine. I have no memories of it being a hardship – was the weather finer then, I wonder?

About halfway to school was the village shop and about twice a week, usually on the way home from school, we used to call for sweets. A penny bought five Bluebird toffees or five liquorice laces – those were my favourites, but my brother liked gobstoppers because they lasted longer.

I would pick, press and mount all the wild flowers that grew along the roadside or in the immediate area, and my brother – dare I say it? - had a wonderful collection of birds' eggs. Here I must make the point that we did not feel we were vandalising the countryside; we loved it, and were very much part of it.

At eleven it was possible, if we passed the Eleven Plus examination, to go to the local grammar school. That meant a cycle ride of four miles night and morning, but again there was always someone for company. It amazes me now that, although we cycled eight miles a day, I cannot recall the wet days; but I do remember the windy ones, and the punctures and pumping up our tyres.'

'As a schoolgirl I remember walking from Uphampton to Shobdon and passing under the wires that carried the cradle transporting wood down from Mortimer Forest to Kingsland Saw Mills; a unique construction. When passing we were alert for movement of the cables and, if alerted, would wait for the next load to pass excitingly by.

Later, aged nine (1920) or so, my sister and I were going to school

131

in Leominster and staying there during the week, having to be up early to be driven by my father in a pony and trap to Kingsland station (four miles). On some mornings I would be awoken even earlier with Father saying, "Sorry girls, it is too frosty for the pony today, you will have to walk."

When older we cycled the distance each morning to join the train crowded with schoolchildren. I remember Mr Tom Evans, a railwayman, keeping a look out for us pedalling towards the station as the train was due. Such days started with breakfast before 7.45 am and we did not have anything more to eat until 1 pm. Then we got back home at 6.15 pm for our evening meal.'

'The parish of Foy lies on both sides of the river Wye, as far as Perrystone. In 1918 the Foy footbridge which had been built at bank level was knocked down by a tree brought down by a flood. The present bridge was built much higher in 1921.

During the summer months children from the west side would be punted across the river from Ingstone to the gatehouse on the east side to school. When the river was in flood the teacher would stay on the west side and teach the children in the Jubilee Room in the grounds of the vicarage.'

'As I moaned and grumbled about the cold so much, my parents decided to send me to school in Ledbury on the bus from the top of the Gloucester Road. It was just before I was six years old, and being the hedgelaying season, my father and I set off across the fields to meet the bus, my father carrying his hacker and hedging gloves in one hand. With the other he helped me over the muddy gateways, lifting me to avoid getting my little black buttoned boots soiled. There were no wellington boots then, or electric fences, so boundary hedges were important since straying animals did not make neighbouring farmers good friends. Father put the tools down where Old Si was to start laying the hedge, and we continued over various meadows, past the next farmyard where cattle turned hopefully and a pony looked inquisitively over the stable door with a polished spring trap outside. The dog barked and the farmer shouted a greeting and I was hurried up the drive and so placed on the bus to school.

On the return journey a dutiful young conductor put me out at the same drive gate where I had been picked up in the morning. My mother was frantic as she watched the bus passing the top of our lane without stopping, and where my father had told them to put me off so that she could meet me.

Alone I was bewildered and desperately frightened, fear driving me through the gate and down the long drive. The dog barked, the cattle again turned hopefully, but the farmer, the pony and the polished trap had gone to visit friends. I ruined my little smart boots by taking no heed of the mud, looking only for a gate or stile to get me to the next field. On I went until I heard sounds of hedgelaying, and off again I went in that direction. There was Old Si with his hat pulled down over his ears to protect them from the thorns, and his rough clothes tattered and torn, but he took one look at me in disbelief and shouted, "Boss!" Pandemonium followed, I was taken quickly home, someone was sent to find my frantic mother.

Later the conductor was told exactly where to put me off the bus, where someone would be waiting to meet me. In the cold weather walking home was a poor substitute, and I missed the company of my father from whom I had learned so much during our journeys together in the horse-drawn milk float. A second class ride was better than a first class walk when I was in my first year at school.'

'From the age of seven in 1929 I travelled to school by train from Colwall and walked from the station at Ledbury down to the town each day, nearly a mile. Tuesday was market day and when my friends and I were walking back to the station in the afternoon when school was over, we often saw cows and sheep being herded along the street to the station where they were loaded into special trucks. One day in the summer we saw several pigs being "persuaded" to take this route. One poor pig went crazy – it made a dreadful noise and started to dash about. We were very frightened and dived through the nearest gate to get away.'

SCHOOLS OVER THE YEARS

'In the 19th century schools appear to have been kept at different places in Bodenham. One of these sites was opposite the millcroft and was liable to flooding. Then there was one at the moat house, which later moved to the weirhouse, and here the salaries of the teachers were entirely paid by the childrens' fees of fourpence or sixpence a week! Attendance was as much as 100. In 1862 the trust deed of the present school was signed, whereby the then Arkwright of Hampton Court agreed to convey land to the vicar and churchwardens for the establishment of a school. And so a fine new school, of which everyone was very proud was erected near St Michael's church, and which is easily recognisable in present day photographs. A resident master was attached and children paid twopence per week. It followed the usual pattern of village schools, in having one large room and one small one, and could accommodate

The pupils of Orleton school in 1910. Pinafores were daily wear for girls – and only a handful of boys can be seen without the obligatory cap!

130 children. The large room was later divided into two. A few years later it was found necessary to build a second school at Maund Bryan because of the numbers of children living far from Bodenham school, but this school was closed in 1891 because of falling numbers, and the children were brought to Bodenham by van.

The school operated on the usual lines of a country school, its holidays geared to the needs of the agricultural community. There were breaks for hay making, harvest and fruit picking, with a long holiday for hop picking. In the early part of the 20th century the school buildings were still vested in the vicar and wardens as trustees, with the Arkwright family taking a great interest in the school, but gradually the Department of Education became involved and later the County Council. Various improvements were suggested, but not always carried out, among them the problem of the school's water supply. This had been a vexed question since 1895, when there was some doubt about the purity of the water. The well was tested and found to be suitable for all purposes but drinking; and though the matter was raised again and again nothing was done about it. Sixty years later the problem was still unresolved!

The school was plagued by staffing problems in the early 1900s, and during the 1914 "strike", the head teacher got into trouble for picketing. Finally in 1922 Mr Mellors was appointed and remained until he retired in 1950 and the school enjoyed a period of stability.

One of his innovations was the introduction of hot malted milk for the children in 1933.

He was an experienced bee keeper and kept an exhibition hive near the school. During the war the school was crammed to capacity with a flood of evacuees from Liverpool.

After 1950 Mr Dance took over and the school continued to thrive. It was during this period that our own Mrs Parker became a member of the staff. The passing of the Education Act in 1944 removed the older children from the school.'

'The mortality rate amongst young children at Pembridge was high. Many suffered from "lung disease" and "brain fever". Infectious diseases were rife – measles, mumps, chicken pox, scarlet fever, influenza and scabies, causing closure of the school for many weeks of the year. Many pupils had medical certificates declaring them "delicate and not to be forced at their lessons". After an outbreak of scarlet fever, both school and homes had to be disinfected. It was the practice to close the school when diseases reached epidemic proportion right up to 1939.

After the introduction of free education, it was no longer necessary to hold the Annual Examination for Payment by Results, but pupils had to sit a Labour Examination to obtain a certificate of proficiency before leaving school at twelve. Sometimes this was held at Broxwood school.

The Diocesan Inspection has been held annually since the opening of the school. It was the usual custom to grant a half-day's holiday after this inspection, but since the Second World War this has become much more informal and no holiday is now given.

In the early days of the school, Pembridge had plenty of entertainments for which the pupils were allowed a holiday from school. Pembridge Fair has always been on 13th May and this was a hiring fair prior to the First World War. Here the older boys and girls went to seek employment, lining up near the Market Hall. If successful in securing a situation, they were given a binding fee of one shilling.

A week's holiday was granted for the fair until 1920, a whole day until 1938, and half a day up to 1947. A day's holiday was also given for Pembridge Races held annually in June up to 1882. The Foresters' Fete was also a great day for the village children; it was held annually up to 1912.

In 1895, when asked, only three of the pupils had seen the sea, so the master took steps to raise money for a trip to the sea. Four years later the older pupils were taken to New Brighton for the day. Nowadays an outing to the sea has become an annual event.

A school cleaner was appointed in 1892; previous to this date the children stayed in turn after school to sweep the rooms, and a sixpenny fine was imposed on those who failed to do it.

The Bible and Prayer Book Examination was introduced in 1908, and was taken at Pembridge in 1925 and 1926. This was not taken again until 1955 and has been taken annually since then, the successful pupils attending Hereford Cathedral to accept their awards. Pupils have always attended church on Ash Wednesday and Ascension Day. The first laundry and cookery classes for girls were held in the village hall in 1914, and woodwork for the boys started in 1927.

On two occasions the school bell-turret was struck by lightning. On the first occasion, on 1st October 1901, "the electric fluid cut through the bell-turret, tearing the rafters, and large areas of tiling were thrown from the roof. The main room was covered with debris". On 7th June 1910, the bell-turret was again struck by lightning and considerable damage was done to the roof. The children were in the building at the time.

During the great storm of 16th March 1947 a chimney collapsed and the large room was unusable for several weeks.

The school had no lighting until the Rector provided oil lamps in 1910. Electricity was installed in 1936. Heating was by open fires until replaced by stoves in 1935.

The playground at the back of the school had no hard surface and rain ran from it into the classrooms, bringing down mud which often formed a layer up to three inches deep. Teachers and pupils were kept busy sweeping it out. In 1932 the school was flooded on five occasions. The floor-boards were continually rotting and having to be replaced. A small portion of the playground was tarmacked in 1939, and the remainder in 1954. Mains water was brought to the village and connected to the school in 1960.

Pupils were first medically examined in 1911, and the first School Dental Inspection was in 1921. There was some opposition to this at first and the school Medical Officer went to the absentees' homes. The first diphtheria immunisations took place in school in 1942.

School milk was introduced in 1935 at a halfpenny per bottle and this was distributed free of charge in 1943. The first school dinners also arrived in 1943 and these were served in the village hall. In 1955 one of the small classrooms was converted into a scullery, since when meals have been served in school.

Pupils listened to the first Broadcasts for Schools in 1935 from a wireless set provided by the headmaster, and the following year they heard a programme from the *Queen Mary* on her maiden voyage to America. Money was raised locally to purchase the school's own set.

From 1933–1939 it was the custom for the pupils to send boxes of primroses, violets and cowslips in spring, and holly and mistletoe at Christmas, to the Children's Hospital, Great Ormond Street, London. During these years, too, an annual collection of goods was made for the Kington Hospital Pound Day.

1939 was an eventful year for the school for it saw the arrival of evacuees from industrial areas. Fitting in the visitors caused a good deal of disruption to the school timetable, but eventually 58 children from Tiber Street, Liverpool were accommodated for lessons in the village hall, and 24 children from West Ham were absorbed into the village school. Gas masks were issued to all pupils, and regular inspections and practice at putting them on were carried out.

The pupils were urged to Dig for Victory and in 1942 the school was able to rent the New Inn garden. Pupils also took over two gardens belonging to the almshouses. Gardening became an important subject on the timetable. In 1949 the school garden was purchased from the Alton Court Brewery.

A further change in organisation took place in 1947, when pupils were transferred to the senior school at Kington on reaching the age of 13. 1962 saw the closure of Broxwood School, when the children from that district were transferred to Pembridge. At the same time the Lady Hawkins' School was completed at Kington and provided secondary education for all children at eleven years. In 1963 a new secondary school was completed at Weobley, and this became the secondary school for the Pembridge children.'

'The original school at Clifford, known as Clifford Charity School, was much smaller than today. By 1846 there were 49 boys and 52 girls attending, taught by a master, Joseph Allbut, and a mistress, along with four paid monitors. The pupils paid a penny a week to attend. The John Smith Charity has long been associated with the school – it paid for two dame schools in 1855, one in Clifford organised by Phoebe Matthews, another in Westbrook run by Mary Ann Davies; they were each paid £10 per annum by the charity.

Attendances were a constant worry, since half the school's grant depended on regular attendance. The weather and illness, ie tuberculosis, scarlet fever and diphtheria, coupled with the need for child labour on the farms, presented the headmaster with problems. The very farmers who employed the children were also school managers. In 1874 the school record book notes children potato planting in April, hop tying in June, harvesting in July, gleaning in August, apple picking in September and potato picking in October.

Some reasons given for absence in 1878 were "gathering acorns" and "crow minding". There were many absences in August when the Cheese and Butter Fair was held in Hay and again in November 1876, when the Great Fair was opened in Hereford. Once again many "skived off" to see the circus in May or watch the Hay volunteers review in August, or to see the Artillery enter Hay in 1888.

One day the schoolchildren were invited to tea at The Moor to celebrate the return after nearly two years of Mrs F B Stallard-Penyore and her daughter, Mrs Napleton-Penyore. The bells of Hardwicke and Clifford churches were rung, and the children carried banners to The Moor saying "Long live Mrs Penyore". Later they ran races and ate tea with plum cake. Sadly, within two months Mrs Penyore was dead.'

THE SCHOOL OUTING

'I remember walking two and a half miles to St Weonards village, each child taking their own mug, then catching a bus to Monmouth to see a silent film. On the return journey everyone had to get out and help push the bus up a hill. Then it was into the village hall for a mug of tea and a bun before the walk home – worth all that energy pushing.'

'Once a year we would go to Barry by train for the day. We would take a few coppers to Bartonsham School every week to pay for the trip. Not all the village children could afford to go. We went from the local station (about a mile from the village), in reserved carriages. We took sandwiches, usually of jam, but before we came home we had a sit down meal at a large local hotel. How we loved that.

The assistant mistress, a tall gaunt woman, came to look after the little ones. She always went paddling with her skirt tucked into her knee-length knickers – usually pink – known as passion-killers. We were all too scared of her to laugh, but looking back, it must have been quite a sight!'

'In about 1934 we set off from Weobley School for a trip to London. We had a lovely day there – guided tours round the museums and a slap-up meal at an hotel. When we arrived at our meeting point to come home there was panic – we were one missing. We could hardly come home and leave one behind, so our bus had to stop until the missing boy (who shall be nameless) turned up. Eventually it was discovered that he had gone to visit relatives without telling anyone. We arrived back in Weobley at eight the following morning, 24 hours after leaving.'

DINNER TIME

'There wasn't much time for childhood in Aston Ingham earlier this century. Girls were expected to help in the home from an early age and boys to work outside. Most children left the village school quite young, often at ten years old. Even so, you had to guard your lunch pack otherwise it would be stolen by the less fortunate child who had no sandwiches.'

'We invariably walked to school at Hampton Bishop, unless we were lucky enough to cadge a lift on a timber waggon. We carried our dinner in our school bags, usually bread and jam, washed down by a bottle of cold tea. Perhaps in the summer we might have lemonade made from some revolting looking yellow crystals. That was a treat.'

USING THE CANE

'We walked two miles to school at Bishopswood before the First World War. The headmaster was cruel, and if someone spoke he would make us fold our arms on the desk. He would then use his cane across our arms. There were plenty of black arms the next day.'

'This was the age of "spare the rod and spoil the child", and that was strictly adhered to at our school in the 1940s. The headmistress kept her cane across her desk and it was used for the most minor offences such as being one minute late to class. Indeed, the innocent also received punishment because of a personal dislike. The more mature boys often rebelled against this treatment and occasionally the village policeman was called upon for assistance, resulting in youths being given sentences of up to five years' probation.'

SCHOOLDAYS BETWEEN
THE WARS

Schools didn't change much throughout the first half of the century. Open fires or tortoise stoves, wet clothing hung to dry on the fireguard, all ages taught together in one or two rooms, an emphasis on the three Rs and religious teaching – all of these would have been familiar to two generations of scholars. Here are just a few town and village schools during the 1920s and 1930s.

BROXWOOD SCHOOL

'I don't remember my first day at Broxwood School in 1921. I was three and a half years old, my sister had started at five, and apparently, so I've been told, I objected to being left at home and so I was admitted. There were no hard and fast rules in village schools then, although by law children had to attend school as soon as they were five and leave school at 14.

I do remember being very scared of a yellow dog at the post office but I never remember that it attacked anyone though it did visit the school on occasions and stole children's lunches from their bags in the porch.

In the little room I remember a large map on the wall called "Animals of the World", and over the fireplace a wall chart of fairy tales. The one picture I recall was Red Riding Hood where the wolf is in bed.

In the big room by the fireplace on the wall on the right was a copy of the "Conscience Clause". Many, many years later I was to learn that this referred to religious teaching in schools and that parents had the right to withdraw their children from religious instruction. In our school there were several Roman Catholic children and they turned in at 9.45 am when scripture lessons were over. Beside it was a small blackboard on which was chalked morning and afternoon the number of children present each day of the week. Our desks were long narrow forms with seats attached which could be let up and down. There were holes for inkwells to be put in. Miss Knowles, our infants' teacher, had a small, very high desk with high chair to match and steps for mounting it. Mr Knowles, her brother and headmaster, had a large table for his desk. There were

Pembridge school in 1929. Schools changed very little for successive generations before the Second World War.

several cupboards for stationery and large bottles of ink, red and black. There were large sheets of blotting paper (pink), boxes of chalk, blue covered exercise books with "Herefordshire Education Committee" on the labels where we wrote our names, boxes of Arnold pencils with HB on them, and boxes of steel pen nibs which were often rusty, the school walls being damp.

Opening off the big room was the cloakroom or porch as we called it, divided down the middle to separate girls from boys. The porch led out to the playground, such as it was, and over the two doors was written "Boys" and "Girls".

There were hooks at various heights for the pupils' coats and bags. In the corner of each cloakroom was a very small wash basin. Water for washing was fetched in galvanised watering cans from the pump at the school house and I think more of this was used for drinking than hand washing, we just drank from the spout. Not very hygienic you may think, but there never seemed to be the cases of tummy-upsets then as there are today. We were tough in those days.

The children came from far and wide on foot, often taking short cuts across the fields. They came from places as far afield as Bearwood, Moorcourt, The Batch Cottages, Bolton, The Mere,

Weston, Nutfield, Sherrington, Brokaly and Bonds Green. Wellington boots were unknown then so often they must have sat all day long with wet feet, no wonder chilblains were so common. Often the children's clothes would be soaked after this long walk in semi-darkness, and sometimes their coats were put to dry on the high guards round the two big open fires. Mr Knowles often stuffed newspaper up the boys' trouser legs to assist drying. I remember that often in the winter we would arrive at school to find our inkwells frozen solid and we put them in the hearths to thaw out.

The toilet block was at the back of the school and was always referred to as "up round". A brick wall separated the approach to the toilets and behind one side of the wall was the boys' urinal, quite open, with a tin roof, with a drain to take away the urine. There were three bucket lavatories for the girls and two for the boys with wooden seats over them. These were emptied weekly by a man from the village burying the contents in holes in the triangular patch of ground beyond the toilets. This area was always known as "out of bounds". A notable event was the periodic visit of the nit-nurse, wearing a white starched apron over a blue dress. She would rummage round in our hair looking for nits and livestock. Anyone found to be carrying such was sent home with some special soap with instructions on how to use it. My mother gave us a vigorous inspection every week with a small tooth comb. I forgot to mention earlier that the toilet paper used was old exercise books, which our teachers insisted must be written even on the covers before we were issued with a new one.

After calling the registers, we had scripture lessons. Much of this was devoted to learning things by heart. Whole passages from the Bible were recited. In Lent we learnt all the set collects. A hymn was sung at assembly but we had neither hymn books nor piano accompaniment. Mr Knowles would strike his tuning-fork and sing, "Doh, take the note", and away we went. We had a very big repertoire of hymns from Ancient and Modern and the small children picked up the words from older ones. Before going out for dinner we sang, "Be present at our table Lord" and before afternoon session, "We thank thee Lord for this our food".

Once a term a school manager came in to check the registers. This job usually fell to my father as he lived nearest to the school. Whenever a visitor arrived at school Mr Knowles would call "Stand!" and then "Salute!" and then "Sit".

In the infants room we were first taught to form letters in sand trays and then on slates. I still recall my teeth going on edge as the slate pencil scratched the slate. Only when we could form our letters reasonably well were we allowed exercise books. I remember that on

Friday afternoons we had "choosing", though there was precious little to choose from – clay, sand trays or building bricks. That is all I can remember.

My sister and I always felt we were cheated by having to go home for our dinner. The children who came from beyond the village brought sandwiches and some of them in winter brought a screw of paper containing a mixture of cocoa and sugar to make a hot drink. I often had a pinch to taste but I never got to know whether they had any milk in their cocoa.

The middle class was presided over by Miss Daisy Murrell who came from Almeley on a motor bike. She had one half of the big room and Mr Knowles the other half.

Once a week we had "Transcription", which was copying a passage from the blackboard in our best handwriting. Another day we had "Dictation", writing down what Miss Murrell read to us.

Whilst we recited nursery rhymes and tables in the infants, Miss Knowles would stand with her back to the fireguard furiously knitting socks on four needles. I am grateful to her for what she taught me and I have never forgotten the right way to patch. We did the lot, cotton patch, woollen patch and flannel patch. We were also taught to darn. Before I left the school at eleven I had made a pink gingham dress for myself, all hand-sewn with a low gathered waist, and I can still remember having to stroke each gather so that it fell in a neat little pleat.

In Mr Knowles' class we progressed to fractions, decimals and percentages and when I went to grammar school in 1929, my maths was far in front of other children's in my form.

In English we did "free expression" which meant making up a story of our own. Fairy stories were the favourite choice of the girls, and we were allowed to stick in pictures for illustration. I felt quite annoyed that my mother used Sunlight soap and not Fairy as some of the girls had cut out the little fairies from Fairy soap packets.

There was neither water nor electricity in the school and I imagine it must have been pretty grim during the dark winter months. There were hanging paraffin lamps with wide tin shades but the only time I can remember them being lit was when Mr Knowles blacked out the big room for magic lantern shows and for the occasional concerts and whist drives held in the evenings.

The games I remember playing were whips and tops, bowling hoops, bowling an empty tin such as an empty Ronuk polish tin with string threaded through, tag, sheep, sheep come home, the farmer in his den, in and out the window, hide and seek and hopscotch. Marbles always came into fashion around Shrove Tuesday and conkers in the autumn. The playground was not surfaced in any way and in winter it became a morass of liquid mud. The roads in the neighbourhood were of rolled-in stones and very rough, and broken knees, sometimes becoming septic, were commonplace.

At dinner times children were allowed to go where they pleased. They played paper-chase and arrows round the fields or fox and hounds. Sometimes they went to the woods and made huts from branches.

On Fridays the hounds met in the vicinity and at dinner times the boys in particular went in search of them. Sometimes they got carried away and failed to turn in for the afternoon session. That resulted in the cane on Monday mornings. Mr Knowles did not resort to the use of the cane very often and I should imagine it was a very painful experience. Mr Knowles always took us up to the Square when the meet was there.

Certain days throughout the year were celebrated. Woe betide anyone who arrived at school not wearing an oak-apple on 29th May – Oak-apple day. The punishment was being stung with nettles by the boys. On Empire Day, 24th May, we marched round the playground, saluting the Union Jack. Primrose Day, 19th April, was the day when traditionally the cuckoo arrived. On Armistice Day we wore our poppies and sang "Oh Valiant Heart" and I remembered my two uncles, my mother's brothers, who lost their lives during that war.

Sometimes in summer Mr Benn, one of the school managers, from Moorcourt, came with his daughter Molly carrying huge baskets of strawberries. We lined up in the playground and as they passed us we took one, and they carried on till the baskets were empty.

Winters seem to have been much colder in those days. A favourite game for us was sliding on the village ponds. We were not allowed to do this until Mr Knowles had asked my father to test the ice to ensure our safety. The big boys were expert and cut long white lines across the ice with their hob-nailed boots. This was known as "cutting fat bacon". To go across in a crouched-down position was called "doing little men".'

HOLMER SCHOOL

'I walked over a mile to Holmer School, taking sandwiches and a bottle of cold tea; pupils sat outside, usually on Widemarsh Common, to eat their dinner. If it was very cold we were allowed around the old coke stove in school. Pupils had to line up in the playground for a shoe inspection, and those with poor shoes were given new ones by the school authorities.

I remember on the anniversary of Armistice Day, marching to the war memorial in Holmer Road for a service. On Empire Day, Holmer pupils went to the Castle Green, the girls in white dresses and straw hats, to march and sing *Land of hope and glory.*'

PUDLESTON

'The local school at Pudleston was a mile walk for us. We would meet up with our friends and pick wild strawberries on the roadside banks in the summer and blackberries in the autumn. Wild flowers were in abundance on the verges.

School was one large room with a glass partition dividing the infants from the older children. Two teachers were employed and they taught the three Rs. Religion was always taught and PT a daily lesson. Twice a week we would go for a nature walk, keeping to the footpaths. We all enjoyed those walks.

Two large coal stoves were used for heating with iron guards around them. In the winter months they were usually draped with children's coats drying out ready for the children to go home. Some of the children walked three miles across fields to school.

Our games were mostly singing ones, such as The Farmer's in his Den, Bobby Shafto, The Wind Blows High, and Sheep, Sheep Come Home. The boys were segregated from the girls so our games were limited. We liked playing hopscotch and tag for a change, or hockey and rounders.'

CRADLEY

'No meals were provided at Cradley in the early days; most children went home to dinner, though a few took some provisions. When the School Meals Service came in during the war, all the children had to walk up the road to the old boys' school (now the village hall) whatever the weather. The hall was warmed only by one tortoise stove in the middle of the room which was no comfort to the children who sat at the edges. The meals came in containers and there is an abiding memory of apples with everything!

It was always a big school, with on average about 100 children. Before the war, everyone stayed until they were 13, and only went on to Ledbury Grammar School if they passed the scholarship. The 1944 Education Act altered that. Children stayed at school till they were 15, but moved at eleven to the council school in Ledbury. After the war a bus was run in to Ledbury to take all the children.'

145

'Memories of my first years at school are rather patchy. The walk to school down Nupton Lane seemed very long and the Crown Pitch very steep. The return journey was easier and children raced down the hill to be first to look for cigarette cards from packets swept out from the buses at Yeoman's bus depot at the Crown House, Tillington. This had been my mother's childhood home and was where Mr Herbert Yeomans started his new enterprise, a bus service with a slat-seated charabanc, I believe.

At school we learned the three Rs and lots of hymns and songs including *All through the night* and *Oh, sing again my pretty bird*. We were also taught to knit on both two and four needles. Turning the heel of a sock was quite an achievement. For many years we knitted our own jumpers, gloves and socks, and I was particularly pleased with the turn-down, below-knee socks which I knitted for my father to go with his market breeches. Usually he wore highly polished leather leggings.

In 1930/31 we moved to a new farm and a new school in Burghill where the teaching staff had the same names as in our previous school – Mr. and Mrs. Cooke and Miss Powell, an interesting coincidence. There was another young teacher, Miss Richards from Aberfan in South Wales. She was pretty, very firm and had a great gift of imparting knowledge and making lessons so interesting.

Such things as "tables" and mental arithmetic with all the short-cuts, and spelling were important subjects. In needlework we learned to make patterns and cut out garments, then smocking, appliqué work, and "run and fell" seams, all useful and well remembered.

Once a year, in January, we had students from the Teachers' Training College (now the College for the Blind) to gain practical experience. They always seemed jolly and more lenient than the permanent staff. There were also annual cookery teachers who spent a month teaching us how to make such dishes as cottage pies, apple tarts and lentil soup.

Literature was not neglected. I learned about Samuel Pepys, Dr Johnson and Shakespeare, remembering well *The Merchant of Venice* and *As you like it*. Ten years later when living and working in Stratford-upon-Avon I was familiar with the works of the Bard, having had my appetite whetted to learn and enjoy more from the early lessons at the village school.

Gardening was a useful lesson and was included in our Nature Studies. Mr Cooke set out allotments with grass paths in the plot of ground in front of the school and whilst the boys did the spade work, the girls stood by, making notes on double digging, rotation of crops and how far apart to plant the rows of seeds. I have been a keen gardener all my life and now that age and arthritis is catching up with me, I would love to just take notes and let some one else do the spade work!'

BOARDING SCHOOL

'I was sent to boarding school in the 1930s as my parents were abroad – I spent half-terms and holidays with various aunts.

I still have the (very dilapidated!) cabin trunk in which all my belongings were transported to school, and also my tartan travelling rug which we each had to have (mostly used for sitting on out on the lawns during the summer months, if I remember rightly). Things were made to last in those days.

In winter we wore woollen combinations – the trade name was Chilprufe I think – topped by a liberty bodice on which dangled the suspenders to hold up our black woollen stockings. Warm navy knickers with a patch pocket on one side were worn over white cotton "knicker linings", which were rather like today's shorts. Sensible lace-up shoes, either Clark's or Startrites – I recall a shop with a little x-ray machine in which one put one's foot to see how the bones aligned to the new shoes. We wore navy jerseys in the winter under our gymslips, with the striped school blazer; there was a thick winter coat which could practically stand up by itself, and a classic gabardine raincoat for the wet days. There was a much-loathed felt hat for winter, with a ribbon in the school colours round the crown, and a slightly more acceptable panama for summer, as well as a pull-on cap for everyday wear; the more battered one's headgear became, the more it was admired by one's friends. Much time was spent kicking hats around the playground (when the staff were not looking). In summer, short-sleeved cotton blouses replaced the jerseys, and dresses in the same material were worn, with white ankle socks, when the weather was really warm.

The pocket in one's knickers was often used to temporarily dispose of unwanted portions of the school meals – later to be transferred to the lavatory!'

WEOBLEY

'We came to live in Weobley in 1933 and I started school at the old school, which is now Edges shop. There were three classrooms – one large and two small. My class was at one end of the large room, near a big tortoise stove which we used to crowd round on cold

147

mornings. At nine o'clock someone rang the bell and we all filed in for the register to be taken, and for explanations of absence.

The playground was on rough, falling ground behind the school, one side for boys and the other for girls. The girls' lavatories were very primitive, but there was a cold tap over the one basin.

There were four teachers. The head was a much nicer man than his predecessor, who was one of the "old school" and caned the boys' palms.

After we had eaten our sandwiches in the dinner hour, we used to go across and peer into Mr Purcell's bakery window and see the loaves being taken out of the oven. The smell was lovely!

In 1934 we moved to the new school, now the primary school. It was light and warm, with radiators in every classroom. How we appreciated them. We now had a hall and stage for our concerts, and one student teacher could dim the stage lights, which we thought very clever. In the spacious grounds the older pupils had garden plots, two to each plot. There was a well equipped workshop for the boys, and new kitchens for cookery classes.'

LEDBURY

'I came to Ledbury from Leicestershire in 1944. School was an experience, three classes instead of one and a council school as opposed to my Leicester church school. By the end of the first week I was fluent in the local dialect – and I had taught them the swear words I'd learned from the army billeted in our Leicestershire village!

Some of the playground games we had never heard of – a round hopscotch? The area was drawn in chalk starting from the centre in squares like a snail shell, the stone was thrown into the circle and you started to hop from that square into the centre. You marked your initials on the square you started from and you could land on that square in following turns but others could not.

Soon after we came I sat and passed the entrance exam to the grammar school; my parents paid £4 a term. We did eight subjects for School Certificate – English (three parts – grammar, literature and poetry), French (written and spoken), History, Maths, Science, Art, Religious Knowledge and Needlework.'

THE WORLD OF WORK

ON THE FARM

It is not surprising that in this beautiful county, agriculture should have been the principal 'industry' for so many centuries. Farm life has changed in so many ways over the past 50 or so years, with the demise of the working horse and the increased mechanisation which has also seen a huge reduction in the number of men employed on the land. No memories of farming life would be complete without those symbols of our county, the Hereford cattle.

THE HIRING FAIRS

'Local farmers at Dorstone still remember the Hiring Fairs. Workers indicated their trade by wool in the hat for a shepherd, straw for a waggoner etc. If a farmer liked the look of you he would ask your age, where you came from, that sort of thing. Once they gave you a shilling, that was the farmer's bond. One boy hired to work at the Llan Farm came from over the border and claimed that he didn't like it in England. Percy Morgan, the farmer, lent him his bike to go home on as he felt sorry for him. He didn't see the boy again, though he did get his bike back.

As for men living in remote areas of a parish, they would often have to walk two or three miles before starting work at six o'clock. Walking long distances was an accepted way of life for farm workers who sometimes preferred it to the restrictions of living in a tied cottage.

Farmers would often help each other in times of haymaking, harvesting and threshing. Then instead of payment, "bread, cheese and cider" was the order of the day. One villager remembers being told about his grandfather who in the 1880s came to be a live-in servant at one of the Dorstone farms and he was paid the princely sum of 13 shillings per year, and in his first year three shillings of that was deducted for a prayer book.'

THE FARM WORKERS

'In the 1920s the weekly wage for a farm worker was £2 to £3, with potatoes and milk given by the employer. On leaving school at 14, a boy would receive five shillings a week wages.

There was a Clifford Ploughing Society in 1912, which today is amalgamated with the Escleyside Agricultural Society. Many local ploughmen won international awards. At the time of the Royal Jubilee in 1935, the British National Championships were arranged at Bourton on the Water. The ploughing was done by horses then and a lorry arrived early in the morning at Clifford to collect the team which eventually won – Daskie and Diamond. The plough itself travelled by car, a Morris Cowley 1926, registration number VJ 1433. The car had a canvas hood which allowed it to be unclipped and the plough sat across the back seat.'

'My father worked for 33 years for Pearman. He won many championships with bulls – the first went to Russia. And lots of championships at ploughing matches. The wage was about 30 shillings a week for 80 hours. No overtime in those days, no day off. You had very little illness because you had no hand-outs, not even a loaf of bread. But you learned the hard way to take care of all your things. There were six of us and Mum would put dinner out and more often than not there would be none for her. But we all had to work on the land to help her, before school and after. If we were lucky we got a pair of boots – never shoes.'

FARMING IN THE DEPRESSION

'In 1934 we used to kill a lamb and take it up to The Crown and sell it, sixpence a pound. We done that a good many times. You couldn't get nothing for it in the market you know. Me and my brother had a few sheep of our own like, and you was only bid about £1 or £2 for one. So we decided to kill one. Jacky Batt used to come and kill it for us and dress it up and then we'd sell it. The farmers kept going through the Depression. I don't think many gave up, but it was bad.'

SHEEP AND THE STOCK FARM

'In September each year large sheep sales were held in Kington, particularly during the 1930s and 1940s. All the sheep were trimmed and spruced up for the sale and, up until the beginning of the war when the custom died, almost all were "coloured". This was done by first sprinkling water over the fleeces and then dusting with a coloured powder which was then rubbed in. The colours varied from pale yellow to deep vibrant orange and each flock owner favoured his own particular shade. About 25 years ago when an old established firm of chemists in Kington was sold and the cellar cleared out, many boxes of this sheep colouring were found, each labelled with the name of the farmer for whom it had apparently been specially mixed. This practice made a lot of extra work, for the sheep would of course rub their faces into each other before the colour was dry and the last job was to wash the face of each ewe as she was turned out. The colour was harmless to the wool and would have disappeared long before shearing time.

Nearly all the sheep were walked to market and it was a great thrill to be allowed to help drive the flock in. I used to feel very proud to be walking behind a hundred or more smart Kerry ewes. There was little traffic to bother us, but as we neared the town we would catch up with other droves, and yet others would appear close behind us till it became difficult to prevent them becoming mixed. The shopkeepers were careful to keep their doors closed – many had a tale to tell of the time they had had a "ewe in the hardware shop". When the sheep had all passed they would be out with buckets of water washing down the pavements. If the prices were good everyone was in a good humour and there would be a few pence for sweets, but if trade was poor it wasn't safe to ask.

I remember driving the eight miles to Builth with old Brown and a gambo (a multi-purpose flat bedded horse drawn cart) laden with sheets of wool. A man in a little gig drawn by a lively cob went sailing past with a small load. My father said, "Never mind, we will make a lot more money when we get there!"

Growing up on a stock farm meant lots of chores. On winter evenings I had to carry a stable lantern and light my father when giving the animals their last feed. The huge shire horses were let out to the brook for water. I was nervous when they thundered back. On one occasion I got in the way and had to jump up into the manger and through a stave up into the cratch. Helping to unload sheaves of corn late one night perhaps a little tired and with the harvest moon appearing over Colva hill, I tripped and almost fell backwards between two high ricks. My husband grabbed my arm and pulled me back on my feet saying, "What are you scared of? You'd have come to sight when we threshed" (in about three months' time).

Men on the farms worked out in wet weather far more than they do today; more jobs were done by hand and tractors had no cabs anyway – but waterproofs were unheard of. Two Gobsel Browns (sacks) provided great protection from the rain. One was tied round the waist with binder twine and the other worn round the shoulders held together at the neck with a nail.

Rabbits abounded in this area and there was great excitement when the corn was cut. As the binder went round and round the field the rabbits were driven ever nearer to the middle until there was no longer anywhere to hide and they would have to bolt. As the excitement was about to start, men, children and dogs from the nearby cottages would appear on the scene and each time a rabbit bolted there were great shouts of "Hi-hi-hi", and people and dogs gave chase. Many escaped of course, but a lot were caught and everyone went home proudly carrying a rabbit or two – tomorrow's dinner provided for.

After the binder, the sheaves were stooked in sixes or eights to harvest for three Sundays. There can be few better sights than a neatly stooked field of corn but few who have had the job of stooking and possibly of turning the sheaves again in a wet harvest can really regret the advent of the combine.'

THROUGH THE YEAR

'I was born on a 200 acre farm at Middleton on the Hill, and as my father died when I was still a small child, the farm was run by my mother. Three men lived in the house and worked the land, with a mole catcher calling in from time to time. My mother kept help in the house and a local woman came in to do the washing, ironing and mangling.

Ploughing and planting was done with horses, and the waggoners

Harvest time at Little Hereford. Horses were still used on most farms until at least the Second World War and the work was still unmechanised and labour intensive.

153

took great pride in their animals, keeping the horse brasses clean and the gears on the waggons well oiled. There was always a special ration of corn for the working horses. Sheep shearing was done with a large hand-turned machine, with men taking turns to wind the handle. Combs and cutters were sharpened on a smaller machine. When it came to haymaking, sharp knives were important for cutting the grass with a horse-drawn mower, then there was the turning and cocking the hay, and hauling it into barns. The timing had to be right, because if it was left too long an iron rod had to be forced into the stack to check the temperature, as clover would sometimes overheat. At harvest time the binder was drawn by two horses with a man in front to lead them. The sheaves of corn would be stooked and left in the field for three clear Sundays before being taken to the barn or put into a rick. When the threshing box came, extra hands were needed to keep the engine stoked up. Several days in the year were taken up with cider and perry making – that was a great beverage! The men had a small barrel to take to work every morning and a horn to drink from.'

'My memories are seasonal, because my father had decided that he did not wish to follow the family tradition of farming, so we spent our holidays "on the farm".

The chief excitement of January was rabbiting. Well wrapped up against the weather we trudged to some distant field where there was a rabbit burrow. The "boy" on the farm who lived in the house, would carry a wooden box containing two ferrets; my uncle carried a gun and the rest of us carried nets and something to eat and drink. When we arrived at the hedge bank the nets were put over the rabbit holes and the ferrets were taken from their box and put down a hole on a very long string. We were not allowed to touch the ferrets as they had very sharp teeth and must be held by the back of the neck.

We might have to wait silently for ten minutes with just a few squeaks from below ground, then one of the rabbits would rush headlong into the nets. Quickly someone had to catch the rabbit and with one quick pull of the neck it would be dead. If it should get away my uncle would quickly shoot it. This would continue until we thought the burrow was empty.

In the 1920s we did not consider this was cruel. The rabbit population was high, they had to be kept down and they provided very good and cheap food.

At the spring break there might be threshing. Two local men had a steam engine which pulled and drove a threshing box. The wheat, oats or barley were fed into the box which extracted the corn and fell into sacks. The straw came from the box and would be used later, cut by the chaff cutter for animal feed or used to bed down the animals. Casual workers came to help, so there were extra men to feed.

Easter holidays and all the thrill of new life brought baby calves and lambs. If there were orphans, or a ewe had not enough milk, they were brought into the house, well wrapped in a box and fed from a bottle. These are called cade lambs. If fed from a bottle these sheep will remain friendly all their lives.

Then came the chickens and ducks. These were hatched by the hen sitting on the eggs. The hen had to be caught when she became broody and placed in a coop with the eggs. She had to be fed and let off the eggs regularly. When the appointed time came a little hole appeared in the egg and often we had to peel away part of the shell for the emerging chicken or duck. As they emerged they were put in a basket lined with old blanket and kept near the kitchen grate. When they had all hatched they were given back to the hen. It was quite a lot of work shutting up all the hens for the night. It was always a hen who sat on duck eggs. I loved baby ducks. My uncle said, "The ducks only had one meal, because I would feed them all day".

The dairy was below ground level to keep the temperature low. I remember my grandmother had large shallow pans and the fresh milk was put in the pans and after the cream had risen to the top it was skimmed off. My aunt had a separator and it is still a mystery to me how the milk went through all the cones and divided into cream and skimmed milk. Every time the separator was used it all had to be taken apart and every piece washed and scalded.

Cream was taken for the house to use and the rest was put in a bowl to go sour. One day in the week was butter-making day. The sour cream was put in the end-over-end wooden churn and someone had to turn it over with a handle. Sometimes it took a very long time for the butter to "come" – there was a small window to look inside the churn. The buttermilk was drained away; some was used to make scones or cakes, otherwise the rest was fed to the pigs.

The butter was put into the wooden butter mitt and worked with a pair of wooden hands until it became a solid mass. Then the buttermaker would take off a lump and weigh it on the scales in pounds or half pounds, pat it into a convenient shape, decorate the top with the butter hand and it would be ready for sale, either to regular local customers or to the market.

Long summer holidays were filled with harvesting the corn. The farm had an old barn with large double doors at both sides. This was to allow horses and waggons to be driven in one side and the corn to be stacked at each end and the horses could take the waggon out the other side. Before the threshing machine came into use, men would thresh with flails and the draught from the two doors would take away the dust.

In the 1920s corn was cut with a binder which bound the straw into sheaves with binder twine and dropped every yard or so. Men followed and picked up four or six sheaves and built them into stooks. These were left a few days to ripen if the weather was fine. A wet harvest could be a disaster. The excitement mounted as the binder came nearer and nearer the middle of the field, to where the vermin and rabbits had retreated. When they started to make a dash for it the boys and men, armed with sticks, would try to catch them. To us it was all good fun.

When the corn was "lugged" off the field, a hen house, plus hens, would be hauled onto the field by one of the horses for the hens to feed on the corn that was left. This sometimes caused a problem as the hens would not return to the hen house. I remember my cousin and I were sent to shut up some hens in a distant field; they were all huddled together the wrong side of the field. We struggled and carried about 50 hens and shut them in their house. When we returned the family were just ready to set out and look for us.

In the autumn cider apples were picked and left in a heap in the orchard. Later the cider mill would come along and I think every farm in Herefordshire would have a cellar with five or six large casks of cider. As long as I can remember we had cider to drink as children. A favourite supper was a bowl of cider with hot toast cut in squares and dropped into it.

Two sporting events took place on my uncle's farm – coursing in the autumn and point-to-point racing in spring. Very different from today – coursing on a November day would have about three "bookies" and less than 100 spectators. Two greyhounds were held by a "slipper" and beaters would find a hare and direct it through a hedge near the dogs. The aim was not to catch the hare but the winner was the dog who turned the hare the most times. Nearly all the hares got away. Point-to-points were unsophisticated. There were far fewer bookies, few cars and a small bar, but no refreshments. It was an occasion when local farmers' wives entertained all their friends after the racing.'

HARVESTING AND THRESHING

'Many men worked on farms. During the war land girls and schoolchildren also helped. Smallholders always helped one another harvesting and cider making. When potatoes were ready for lifting I remember my father running a 'mooter' down the centre of the rows and my sister and I scratching out the potatoes by hand to be able to pick them up. These were stored in stacks in a field covered with bracken and soil until required.

We had to pick stones, lugged out with farmyard manure, off the grass fields intended for mowing, so that no damage would be done to the mower. Tying corn into sheaves after Father scythed the crop on a fairly steep field was quite difficult work. These had to put into stooks to dry before being lugged into the barn to await the threshing machine. This was a heavy horse-drawn machine, so each farmer was responsible for finding sufficient horses to pull it to his farm from the previous site. A steam engine actually worked the threshing machine. Now all the sheaves were thrown onto the threshing box, cut open, and shaken out as they were dropped into the drum. Here the grain was separated from the straw and husks and came out into bags at the back of the box. These were carried to the granary and tipped onto the floor. The loose straw was made into boltings and put back into the barn to be used as fodder and feed. The husks off the corn soon piled up and had to be continually moved.

The farmer's wife supplied substantial meals to all those helping. I well remember Mother's spotted dick pudding wrapped in a cloth and boiled. It was delicious and filling.

Haymaking time saw father harness the two horses to the mowing machine at daybreak, before it got hot, and set off for the field to be cut. Prior to this he had scythed an entrance to the field so as not to have any of the crop wasted. After cutting a few swaths around the field, the back swath was raked out, so that he could cut nearer to the hedgerow. The swaths were turned over with a rake, or shaken with a "pikle" to enable the grass to dry, when it was horse-raked into rows then made into cocks and eventually loaded onto horse-drawn waggons. It was put into stacks and thatched, or taken into the barns. When crops were brought down the steep roads the waggon's one back wheel was tied to stop the load pushing the horses too fast. Picnics in the hayfield were fun.'

'I was born and brought up on a Herefordshire farm. One of the most exciting times of my childhood was at harvest time.

First there was the cutting of the corn by my father riding on a machine called a binder which was pulled by two horses. This was driven round and round a field, tying the sheaves of corn and tipping them on the ground. These were usually collected by my mother and us children and stacked into sheaves of six called stooks, and these made quite good hiding places for the children.

These stooks stayed in the field till the straw was dry, not long

157

if the weather was good, but sometimes for weeks if there had been rain. When dry the sheaves were carted into the farmyard and stacked in the barn or made into large ricks. Later the corn would be threshed out and the straw made into ricks to be used for bedding the cattle down in the winter, and if it was barley or oats it could be used as feed.

When the time for threshing arrived my father and the waggoner would take two or more horses to a neighbouring farm where the threshing had finished and bring the threshing box, then go back and get the engine which drove the machine. The engine was a very large one and very heavy. It did not travel on its own, so the horses were taken to pull it along the roads. I can well remember them pulling it up the hill to the farm, and there was much shouting and whips slashing to get it through the gateway. The engine was fed with coal and a great deal of steam was made. A very big long belt was attached from the engine to the threshing machine. When the engine was started up this put all the parts of the threshing machine into motion, and a shrill whistle from the engine told the men it was time to start work.

The threshing tackle was owned by one man, and he travelled from farm to farm, and it was often winter before he reached us. It was a busy time then as usually eight or ten men were needed for the job.

The sheaves of corn were brought off the rick onto the threshing box, the bands of string were cut by the bandcutter and passed onto another man who would feed it into the machine, which threshed the grain from the straw. The grain came out at the one end into sacks which were taken off by my father. Other men did various jobs such as ricking the straw and hauling the chaff etc away. Today with the coming of the combine, harvesting is much quicker and easier.'

THE FARM FOREMAN

'I came to Ledbury in 1944 when my father was appointed Farm Foreman for E B & D H Thompson. We came from Leicestershire and after Dad's new boss had got all the permits to move our furniture on the railway, it took us a week to move. The furniture was packed into a railway truck and then transferred from a lorry on to a waggon. We were to go when Dad sent to say the furniture was at Ledbury. Mother had not seen the house, and my sister and I thought we were going to a foreign land. We would be neither fish nor fowl; foreman's children were rare folks and we didn't know any.

It was a large farm of 800 acres, with 16 men, two boys and three pensioners, three pairs of horses and four tractors. Today the tale is still told of how Dad had never seen a hop before and didn't know how they grew. The men could not understand that there were folks who lived without hops – we soon learned to live with them!

Dad as a Union man sat on the Agricultural Wages Board to represent the men, against his employer who represented the farmers. In the 1940s each county still set its own rates of pay. The farmers thought Dad would toe the line and vote with his employer but he didn't and there was uproar at the meeting. Dad's boss told his fellow farmers that outside working hours Dad was his own man and he was elected to represent the men – that was what we fought a war for. The wage rise consequently went through that year on Dad's vote.

Mother never worked outside the house and garden except for hop picking, when everybody worked, and we as a family picked up cider fruit. Each house on the farm had its own orchard. It belonged to the farm but we had all the boughs and dead trees for firing and the picking up of the fruit – piecework at so much a ton. Hop picking money bought shoes, boots and wellingtons for Dad.'

FARMING DURING THE WAR

'In 1943 we began farming on our own as a newly married couple. Needless to say, our first and oft-recurring problem was money. Post Office savings were to be used to buy cows, and then we would sell the milk and buy more cows.

Five cows were bought at £50 apiece (today, that would probably be £300 apiece). All milking was done by hand, there was no electricity. We had Tilly lamps in house and cowshed and the lamps were moved around according to need. Electricity came to the farm two years after it came to the village, and that was long after the war, in 1954.

Then there was the awful long wait for the money from the Milk Marketing Board. Then more cash, then more cows to milk!

By then Madley had its wartime airfield and an additional source of income came from billeted airmen. I took in their wives and children as well. I remember I was pregnant with my second son, and still hand-milking ten or eleven cows, when I decided it was time to go to hospital. No telephone, of course. Someone had to cycle to the village to order Enoch's taxi, and in time he came, and all was eventually well.

Transport was always a problem: I remember borrowing a float to send some pigs to Hereford Market. With a net over the pigs and our own mare in the shafts, we set off. As soon as we reached the main road we met big RAF lorries and the mare, terrified, bolted all the way to the Wye Bridge!

In our fields we at first grew roots, using a horse-hoe on the flat. We sold what we could and stored the rest for winter feed in a tump. This was covered with hay, hedge-cuttings and fern to keep out the weather. Another farmer had a binder – he cut for us, and we would help him. The sheaves were stacked in stooks of six – two that way, two that way, and two at the ends, and they stood out for three Sundays till they were absolutely dry. The sheaves were unloaded into the barn and pitchforked up so that a man standing atop the stack forked them in circular fashion, each with its head facing inwards. When thrashing time came, the pattern was unravelled and they were pitchforked out in reverse order. I remember having blisters on every finger of my hands when I was pitching.

The thrashing box passed from farm to farm and with it along came "Darkie" George, "Cuckoo" Tom and "Old Poll" (who always smoked a clay pipe). These three dark-skinned, long-robed characters spent their winters in the "Union" or workhouse, perhaps at Weobley, or even sometimes at Madley. They came out to do casual labour throughout the summer, and were regarded with considerable suspicion.

Thrashing was done by traction engine hired for the purpose. Safety measures were virtually non-existent. The driving belt flapped loose and free. I remember an occasion when the heavy metal joint which was supposed to secure the webbing bands flew off and hit me in the back, on my right shoulder. It cut the skin and caused a bad bruise. I knew something had hit me worse than the kick of a cow! I then walked the half mile to the house to fetch the tea.

We needed more help on the farm and through the good offices of the "War Ag", as it was known, it was possible to hire a prisoner of war, usually a German. These were delivered by lorry in the morning and collected in the evening to return to their camp. They brought with them a packed lunch provided by the camp. I remember one of these men was so good and friendly I used to give him his midday meal with the family in the house. He was a good worker. Another one only inspired fear and caution, and when I decided to take him a hot dinner out to the barn he refused it saying, "I will not eat unless I can have it in the house".'

FOOT AND MOUTH

'I remember well the outbreak of foot and mouth disease at Clearbrook in 1942, on the county council dairy holdings near the station. It appeared to be an isolated outbreak, but all the cattle on both farms were slaughtered and put in a very large and deep pit, then covered with quicklime and finally soil. The mechanical digger that did the job belonged to Mowlems, who were employed on the newly constructed airfield nearby. All the cattle at Middlebrook, just up the main road, were also slaughtered, but these were used for food.'

THE HEREFORD CATTLE

'Because of its close proximity to the river Lugg, the Bodenham soil is rich agricultural land, a mixture of clay and loam with a gravelly sub-soil. It is well watered by the Lugg, several streams, and an abundance of springs. Unfortunately, for these reasons, and because so much of the land is low-lying it has been subject from time immemorial to flooding, and almost every winter after a spell of heavy rain, large areas disappear under water.

In the last century much of the land was owned by Mr John Arkwright of Hampton Court, but the estate was sold in 1911 and many tenants then bought their own farms. So up to 1960 there was a mixture of owner and tenant farmers, with some of the latter renting their land from Broadfield estate. Most of these carried on mixed farming with a smallish number specialising in milk production. The milk was originally taken out from Dinmore station, but later it was sold to Cadbury's. Many farmers also kept small flocks of sheep and grew potatoes. Several flocks on the larger farms were over 200. During the Second World War much land disappeared under the plough, but after hostilities ended it reverted to pasture again.

However Bodenham's greatest claim to fame is its long association with Hereford cattle. Indeed from early records of the breed, it appears that a large number of early improvers farmed at Bodenham. Some of the names that come to mind are J Hewer, W Price and the Medlicott brothers. It is not too much to say that the breed of Hereford cattle owes a large share of its popularity to farmers of Bodenham. One of the most famous was Capt R S de Quincey who bought the Vern and its herd of Herefords from Mr Richard Medlicott in 1922. Other breeders were Mr J Weyman-Jones of Bodenham Court and Mr Donald Vaughan of Upper Moor. Mr Weyman-Jones started his own herd – the "Bodenham Herd" in 1925 with the purchase of Oyster Girl, a descendant of a previous Oyster Girl bred by Mr J Arkwright. Mr Donald Vaughan started his herd at Upper Moor about 1940. But one of the greatest of all Hereford bulls lived at the Vern and was called Vern Robert. He was born five days after the outbreak of war in 1939, and as a result never left the Vern, and never won a show prize, because no shows were held during the war and for some time after. He died and was buried on the farm. But he was a great stud beast and as far as we know, his male descendants have sold for £135,000 – a lot of money before 1960.'

HOP PICKING

Every year the hop pickers arrived in force, some local, others from many miles away, all keen to earn some extra money and help them through the winter ahead. Whole families picked together and it was a sociable and goodnatured time, now gone forever.

THEY CAME FROM MILES AWAY

'Talking to the older generation about their memories the first thing mentioned is hop picking. Indeed throughout north-east Herefordshire and beyond to the Black Country of Birmingham and in the valleys of South Wales, the name Bishops Frome was synonymous with hops. It conjures up a picture of great activity everywhere, in shops, pubs, farm kitchens and doctors' surgeries and even churches, all preparing for the annual arrival of people from the poorer areas of towns and of course the casuals, the roadsters and in those days many of the true romany gipsies with their caravans and their dogs tied to the back axles. The years fall away as they see in their mind's eye the hopyard weighted down with the bines and the smell, the unmistakable smell of hops. It was such an all-embracing crop for though the actual picking was confined to September and October, before mechanisation hop farming was an all the year round activity and most of the men and quite a few women earned their living through hops.

People remember the waggon loads of pickers arriving from Ledbury station and Bromyard too while the railway there existed. Before the First World War and throughout the 1920s and 1930s the population of Bishops Frome increased from about 700 locals to over 5,000. Here must be mentioned the name of Farmer Pudge, a legend in his time and some said a millionaire. He was certainly a shrewd businessman for he owned and planted up with hops the whole valley of the Frome in this area. He died in 1938 but his daughter,

Mrs Woodward, carried on until it was wound up in the 1960s. She is spoken well of by people in the village and some remember her with affection, but like her father she expected good work from her employees and they say that she used to be driven by her chauffeur to the top of Fromes Hill where she would sit and look down on the valley to judge how the tying and leafing were proceeding. Many of the Pudge pickers brought their own accommodation and she allocated one side of the Burley Gate road to the hedge crawlers and the other to the true gipsies who kept themselves to themselves, were first class pickers and caused very little trouble. Those pickers who came from the towns were accommodated in buildings around the farm which became known as Tin Town. Almost everybody spoken to remembers the horse-dealing on Sunday afternoons outside the Chase Inn and the gipsies running the horses up and down the road to show them off.

Farmers' wives remember the business of feeding the men in the hop kilns whose work went on throughout the night. But they had to hold vast stocks of food for the pickers to buy and during the war they were allocated extra rations. Most farmers treated their pickers well and made sure they were well fed, sometimes providing tea in the hopfields, and potatoes and other produce free, and always there was ample fuel for their braziers locally known as "hop devils". One lady did tell me she knew one farmer who tried to charge his pickers for water, but he certainly would not have got away with that.

Although pickers lived in very poor conditions, in buildings called barracks, the remains of which can still be seen cluttering up areas around farmyards, on the whole they kept surprisingly healthy. The District Nurse was kept busy attending to accidents and minor ailments and confinements, which seemed to be quite common, especially among the travellers.'

'During the 1930s and also just after the war, the Welsh mining valleys were very depressed, work was scarce and when found very hard, so the summer months would see a mass exodus of unemployed labourers with their families heading towards the fertile fruit and hop fields of Herefordshire. They would travel by any means available to them, horse and cart, coal lorries etc, complete with most of their possessions. They were often housed in very primitive conditions, sometimes in pig sties, but this didn't seem to worry them in the least so long as they could earn a few bob so that Father could spend Saturday night in the pub and Mum could buy the kids some shoes. The local hops and apples often proved too strong for the visitors, but should their goodnatured singing and carousing turn to fisticuffs, the local bobby would be waiting outside

Hop picking brought people to the villages from far afield for a few weeks' hard work and a happy social occasion. This photograph shows the crib and measuring basket in use.

to sort them out – no questions asked. It was the sort of rough justice they respected and no doubt deserved.'

'1960 coincides with the end of an era as the invention of the hop-picking machine changed the whole pattern of hopping.

The hops needed workers all through the year. The frames and the wires had to be mended in the spring, followed by stringing, tying and weeding. This was done by the farm workers employed on the farms, a considerable number of people.

In September and October these workers at Cradley were greatly increased by pickers who came from the Black Country and Wales for their summer holidays, and to earn some extra money. The same families tended to go back to the farms year after year. They were joined by gipsies, and the local school children also had their holidays then. They all lived in barns or mobile homes especially kept for them. The local shop ran a mobile van round the hopyard selling their goods, a very profitable enterprise. Each group supported one of the local pubs, The Crown, The Red Lion or The Seven Stars, who mostly sold a very potent brew of home-made cider. Pay day was on Friday so the men took down their wages and after a convivial evening a right royal row would break out. If the police were called the men could be seen running for home as fast as they could go. One night after a particularly vicious fight the Black Country men set off for home at the Nupend by going down the Bean House drive, but unfortunately for them the owners locked the gate at the far end of the drive and they were all caught and taken off to cool their heads.

The fires in the hop kilns were kept burning night and day for the whole period of hop picking, as soon as one load was dried another was brought in. There were usually three or four kiln men who were regularly employed all the year and who lived in the farm cottages. The bushels were brought in from the hopyards in big canvas bags, on horse-drawn waggons.

At the end of the season the Welsh people who picked on the Hope End Farm always gave a concert, singing, dancing and playing their guitars.'

SCHOOL HOLIDAYS

'In 1935 the school managers at Pembridge recorded that "a large number of parents wish that the summer holidays should take place during the months of July and August. On the other hand eleven families having children at the school wish to go hop picking, and the County Council has issued an official letter stating that parents withdrawing their children from school for hop picking during the time that school is at work will be prosecuted".'

HAPPY MEMORIES OF HOP PICKING

'I was four years old when our family first went hop picking. There were eight of us, Mum, Dad, four girls and two boys; at that age I can just remember being put to sit on a sack and pick hops into a cornflakes box. As I became older I graduated to pick into an upturned umbrella, and then I was put to sit in the corner of the crib. By the time I was seven I was tall enough to stand and pick.

I can remember the first morning of the season. When our bus arrived it was crammed full with adults and with children of all ages, together with stools and boxes for sitting on, kettles, water cans and stoves, all of which would be left at the hopyard until the last day. There were several buses of pickers from Hereford and there were the home pickers who lived near the farm. Then there were the

Welsh pickers who would come for the start of the season and live in huts on the farm until all the hops were picked. Sometimes they would fight amongst themselves and at other times they would sing beautifully.

When I was about ten years old my mother was asked to be the leader of our bus, and I felt very important. By now there were only two of us girls and one brother still at school. We were able to go with Mum during the week whilst on Sundays Dad and the others would come too. These are the times I remember best; the journey to the hopyard was always happy with everyone singing at the top of their voices, but on the way home most of the children would fall asleep.

On the first day in the yard you would choose your crib which was already standing in a "house". There were hop bines on each side of the crib which had to be cut, pulled down and all the hops picked. Sometimes when a bine was pulled part would get left on the overhead wires, then the cry would go out for the pole puller, and along came a man with a long pole which had a hook on the end which he used to pull down bits of the bine.

When all the bines in the house had been pulled down and picked another call went out for the crib carriers, and two men would come along and carry the crib to a new house where you began all over again.

At about 11 am and 3 pm each day the busheller came round with his sack carriers and bookie. Two men would hold the sack at the end of the crib and the busheller would scoop up the hops into his measuring basket and tip them into the sack. Then the bookie would record it in the big book and on the picker's card. Pickers were paid by the bushel, I can remember it being about ninepence a bushel. Sometimes the busheller would pack down the hops in his basket, and you would get less pay than you thought.

If we were in a yard where the hops were not very good the leaders from the buses together with the leaders from the Welsh and home pickers would all go and talk to the farmer to get him to pay more per bushel.

When we were young we had to pick hops in the morning, then at about 11.30 am we were allowed to light the methylated spirit stove and put on the kettle. When it boiled we stopped for dinner which was an assortment of sandwiches, cheese and pickle, tomato or meat, and best of all egg and bacon pie which Mum would make each evening. That was always followed by slabs of home-made fruit cake, tea and orange squash. When all the tins had been shut and the stove and kettle put away we children were allowed to play all afternoon. It was a lovely time when we would explore the woods

166

and streams (someone usually fell in), make pipes with grass tobacco and try to smoke them. Or we would go into the orchard and pinch the apples; woe betide us if the farmer caught us. Or we would help the pole puller or crib carriers.

Looking back it seems as if it was always hot and sunny, but of course it wasn't. It was often very wet and muddy, walking from the bus to the hopyard would take a long time when children would get stuck or fall over in the mud, or someone would lose a boot and everyone would try to help. At times it rained so hard that the grown-ups would be picking into their cribs with a sack over them and the children would be huddled under umbrellas or under the crib to try to keep dry. But all that would be forgotten when the sun came out again.

It was such a happy time but alas, just a memory now.'

'Early in the morning at Acton Beauchamp the pickers wended their way to the hopyards, hoping to pick a good many bushels of hops before we came round to collect them. At ten years of age, I rode high on the dray pulled by lovely carthorses, with the book under my arm in which to record each person's crib-load. I had to walk back home because the dray would be full of sacks of hops. They were dried in the hop kilns and then pressed into enormous hop-pockets, higher than the room itself, before being sent off to the brewery.

The cow-houses were all whitewashed, cleaned out and laid with fresh straw for the hop pickers. We also kept the milk, eggs etc and they would come to the house and buy whatever they required. Oh, it was such a happy time! On Sundays, the women pickers came in and peeled a large sackful of white potatoes which were cooked in the furnace, and we roasted a *huge* joint of beef, and after the gravy had been put on the plates it was my job to carry them out to the wall in the courtyard, and all the pickers came and collected their lunch.

There was one Cockney chappie who always stopped at the village shop on his way, to buy me a box of chocolates. The last I heard of him was that he was in jail!'

'Many women and their families went into the hopfields around Leominster in the 1930s to pick hops, sometimes getting up at six o'clock and picking until dark. They would earn enough money to reclothe the whole family and put some towards Christmas gifts and luxury foods, which to us then included chicken, sugar pigs, oranges, dates and figs, and if we were lucky a large box of chocolates.

I used to accompany my father, who was a baker, into the hopfields each day with large four lb batch loaves and the ever popular "Lemster Bread Pudding" which my father made trayfuls of every day during the hop season.

Many families came from all over the country, staying in caravans and farm buildings for as long as six weeks. What a happy time they had as they could combine a holiday within a working community. They held sing-songs round large bonfires whenever the weather allowed, and had smaller fires on which they boiled kettles and stews, and roasted rabbits and poultry on fixed spits.'

'I have very happy memories of hop picking in the 1940s, as it meant an extra two or three weeks away from school and days spent in the open air. My parents' main reason for going was to earn money to buy new winter coats and shoes for the family.

The lorry arrived at about six o'clock to take us to the hopyard at Madley, we sat on bales of straw in the back. The mornings always seemed to be misty but by about nine o'clock the sun shone through and the mist cleared (these sort of mornings are still called hop picking mornings). The first job of the day was to search for wood to light the fire to boil the kettle and cook bacon and eggs for breakfast. After that the women got down to the serious business of picking.

There was real rivalry between families to fill their crib first. Older children would either help with the picking or look after the younger ones. The babies were put to sleep at the end of the crib. At five o'clock we all piled into the lorry again for the homeward journey.

I will never forget those times in the hopyards with the sound of people singing as they worked, the voices of the children and the mingled smells of hops, frying bacon and wood fires.'

IN SERVICE

For many young girls, right up to the 1940s, going into service at the big house or the local farmhouse or rectory was the only option available to them when they left school. It could be a good life with the right 'family', but it was hard work and long hours for little pay. Men too worked both inside and outside, such as on the gardening staff.

ON THE HOP FARM

'I recall being in service on a hop farm around 1920. Wages were £20 per year. I washed in the wash-house, lighting the copper with wood, scrubbed the floors and tables, blackleaded the grates and helped in the kitchen.'

THE 'TWEENY'

'Mother coming from a Welsh Valley and sent into domestic service, thought it was the work for me to do, so when I left school at the age of 14 in 1937 a situation in domestic service was for me. My employer-to-be came to our house to look me over, and thought I was too small to do the work required of me but decided to employ me anyway. My wage would be £10 per year with uniform and food, half day off each week 2 pm until 9.30 pm. My employer thought my name, Pearl, was too "posh" for a between maid so I was known as Mary, my second name. This I objected to and so would not call her Madam. She constantly complained to my mother who chastised me but I pointed out I was not rude to her.

My day started at 6.30 am scrubbing the nursery floor, then helping Cook to prepare breakfasts for the nursery, dining room and servants hall (four servants – cook, parlourmaid, housemaid and myself). Behind the housemaid's pantry door would be a list of work for every day of the week. Very often I would not finish until 7 pm as there was so much to do. No hoovers, so all carpets were cleaned with dustpan and brush, old tea leaves and newspapers dampened and torn up and spread on the carpet to help damp the dust. It was not uncommon for coins to be put under rugs or cigarette ends put on top of door frames to see if we did our work properly. All wooden floors were polished with polish made from beeswax and turpentine which we had to make. No wonder we developed housemaid's knee.

When the family went away, mostly to Scotland, the whole house would be springcleaned, carpets taken outside and beaten, curtains cleaned, paint washed and all furniture moved. When the family returned the pantry would be filled with pheasants, hares, snipe, woodcock and quail, which would be hung until ready, then there would be many house parties and lots of entertaining. One was always in awe of the front of the house and did not speak until spoken to.

Evenings were taken up doing household mending, one evening each week allowed for our own personal mending. When I collected my first month's wage of 16 shillings and eightpence I was given an extra sixpence and told never to spend it, so I would never be without some money. Needless to say I did not keep it long.

After 22 months I took up another position at Ledbury at £12 per year with twelve in staff, and having each afternoon off. My father bought me a bicycle for 30 shillings so that I could get home on my half day off.

In spite of a bathroom next to my employers' bedroom, they insisted on bathing in hip baths in their bedroom which involved carrying in large brass cans of hot water. When the war broke out in 1939 the grandchildren were evacuated from London with their governess and it was my duty to bath the little boy. He was a mischievous child, who often soaked us with his water pistol and was always singing wartime songs like *Roll out the barrel* etc, of which his mother disapproved. One night while in the bath he called down the overflow pipe which led into the sink of the butler's pantry to listen to him singing. Before I realised what he was doing, he poured a jug of water down the pipe into the butler's ear (he was not amused).

A room was later put at the disposal of the Red Cross and we used to help them one afternoon a week to make bandages from sheets, rolling them and packing them for the troops.'

THE COOK

'I started in a large house which is now a school at Aylestone Hill, Hereford. My job as a scullery maid was clearing up for everyone else, all dirty work. Then I had a promotion to kitchen maid, when I had to prepare vegetables, wait on Cook, and wait on the servants' hall staff.

After three to four years I trained for a cook's job and travelled round the country as a temporary cook. I worked in some very nice homes and had lots of perks. I always saw the lady of the house to arrange lunches, and dinner parties, each day. Wages were very poor, but we had good food and warm beds. We had to buy all our uniforms – one for morning and a different one for afternoon. I started work at seven in the morning till half past nine at night, six and a half days per week, with one half day off.'

'Lifestyles alter greatly with the passage of years. The household duties and conditions commonly imposed upon a teenage girl entering service in the 1930s would not be tolerated by today's standards.

I entered the employment of a retired vicar, Rev Vincent Gressley, and his two sisters Eleanor and Margaret, at Burcher Court in Titley in 1936, when I was 17 years old. My duties as cook-general were many and varied, and some are described below.

Uniform for rough work comprised a cotton dress, apron, and a large cap, with a hessian apron for dirty jobs such as lighting the kitchen range and blackleading. The working day began at 6 am. The vicar's hipbath had to be filled, and the water for this, and the ladies' requirements, had to be heated and carried up to their rooms.

Before breakfast, the family and staff assembled in the dining room for morning prayers. The other servants were a parlourmaid, and a gardener who doubled as boot boy. In addition, a woman was employed part-time to perform extra duties including any necessary sewing.

After breakfast, the elder Miss Gressley decided on the meals for the rest of the day, and exact rations for these were issued. All vegetables were home grown, and deliveries of groceries and domestic items came from Kington three times a week. Cows and chickens kept at the Court had to be tended, and butter had to be made twice weekly. In summer, everyone was also expected to help with the haymaking.

In the afternoons, uniform was a black dress, lace apron, and a head-band threaded with ribbon. The cost of these service clothes was deducted from the weekly wage, which was ten shillings initially. By 1939, this had risen to the dizzy height of twelve shillings and sixpence. My free time was one half day each week, and a half day every alternate Sunday. My employers set strict rules, including curfew at 10 pm, and boyfriends were discouraged.

Very little entertaining was done in the evenings, but the Gressleys regularly had guests for afternoon tea and, on occasions, their brother Sir Nigel came to stay.

I cooked for the whole household, cleaned and filled the oil lamps, and checked the candles. I washed up, scrubbed floors, and also cleaned and polished the silver and brass twice a week – and all without the aid of modern household cleaners.

I shared an attic bedroom with the maid, which was very hot and stuffy in the summer. We slept in feather beds laid on palliasses. On the warmest nights, we dragged the beds onto the roof. On one occasion a storm broke, and we scuttled back inside to escape the heavy rain, leaving the beds behind. This resulted in rainwater collecting, and seeping into the house. The gardener, who was sent to investigate, removed the offending objects, but maintained a discreet silence.

During my years of service, Titley was a busy little village. Four of the largest houses each retained several members of staff, and every morning one would see a bustle of people setting off for the day's work.

Despite the restrictions on my social life, I married a young farmer in 1939. Soon after, I left my employment to settle down to family life in the village.'

THE GARDENER

'It was about 1930 when I first went to work up at the house. I wasn't in the gardens then. I was labouring for the firm putting in the central heating. They paid us a shilling an hour, which was good money in those days, and they offered me more to go and work up in London when the job was done, but there was a chance to work in the gardens here, so here I stayed.

There were about eight or nine of us, working under the Head Gardener. The gardens were beautiful then. There was a great terrace behind the house, and different gardens divided off with yew hedges. The house was famous for its yew hedges. There was the rose garden, and the Italian garden, all divided into little beds with box edgings, and the herbaceous borders. Beautiful delphiniums and foxgloves and such like. Then there were great stretches of grass right down to the lake. It all had to be mowed with hand mowers. Many a tumble I've taken trying to mow some of the steep banks. I can remember when I was a child they were mown by horse-drawn mowers. The horses had special leather shoe covers on, to stop them leaving footprints.

There were grapes in the hothouses, and the walls of the orangery were covered with peach and nectarine. Wonderful fruit we grew in there.

The vegetable garden was in four separate sections, walled-in, of course. Everything was done by manual labour, digging and forking and raking. We didn't use any artificial fertilizers, only farmyard manure. This was dumped in a huge pile in the yard, and we had to load it in wheelbarrows to take it to different parts of the garden. We did use weedkiller, though, especially on the paths and terraces. There were large drums of arsenic in the shed, which we diluted with water and ladled into the watering cans. It's a wonder nobody was poisoned.

In the 1930s the house passed from private ownership and became a hospital. The grounds were still kept up but in a less lavish way, with dwindling staff. Then came the Second World War, and nothing was ever the same after that.

It's a vanished world.'

172

CIDER MAKING

Though cider was home-produced in most farmhouses in Hereford-shire, which belongs more properly to an account of our food and drink, the county has also produced some of the finest commercial brands and many men and women have been employed by companies such as Bulmers and Westons on growing and production.

WORKING FOR WESTONS

'Henry Weston first took on the tenancy of The Bounds Farm at Much Marcle near Ledbury in 1878. There was a general agricultural slump at the time and Henry decided to turn his attention to the commercial production of cider and perry, using the apple and pear orchards already on his land. With the railway coming to Dymock as well, he chose a good time to start his new business. The family firm went from strength to strength over the following century.

I started work at Westons in 1921 straight from school at 14 years old, starting at 7.30 am until 6 pm, working in the Bottling Department, where all jobs were done by hand, moving bottles and cases. Only the cider mill and presses were driven by a huge oil engine, also the pumps, but all other work was manual and very different to today when all the work is done by machinery.

The cider was taken to Dymock station five days a week by horse and dray, and all the apples were brought in by horse and waggon. The work was hard and the hours were long, but despite this I enjoyed many years at Westons. Not many holidays – Saturday half day and six Bank Holidays a year.

The cider making was a very busy time from September to the end of December. Westons had their first motor lorry in 1921, with all the unloading and loading done by hand. I started driving lorries in 1925; I did five years in the Army during the war, then came back to Westons in 1946 and finished driving their lorries in 1972, when I went over to attending the boiler and assisting in the Barrel Department.

I really enjoyed my years working there, they were very good employers, very considerate and understanding. I have lived in their houses all my life, and I'm happy to say the old firm is still going strong, but I'm sorry to say that at the age of 85 I don't take any part in its activities – I wish that I could.'

HAMPTON BISHOP FIELD FARM

'Bulmers started growing cider trees at Kings Acre, Hereford, somewhere around 1935–1937.

My husband started there after the war in 1946, and we lived in Kings Acre for 20 years working in the orchards. I used to pick apples for cider, at £1 a ton (20 cwt bags); that's how we saved up for our first black and white TV. I also had two children in a pram and one helping me.

When we came back to Hampton Bishop Field Farm in 1968, Frank was made manager. What he knew about cider trees could fill a book!

The Field Farm, situated just over two miles from Hereford on the B4224, was acquired by H P Bulmers in 1968. The farm of about 230 acres was to be used as a nursery and experimental fruit farm as part of a general planting scheme started in order to produce enough high quality cider fruit for increasing demands.

The actual landscape of the farm was changed considerably, with grubbing out of old hedges to be replaced by fast growing evergreen Cupressocyparis Leylandii in rectangular blocks for easier management and as a more regular and effective windbreak system necessary for good tree and fruit production. A vermin fence was placed around all the areas to be used for nursery and orchard purposes. This was necessary to keep out mainly rabbits and hares who seem to have a liking for young tree bark. Unfortunately some hares and rabbits were naturally fenced in and did do quite a bit of damage to the first planting of trees. These had to be cleared out by numerous shoots and other means. Another early problem was that the fence had crossed and blocked routes used nightly by the local badger population. This problem was overcome by the use of badger gates which had to be placed exactly on the badger routes for them to use. Later on the badgers must have thought it to be a good thing as there was evidence, namely trails of straw taken from around the young trees where it was being used as a mulch to retain moisture, and then through the badger gates to their sets.

The areas which were not plantable, the majority being river meadows liable to flood, were later sold off and used as cattle grazing. The nursery area mainly to the south of the main road was to be about 50 acres, to allow for the growing of trees on a rotation basis combined with a two year cycle. The remaining acreage of about 100 acres was to be used as mentioned before on an experimental basis, to test the results of cider apple production, on different rooting and planting systems, and management technique.

Due to the large areas that Bulmers intended to plant up with cider apple trees in Herefordshire and Worcestershire, the Field Farm Nursery was called upon to produce large numbers of trees, in fact producing 150,000-plus trees at its peak. The actual process of tree production is mostly the same as for the production of dessert and culinary varieties, the only difference being that the majority of trees were to leave the nursery as maidens, ie with one year's growth, although a certain number of standard trees were still being raised for farmers.

Cider apple trees are usually propagated by budding or grafting onto a rootstock. This is a very old method of propagation which was originally used because of the difficulty of propagating the cultivated varieties by cuttings or layering. The rootstock used have over the years been bred and improved upon at various research stations.

All these rootstocks have different characters and they impart less or more vigour to the varieties grafted on to them. So by using different rootstocks, different sizes of trees will be grown. These rootstocks are divided into four main groups; dwarfing rootstocks, vigorous rootstocks, very vigorous rootstocks and semi-dwarfing rootstocks.

The chosen rootstocks are planted in springtime and left until late July, early August when budding takes place. The following year buds are checked to see if they are alive, in which case grafting is applied. Finally they are undercut and lifted that winter for planting out.

In latter years the nursery turned its attention from mainly tree production to raising government certified rootstocks for sale to the nursery industry. The rootstocks can be raised by three main methods, of which all have been at Field Farm. They are by layering, stooling and hardwood cuttings.

Major improvements were made to the farm buildings, which included a refrigerated store and farm workshop. The old water tower which supplied the gravitational feed to the top areas of the farm was taken down, water now coming from the main. An area was set aside for a cider folk-type museum.'

OTHER WAYS OF MAKING
A LIVING

There were of course dozens of other ways in which we made a living over the years, from making clogs to working in the tile works. These are just a few examples.

EMPLOYMENT IN THE VILLAGE

'Dressmaking was done by several women at Fownhope – from the expert who took apprentices to the woman who did a bit of sewing. One lady managed to bring up a family on knitting and smocking! There still are people who make dresses and are kind enough to give amateurs a little help and advice, but generally speaking, no one makes a living at it these days.

Beautiful laundry work was done by several people and one person I know still picks up very lovingly a little collar iron and her goffering irons and sighs for departed days.

The flourishing saddlery business has now gone, as also has the home brewing. The Highland Home brewed its own beer which was considered to be exceptionally good. The Green Man brewed too and a brewing business was carried on at The Green. Most people made their own cider.

Farms have always given work to many men full time, and women work in the fields at all seasons.

At the beginning of the century, both the Nupend Mill and the Pentaloe Mill were working. The Nupend Mill was only working about two days a week when local cottagers could be seen carrying sacks of gleaned wheat upon their heads, returning later with their sacks of flour. The Pentaloe Mill catered for the farmers who arrived with carts filled with sacks of corn. In the 1950s Mrs Mason, who was the wife of the miller, related how she could "knock a sack of wheat about like steam". She remembered that old Squire Hereford always wanted wholemeal flour as he liked a good wholemeal loaf.'

'At Colwall people usually worked as near to their homes as possible, the men as gardeners, quarrymen or farm labourers. Some from this area worked in the South Wales coal mines. A local builder and undertaker also had a pony and trap in which he gave rides

176

The wheelwright was an important figure in village life, making and mending farm equipment and also often acting as the village undertaker. Ephraim Pikes is shown in his workshop at Dorstone in 1935, with 'Chip' Dawe powering the hand-turned lathe.

round the hills to tourists, and acted as a taxi service. Women worked mainly as domestics in large houses. Everyone knew their place. Most wages were very poor. The quarrymen worked under very hard, dusty conditions and were quite well paid, but most of them died young. Quarrying ceased in about 1960.

A prominent local family, the Ballards, provided much employment for village people, having started a brickworks, a vinegar factory and a nursery specialising in Michaelmas daisies, varieties of which were often named after female members of the Ballard family. They were also responsible for developing the Colwall Spring into the bottling plant now owned by Schweppes.'

THE DISPENSER

'When I take prescriptions into the chemist and see the ease with which they are dealt, I think back to my father's job which was that of a true dispenser. Having had a leg amputated when 19 years old, the doctors were impressed with his fortitude and offered to train him as a dispenser.

He had left school at 14 but obviously had a good brain. He learned shorthand, typing and book-keeping at night school, taught himself Latin, then went on the train to Birmingham University twice a week to study for his diploma in dispensing. He achieved this in the early 1920s. His dispensary was a magical place with huge glass bottles of coloured medicines to be diluted. I still have the pestle and mortar he used to grind powders, which were put into neat paper packets. He was looked upon as an honorary doctor, often being asked for free advice. Everything had to be paid for then, and a half-crown bottle of medicine was often paid for at sixpence a week. People on daily injections came to our house on Sundays when the surgery was closed. He gave loyal, unstinting service to eight doctors during 35 years, until his early death at the age of 55.'

DROVERS AND ROADMEN

'Cattle droving was a memory at Aston Ingham – long distances were covered and often entailed an overnight stop. There were several old drovers roads through the village. Cattle also grazed the sides of the lanes.

Road workers brought loads of stones in a horse-drawn cart and piled them on the side of the road. Another gang would then break the stones and lay the surface of the lanes. The council also employed roadmen to keep the verges tidy. These men had a real pride in their work and kept the grass cut and ditches clear. They were a fund of local knowledge.

Some men walked miles to work and therefore didn't come home for lunch. Older villagers can remember how indignant one wife was because her husband wouldn't walk home for lunch – a round trip of some two miles! This particular chap always had an ounce of tobacco as part of his pay. "Don't matter how much it weighs," he'd say, "so long as 'tis a heap as big as May Hill."

All the local crafts were connected in some way with the rural way of life. Two families were engaged in hedge-laying and ditching, and there were wheelwrights, spoke-makers, basket makers, gate makers, those who made wicker chairs and tables, and cobblers. There were two blacksmiths.'

THE TILE WORKS

'The tile works at Withington was established by William Godwin in 1848, who majored in encaustic tiles which came to adorn many fine churches, cathedrals and imposing Victorian civic buildings across the country. Through marriage, I believe, the company passed into the hands of the Thynne family.

The factory brought much needed employment to the village. A bonus, too, was that the site was adjacent to Withington station and the railway line, for which a "new fangled" electricity cable was installed, bringing a welcome electricity supply to benefit the rest of the village.

Mrs Millie Eckley recalls working at the tile works in the 1940s, when it was managed by a Col Tomlinson. Mrs Eckley's principal tasks were the making of "angle beads" which fitted down the sides of the tiled fireplaces. Her lasting memories are of the thick layer of clay dust which seemed to overlay everything, the large lorries delivering flint supplies, and the imposing portrait of Col Tomlinson in the staff canteen. Three or four large kilns fired round the clock, and there was an immensely tall chimney on a site near the centre of the village. This was finally taken down, brick by brick, in the 1960s.

Lloyd's tile works came later, and this was taken over in the 1950s by the Bell Fireplace Company of Northampton. Several houses built in the early 1950s had Bell fireplaces installed. Sadly, Lloyd's failed in the 1970s and their successors Hereford Tiles went into liquidation in the early 1990s.'

ELECTRICAL AND RADIO

'My husband started his business in 1925 – Electrical & Radio. In those days there were very few electrical goods and most wireless sets were powered by batteries which had to be charged. We made our own electric power and recharged batteries before delivering to customers all over the area. These accumulators were collected, brought back in the van to be recharged, often 600–800 weekly. They were then charged for about 36 hours and taken back to the different homes. Each battery was handled five or six times, and the price for all this was sixpence each. About every three months the larger high tension battery in all sets had to be renewed. The accumulators had to be delivered in all weathers, especially during the years of the Second World War, as so often this was the only means country people had of learning how things were progressing. It was quite a colossal task to get to the outlying districts, as we had very little labour owing to the men having been taken to help in the war effort.

Before we retired in 1965, everything had indeed altered. Electricity had reached most of the outlying areas, and so the nature of our stock changed. No more batteries to be charged – mainly electric radio sets, and television too had become widely purchased, also electric fires, fridges, washing machines and so on.'

WOMEN IN THE OFFICE

'In the 1930s women were not allowed to work after marriage in banks, teaching and the Civil Service. No overtime was ever paid to office workers, and starting pay for a qualified shorthand typist was 15 shillings a week.'

'In 1939 I was employed as secretary to the Consulting Engineer of the River Wye Catchment Board. A self-styled "squire" of Hampton Bishop was a member of this board, and one day he was visiting my boss when he spotted me sitting at my typewriter. "What is she doing here?" he asked my boss. "Miss Tayson is my secretary," was the reply. A snort from the "squire". "She should be in service, not sitting in an office." Words failed me.'

TELEGRAM GIRL

'After leaving school in 1919 I worked for the West Malvern post office, delivering telegrams to the Wyche, Mathon and West Malvern. For this I was paid five shillings a week. While I waited for the telegrams I did housework and mending for the postmistress. As I got older I was able to learn the work of the post office, including the weekly accounts, which was very interesting as I was then allowed to go to another office as relief when required.'

THE BRICKIES

'Since the Second World War the "Bricky" at Tupsley which made the beautiful smooth red bricks has run out of clay, and it has now been built over. It is now called the Quarry, but the original clay pits were worked by the men who had first come to build (dig) the Hereford Canal, which was rather a late development, as it opened just in time for the advent of the railways in the 1820s. The canal diggers were thus able to dig the cuttings and make the embankments for the railways, and their descendants were able to make the new bricks. There were a great many Irish names among them. I was told that a lot of the "brickies" found jobs at the filling (munitions) factory at Rotherwas during the Second World War. They could walk to Rotherwas along the side of the railway line, crossing the river at Eign Road.

180

I was told that the girls who worked at the filling factory in the First World War used to turn bright yellow; that they slept all day and worked all night – but they also bought new hats for themselves every week, broad-brimmed hats transported in hatboxes. In the Second World War the factory was extended, but by then everyone seemed to wear berets or headscarves!'

THE CLOGGERS

'Until the start of the Second World War, every ten years or so the cloggers visited the Preston-on-Wye area. These were men who came and camped beside the brook to cut down the alder or awl trees and make the wooden soles of clogs, which were worn in Lancashire by the mill girls. They were cut from the fresh, orange wood using a long knife which was fastened at one end to a big, circular block of wood. The knife was moved up and down to shape the wooden soles which were then stacked in a circle to dry, and the cloggers moved on to the next tree. The stumps of the trees were left to grow again for the next cutting. I used to pass the cloggers as I walked from my home to the village and they would always give me a greeting.'

A POLICEWOMAN'S LOT

This is an account of a policewoman's life in Hereford in the 1940s, when women were admitted to the ranks for the first time. It proved to be an educational, if not entirely happy, experience for one young recruit!

'At the start of the war and already operating with eight men short of their full complement of 49 officers and men, the Hereford City Police Force suddenly found itself decimated as the men immediately signed up for the services. Men who'd just retired were brought back as reserve constables, but by 1941, the force was so understaffed they admitted defeat and recruited the first women police officers! Affectionately (?!) known as WAPSES (Women's Auxiliary Police Corps), they were untrained in police law, but acquitted themselves well as drivers, telephonists, clerks and female prisoner escorts.

Disbanded at the end of the war, three of the women went on to join the force proper.

I think I was the first Hereford City policewoman to be sent to the training college at Ryton on Dunsmore, near Coventry. There I was to learn law according to Moriarty (the police "bible"). First, I had to pass the physical and be examined by the police doctor, Dr Ward-Smith of St Owens Street. He took one look at my five feet three inches, seven stone three lbs frame and said, "She'll never make it!" The escorting sergeant laughed and responded, "You won't recognise her by the time they've finished with her at Ryton." How true that was! The first fortnight after toughening up treatment, square bashing, swimming and life-saving, first aid, accident procedure etc, as well as swotting up the legal side, I was convinced Dr Ward-Smith was right: I was never going to make it! I cried myself to sleep most nights, trying to get my aching body comfortable on my hard little straw palliasse, and yearning for the comforts of home. I could have been a junior schoolteacher on £4 6s a week – why was I putting myself through this for a measly extra 15 shillings a week – not forgetting torch allowance and the doubtful privilege of getting free black silk stockings from Augustus Edwards, then Hereford's swankiest store.

On arrival at Ryton, all gentlemanly niceties flew out the window: on my first day, aged 22, I lined up at assembly with the 27 other female officers and 500 men to hear the Inspector spell out the rules and regulations of the college. Here, we learned, the women were treated exactly the same as the men, except we were to be excused swimming one week in each month . . . "anyone trying it on more frequently would be severely punished."

This apparent equality and "all boys together" message from the officers was not exactly taken on board by our fellow recruits who scoffed at our drill efforts and poured scorn on our PT but never stopped trying to chat us up. We were obviously fine to socialise with but, in their eyes, useless for anything else! My three months at Ryton were the most miserable of my young life. Passing out parade couldn't come quickly enough, but all I remember of being reviewed by the Home Secretary of the day (Mr Chuter Ede) was to respond to his enquiry as to how I'd enjoyed my training with, "Sir, my bed was very hard."

Upon my return to Hereford, I was discovered to have grown half an inch and put on over a stone in weight! I entered my new job full of apprehension – training was all well and good, but how was I to put this into practice? In my first week I was sent to arrest a drunken woman causing uproar at the bus station, indecently exposing herself to the queuing passengers. She was not about to "go quietly" and proceeded to punch and kick me as I tried to take her under arrest. Without handcuffs (WPCs were not issued with them . . . they probably thought we'd lose the key!) I could do little, as the duty sergeant surely knew, when he sent me. I called for reinforcements which turned out to be one inspector, one sergeant, two constables and a police van. The woman was held overnight at the station. I can remember exactly what she looked like, what she wore and her name as if it happened last week: she was about 60 and drunk on methylated spirits. This was her 108th arrest so she took it all in her stride; not so WPC Elias who went home that night reeking of meths and sick to the stomach!

There's no doubt my male colleagues found it hard to accept WPCs and it seemed as if they went out of their way to make our lives difficult. Many of the older constables seemed to think we were Dracula's daughters judging by the quantities of onions which were always being consumed in the staff room. Daily conversation revolved around how many pints they'd sunk or girls they'd pulled the night before and they were damned if they were going to change their conversational habits just because women had the temerity to invade their staff room!

Most PCs worked three duty shifts but women worked two – 8am till 4pm or 4pm till midnight, though the evening shift quite often extended to the early hours of the morning. Duties varied from point duty to escort, beat duty and special duties, for instance when there was horse racing. Market duty involved issuing livestock licences and overseeing the transportation of pigs etc! Welsh farmers bringing their wares to market found female officers quite a novelty and felt quite at liberty to run a hand over my fetlocks to "check out the stock" . . . talk about undermining the authority of the law! Quite often WPCs would be involved in plain clothes duties with CID officers. This sounded exciting to me, but more often than not I was used as a decoy to catch sex offenders.

One of my first cases found me paired with a young policeman with whom I'd been sworn in at the magistrates court. As Jeff stood six feet four inches in his stockinged feet and I five feet three (and a half!) in my regulation shoes, we looked a right pair and were immediately christened "Mutt and Jeff"! We went off to investigate late-night noise and an unusual number of visitors at a house in the city. Jeff and I spent long hours together in the bushes, lying under the lounge window dutifully noting down the number of men who came and went until a cold, damp and decidedly stiff dawn broke! The following night we sensibly commandeered a neighbour's garden shed and fortified ourselves with a thermos of tea. We soon gathered enough evidence to prosecute the lady of the house for

Hereford women police in the 1940s. It was not an easy life for these pioneers in a male-dominated occupation.

running a brothel. Most of her clients were the American soldiers who were still stationed at Hereford.

One of my favourite persistent offenders was called Hilda. I remember escorting her to Winson Green Prison in Birmingham on more than one occasion and each time she was released she'd bring me a bunch of flowers (undoubtedly stolen from someone's front garden) and I'd buy her a cup of tea in the milk bar where she spent most of her days. Night time would find her in one of the derelict houses in town . . . today's squatters are hardly a new phenomenon.

Another "character" with whom I had a close encounter was Bridget. I'd been called to a disturbance in a pub in Commercial Road. A drunken woman was holding the landlord and customers at bay with a broken beer mug. I entered the scene, resplendent in uniform and ready to wield the full weight of the law (gulp). Whether Irish Bridget was entranced by the uniform or me I don't know but she accompanied me to the station like a lamb, lugging all her worldly goods tied up in a large sheet. She smelled to high heaven of mothballs, and the reason for this became clear at the station, when we undid her bundle to list her personal effects: hundreds of mothballs rolled across the floor. Bridget let forth a stream of very colourful abuse and it transpired that this was her livelihood: selling mothballs door to door!

Though a minor offence, it was far from her first and she was remanded in custody for two weeks. This meant another trip to Winson Green, but by train this time as there were no vehicles available. In civvies with another WPC colleague we duly boarded God's Wonderful Railway at Hereford station but failed to find an empty carriage (Bridget still reeked of mothballs). Opting for a carriage with only two other briefcase-carrying passengers, we installed ourselves, me next to the window, Bridget and her bundle (from which she refused to be parted) in the middle and my colleague on the other side of her. Bridget had a nasty cold but an aversion to handkerchiefs, and now proceeded to embarrass us by blowing her nose on sheets of torn-up newspaper which she pulled from her bundle. After trumpeting loudly she'd lean across me to jettison the offensive "rag" through the window, much to the horror of our fellow travellers.

As we neared our destination Bridget loudly announced her need to go to the lavatory so I accompanied her down the corridor. On our return I found that our compartment companions had overcome their curiosity to strike up a conversation with my colleague, intrigued to discover the relationship between us girls and this mad Irish woman. They simply refused to believe that we were policewomen, who they expected to be twelve stone, bearded Amazons! We duly escorted Bridget to Winson Green and bade her a fond farewell. I must say that I always found visiting prison a chilling experience, and hated the clang of iron as each door banged shut and locked behind you. This "prison claustrophobia" disappeared the moment I stepped through the gate and onto the street again. Police and released prisoners alike usually headed straight for the dingy cafe on the opposite side of the road for a decent cup of tea and a fresh look at the world.

It's funny how often Withington, where I was to live when I married, featured in my life. I remember being called out during the hop picking season to a serious road accident at Whitestone corner after two lorry loads of gipsies had crashed. When we arrived on the scene we found one lorry on its side right across the road and blood apparently everywhere. Dead bodies, the injured and the result of their Saturday shopping in Hereford were all strewn across the highway. One old lady was put into the police ambulance with me in attendance, but she promptly expired before my eyes, while other injured, including the baby she'd been nursing, were loaded into the waiting Hereford ambulance. Within minutes, dozens of gipsies from nearby farms arrived and were sitting in the middle of the road, wailing and beating their heads in grief.

I went with the dead woman to the mortuary where the resident doctor took a brief look at her and casually pronounced, "She's dead alright; strip her and tie her ankles and wrists together." My first dead body and I was paralysed with fright! Sergeant "Chalky" White came to my rescue and explained that we had to list all her belongings for the records and in front of witnesses for our own legal protection. Her hands were laden with gold rings, many made from sovereigns or half-sovereigns, as were her earrings, one of which, I remember clearly, had been virtually torn off by the accident. We also removed dozens of bracelets and several necklaces, but what gave me the greatest shock was the quantity of pound notes we discovered as we removed her many layers of clothing. She wore no knickers, but four different corsets, and between each layer of clothing was stashed a small fortune in notes! The members of her family were furious that we'd removed her jewellery and insisted it all be put back before her burial.

On one occasion I was patrolling High Town with another WPC when we were literally overrun by "gentlemen of the press". A glamorous actress was thrust between us and before we knew what was going on we found ourselves in the middle of a publicity photocall. The Chief Constable was far from impressed to see "An Arresting Shot of Beryl Baxter, the Actress" featured in the local paper to publicise her film then showing at the Odeon cinema. We received a severe reprimand for allowing the force to be used in this way! It was another matter when there was a feature on the police force in the same paper at a later date, when I was called upon to pose with a young reporter in a ju-jitsu grip, captioned "Policewomen are now taught how to throw strong men to the ground!"

In 1947 Hereford City Police Force joined with the County Force and gradually WPCs became much less of an oddity, with two each stationed at Leominster, Ross on Wye and Ledbury as more women were recruited. I left the force in 1949 to be married – not, I hasten to add, to a policeman! I look back upon those three years with mixed feelings. There were some very black moments, but it was certainly an educational experience in more ways than one. I remember my mother's sad reflection on this period of my life was, "And you used to be such a nice girl!"'

WAR & PEACE

THE GREAT WAR 1914–18

Though the war itself was fought far from Herefordshire's still peaceful rural countryside, the sight of German prisoners of war and other 'strangers', and the wounded in their hospital blue, brought the war home to local people. To children who grew up during the war years, their absent soldier father was often the 'fly in the ointment' when he returned home and disrupted their day to day life.

STRANGERS AND SHORTAGES

'I was born at Leintwardine and my earliest memories are of the First World War, which seemed to go on forever. There was no radio, but daily newspapers gave the grim news, and almost every family was affected as men were called up and the awful casualties mounted. A large house in the village was taken over as a hospital, and we saw the wounded soldiers in the hospital blue uniforms when they were able to walk around.

The item of rationing I remember most was butter, when at tea time we were allowed one piece of bread and butter, and then of bread and jam.'

'During the war a Belgian family was received, housed and maintained at Pembridge. A cottage was lent to them, various people supplied money, furniture and equipment, the children went to the village school and the young men learnt a trade.'

'Thinghill Mansion, at the top of Thinghill at Withington, was used to house prisoners of war during the First World War. It was like something from the Austrian Alps, its pretty painted turrets outlined against the sky. It was demolished in the late 1920s, but some parts of it were carefully preserved and shipped to the United States, where it was rebuilt.'

'At the outbreak of war I was three years old. I overheard my parents and our postman discussing the war and feeling that something terrible was happening, I shrieked, "What shall we do now?" Afterwards they were more careful when I was around.

A naughty servant boy used to point to bushes and small trees and tell us young children that Germans were hiding there and about to attack us. Oddly, we never told our parents about this.

One day when going down the hill to a little shop I met a party of escaped German prisoners of war. They spoke and smiled as they hurried by; I heard later that they had been recaptured.'

'During the war schoolchildren at Cradley were given a day off to go blackberry picking. The blackberries were used as a dye for wool, not for consumption. The children would take them to the local shops and be paid for their efforts.'

'I remember my schooldays at Peterstow as a period of poverty – children in ragged clothes, holes in their boots and stockings, picking up sticks on the common for their fires. I remember the pools being frozen, and seeing soldiers riding through the village, and tea and sugar being in short supply. My father was making horseshoes for the Army. When he was working in Cardiff he sent us a box of bananas. My cousin brought the news that the *Lusitania* had been sunk – that was 1915.

Father was sent to France and then to Mesopotamia as Chief Farrier, and then had a month's leave in Jordan from where he sent us a parcel containing shoes, silks, shawls etc. I remember the Peace celebrations in Ross and Father's return home, and then a new chapter in my life began.'

THE FLY IN THE OINTMENT

'I was born in 1914 a few months before the outbreak of the "Great War" as it was called, the first child of a couple living on the estate village of Stretton Grandison. All the farms and cottages were part of the estate and rented by the tenants and all, including quite small cottages, had a few acres of land on which they kept cows and pigs, often a horse and always poultry. So they were all virtually smallholdings of various and different sizes. Apart from the post office, the blacksmith and the cobbler, the only other dwellings were tied cottages where farm labourers lived and even these had large gardens, often an orchard and always a pig run. All had outbuildings, sometimes attached to the house, such as a barn, cidermills, woodsheds, cowsheds and pigscots – and, of course, the outside lavatory sometimes coyly called "the privy". At that time no house in our village, not even large farms, had any type of indoor sanitation. Everyone's water came from wells or more fortunately a pump in the yard. As time went on most of us acquired a semi-rotary pump in the kitchen and eventually in a very primitive sort of bathroom – only cold water! All the cottagers had a trade and were employed by the estate – wheelwrights, masons, carpenters (these were also the coffin makers), glaziers, painters and decorators and plumbers who were mostly well-sinkers and often roofers. Each would have "the shop" almost always joined to the house where he carried out his trade.

By the time of my first birthday my father had joined up, first in the Yeomanry where the sons of the owners of the estate were until they all got killed, and then because he had some aptitude for gunnery, in the Machine Gun Corps. The basic training was short and he was soon sent out to France. So during my early years he was no more than a name to me except for those brief periods when he turned up on leave, just out of the blue having walked the four miles from Stoke Edith station. My mother, a farmer's daughter, managed the smallholding quite easily with the help of Tommy who came before and after school to help with the milking and pig feeding and chopping the morning wood. Tommy was part of my life and sometimes took me round his mole traps and showed me how he skinned them and stretched them on a board to dry. He must have sold them somewhere and I suppose Mother paid him a few pence – certainly she fed him very well and to the end of his days he treasured her memory – "the best friend I ever had" he told me not long before he died. We also had the backing of my maternal grandfather and his son who farmed nearby, and my Auntie Nell who kept house for them. Just up the road my other grandparents lived, also an aunt who was a teacher through the old pupil-teacher system. So, looking back across the years, I suppose we were in a better position than most.

As far as I was concerned, a spoilt and solitary child, the fly in the ointment was this soldier called Daddy. For one thing my mother sometimes baked some specially nice cakes and packed them in a shoe box to send "out to France". (Years later I asked him if they ever arrived and he said they did within the week in good condition.) But worst of all were the "leaves" when suddenly this soldier would arrive, unexpected and unannounced. I think my earliest recollection is of his arrival in the dim light of a winter morning while Mother and Tommy were milking and I, warmly coated and bonneted, was happily playing in the barn with the cats. He picked me up and then as Mother appeared in the doorway dropped me down in the hay to embrace her – and that night I was firmly put in my own bedroom and told to stay there.

I wonder now, how many or rather how few home leaves he could have had during his time in the trenches. Actually machine gunners were usually behind the lines so he may have been spared some of the worst horrors. But he did have to "go over the top" sometimes for the fighting surged backwards and forwards over the same countryside. He was in all the big battles, Ypres, the Somme where he saw the first tanks go into action and the battle of Arras where he must have got his "blighty". As far as I know his only injury was caused by the shrapnel in his leg, a piece of which he carried to his grave. He was in a gas attack at one of the Ypres battles and he blamed it for his bronchitis in later life but in fact he lived into his 94th year mostly in extremely good health. In his old age he mourned the comrades who had been killed so long ago and wondered why he had been spared. He seldom talked of the war except in a lighthearted way, such as the fact that some of the men were poor scholars and unable to read letters from home let alone write to their wives and they gave him their rum ration to do it for them. I think he drew a veil over the war years and in any case it was part of his life that had nothing to do with us. But during his nineties in his maudlin moods he would fight the battle of the Somme on the tea table, moving the cutlery round to explain where the lines were and picking up the tallest object on the table he would carefully position it to represent the tower of St Quentin which was a landmark for the gunners. Then he would recall that once they received an urgent message to stop firing as their shells were falling on their own forward troops.

There is another memory which is indelibly engraved on my mind. Sometimes in the morning, I suppose after one of the big battles that people would have heard about, Mother would take me in her arms and stand at the garden gate waiting for the postman. At each house down the road a woman would be standing waiting for the postman to hand out the letters – all dreading the one from the War Office. In the spring of 1917 my mother was given one, the buff coloured letter form I have before me as I write. It told us he had been wounded on the 11th of April and was being sent to a military hospital in the North of England. This was considered very good news as he was now safely away from the Western Front where so many young men had lost their lives and from where already the maimed and crippled were returning to the villages.

It seems we had some relatives in the Manchester area and Mother and I arranged to visit them and they said we would be able to make the journey by tram to where the hospital was. I do not remember my first train journey, perhaps because I disliked the whole thing. But I think it must have been the occasion I do remember well of sitting with the luggage in the back of our neighbour's pony trap with my feet dangling over the tailboard as we jogged along the country lanes to Stoke Edith station. The town where we stayed was

Rawstenstall which manufactured cotton materials and I remember the factory chimneys. I hated it and was afraid of the noise, the people and the awful clanging trams. I was sent out to play in the park with my cousins and disgraced myself by picking the flowers, rhododendrons I think. The military hospital with all the rows of men, many with bandaged heads, all sitting up waiting for a visitor was even more unpleasant to my childish eyes and I can't think that I did much to cheer them up. I was so pleased to get back home to the country, I remember running up and down the roadside picking the buttercups and taking them in and filling all the jam jars I could find. Over 70 years on I'm still pleased to see the buttercups and much regret that the tall, branched common meadow buttercup, so common a sight in the lanes of my childhood, is now very hard to find.

After the Armistice my father did come home and strangely I seem to have a memory blank. I don't think I was an easy child to contend with and I went through a period of poor health. I'm sure a modern-day child psychologist would have no difficulty in explaining this. My father used to call me his "White-faced Hereford" in reference to the Hereford breed of cattle which were at that time becoming of international importance. Then with my fair flaxen hair "as straight as a yard of pump water" (it doesn't sound very pretty!) and as there are several snaps of me at that time I must say I look a bit sullen. However, it all ends happily as in due course my mother had three more children and I suppose I had perforce to do a bit of nurse-maiding. In any case we did become a happy and well integrated family and have remained so ever since.'

THE SECOND WORLD WAR 1939-45

Just 20 years later war came again, but this time it brought real hardships and dangers to the county. Rationing and shortages made Digging for Victory a must, and making do and mending became the norm. American soldiers became familiar and welcome in towns and villages, especially to the children, and once again we saw prisoners of war on the land. Herefordshire did not suffer the heavy bombardment of some other unfortunate counties, but bombs fell here too and gas masks and air raid sirens were an ever present reminder of the possibility of sudden death. The bombing of the Royal Ordnance Factory at Hereford in 1944 was one catastrophe that has never been forgotten.

WHEN WAR BROKE OUT

'On a Sunday morning in September 1939 lunch was being prepared, cakes and pies were being baked and we were carrying on with our usual Sunday activities, but the radio was on and everyone was on tenterhooks to hear what was happening in the country.

At eleven o'clock the news was broadcast – war had been declared. Everyone at home seemed very upset. Within an hour of hearing the news there was a roar of lorries in the road, loaded with soldiers. Everyone waited with baited breath to see what would happen. After a short while the Commanding Officer and Sergeant Major were around the streets, knocking on everyone's door to get information on how many people were living in the house and if it was possible to take two men to each house to be billeted for a while.

We had a double room, so my sister and I had to move to a smaller room to accommodate these men. I thought this was very exciting, but my father soon let me know how serious it all was. I shall never know how my mother coped with it all, but even with ration books she was able to make a meal for us all. We used to sit in the evening and hear lovely tales from these boys; later they were posted to Ireland. We kept in touch until after the war, then they went their individual ways.'

'At the time when I was about to leave school I had heard a lot about war, but could not imagine what it would be like. On holiday in Aberystwyth, I remember that Saturday 2nd September 1939 was a miserable day with the town packed with mothers and children evacuated from Liverpool, all arriving by train and being taken to a reception centre before being detailed out to different homes. Some arrived in an appalling state and there were appeals for clothes and blankets. Hotels and boarding houses were trying to clear the rooms as they, too, were allocated evacuees.

On 3rd September, the fateful day, I was in chapel when at 11 am war was declared, and after the service a gloomy crowd gathered outside W H Smith's shop in Terrace Road where the news had been posted. Like a good many other people I tried to phone home, but I had to book a call and then wait five hours for connection. Loudspeakers called all men on the reserve to report for duty, and everyone seemed to be rushing about in turmoil. When I arrived home on the Tuesday there had been a few evacuees in Little Hereford, but they did not stay long because it was "too quiet"!

That first winter of the war was the worst people could remember, the trees cracking and breaking with ice. It was said to be a "glacier" frost with deep snow, too. The troops also suffered a very severe winter in France. Shelters were dug out in our field and lined with chestnut paling. Steps were made, but no roof, so just what good they would have been if the enemy had arrived I don't quite know! Traps were set on our bridge over the river Teme, and to the fury of many local folk the Army blew up the aqueduct which had carried the short-lived Kidderminster to Kington Canal. Church bells were silenced during the war, to be rung only as a warning of an enemy landing. However, one night, about midnight, the bells rang out to test the Home Guard, and as no one was aware that it was an exercise it caused a great sensation! The only real action in the parish was the dropping of a screaming bomb into a ploughed field by the river.

Like everyone else we had to cope with the black out and the rationing of food and clothes. We had to make do and mend, which to this day I think was no bad thing. If people adopted that attitude today life would be a lot happier instead of everyone trying to reach goals they cannot afford.'

THE AMERICANS CAME

'The Americans came and they were stationed up on Wigpool. They had the field right opposite our place as a little plane place for dropping their planes down and taking off like. We used to go up the White Hart then and never pay nothing there. The soldiers, they'd say, "What'll you have to drink?" and they'd leave the change on the table. And foodstuffs, we had any amount of stuff from them.

They used to come down to the farm and have a walk around. One of them, his father used to come and buy a bull off the farm next to ours before the war. But we never heard nothing of those Americans after they left. They said they was all going to write, look, but we never heard a word. Whether they all got wiped out on D-Day I don't know. Never heard a word from them.'

'It was in November 1940, just after the Battle of Britain, that my mother, brother and I left war-scarred London to settle on a farm belonging to a cousin, in the tranquil Herefordshire countryside (my father and elder brother were in the Merchant Navy).

How I loved to feed the "tiddler" lambs, fetch the cows to be milked, feed the chickens and collect the eggs. I mastered the art of milking by hand, but I never really trusted those hind legs!

It was a new experience having only oil lamps by which to do my homework; and having to walk half a mile to fetch the drinking water from a spring in a very, very muddy lane! Swimming in the river, in summer, was great fun – as was sledging in the winter when the snow was so deep one couldn't get to school.

The highlight of the week, during the holidays, was catching the bus on a Tuesday, market day, to go to Kington. Climbing over baskets of eggs and chickens was like an obstacle course! How the eggs remained intact I shall never know.

In 1942 my family and I moved to Kington. Later, I joined the Kington Pantos Concert Party. This comprised all local talent, that included vocalists, dancers, instrumentalists and comedians. My contribution was a song and tap dance routine. The Concert Party put on variety shows in many village halls throughout Herefordshire, and over the border into Wales. Also, we entertained the troops at several places, including Hergest Camp – firstly British soldiers, who were then replaced by the Americans. The comedians in the show had great difficulty in making the Americans laugh, because their sense of humour was quite different from the British. I can visualise them still, sitting in the front row, legs sprawled, faces expressionless and chewing gum! Fortunately, they appeared to enjoy the rest of the show.'

'Bomber Harris organised the first 1,000 Bomber raid on Germany, but the whole operation could have ended in hopeless confusion over the Welsh hills. One evening two teenage boys were stopped by a US army lorry, pulling a trailer. "Are we on the right road for Urishay Common?" they enquired; they had been ordered to set up their equipment and get it working by nine o'clock. The boys suggested the GIs' map was out of date because Urishay had no common, but maybe a nearby field would be big enough to accommodate the huge vehicle and trailer. The boys were invited aboard, and with haste they all made their way to the aforementioned field.

The GIs handed the boys some chocolate bars, and the adventure began. They roared up the King's Pitch, only to find the field gate had rails securing the gate post, so out came the crowbars and they ripped off the gate post then drove into the field with great urgency.

When the covers were taken off, a huge powered generator was revealed. Its purpose was to drive a revolving beacon with shutters numbered to be greater on a certain sequence. Except for a few written instructions the Americans seemed to have no idea how to start the generator. As the seconds ticked away, there was still no response from the machine and the deadline to get the beacon shining was fast approaching.

In desperation one of the Yanks said, "Do you know anything about engines, boy?" The lad realised that the taps were similar to those on the Fordson tractor on the farm, which wouldn't start on vapourising oil unless the carburettor was drained of TVO and the engine turned over to petrol; all this the lad did. "Give her a swing", said the GI. The whole countryside was suddenly lit up with a blazing light from the revolving beacon.

Before long the special constable arrived enquiring, "Don't you know there's a blackout?" "Fellah," came back the reply, "You'll see more light than this soon." Within five minutes the sound of heavy bombers could be heard in the distance and before long the raiding party flew round the beacon across the hills to the Channel and to Germany.

Those two local lads had a very important part to play in the war effort that night.

Life took a sudden jolt in the countryside with the arrival of evacuees from Bootle, American servicemen at "The Moors" and later Italian and German prisoners of war.

An Italian prisoner of war billeted on a local family was sent to Green Sidings, an unmanned halt, to collect a new hen house for his employers. He saw the hut there ready for collection, he dismantled it and took it to the farm. The next day the farmer received a communication from the firm apologising for the delay in dispatching the hen house. The farmer decided to have a look, and realised the Italian had dismantled the plate-layer's hut from Green Sidings.'

RATIONS AND MAKING DO

'The weekly rations per adult from 1939 to 1953 were as follows, though there were occasional variations:

Bacon or ham	4 ozs (100 g)
Meat	to the value of 1/2 d

(Sausages were not rationed but hard to get; offal was usually unrationed, but not always.)

Butter	2 ozs
Cheese	2-8 ozs
Margarine	4 ozs
Cooking fat	2-4 ozs
Milk	⅓ rd pint daily (more for babies and nursing mothers)
Sugar	8 ozs
Jam	1 lb per month
Tea	2 ozs
Eggs	1 shell egg per week in good times, sometimes 1 every two weeks.
Dried eggs and Dried milk	1 pkt every 4 weeks.
Sweets	¾ lb per month

Points were required for other goods such as tinned goods, dried fruit and pulses: eg 18 for a tin of fish or meat, or 2 lb dried fruit or ½ lb split peas.

No imported fruit like oranges or bananas.

Dockets were needed for furniture, bed-linen and curtains. Clothing coupons for anything else. They were used as currency among the young, and were valued gifts at times of weddings and new babies. If grannies had not been thrifty many a new babe would have had a skimpy wardrobe.

And the fact of the matter was that the general health was good, while children and babies throve with their ration of orange juice and codliver oil.

A food office was opened in Weobley, employing about eight people, issuing ration books and petrol coupons. As not many people owned cars, most shopping was done in the village, and at that time there were four grocers, two butchers and two drapers. The postmistress operated the telephone exchange, letters and parcels were sorted there, and postage was a penny sealed and a halfpenny open and postcards.

American soldiers were stationed in the village; there was a team of local firemen and the engine was kept in the garage at The Gables. There was a detachment of the Home Guard, and the young ones joined the junior training corps. Everybody was issued with a gas mask, and we had to take them to school, where we were taught what to do in an air raid. There was only one school at that time, and pupils were aged between five and 14; dinners were cooked in the canteen. A number of evacuees came to the district and lived with local families. Land girls lived at the hostel in Kington Road and went out to work on the local farms.'

'The war brought people together; rationing made things difficult, clothing coupons were saved and friends helped each other out by loaning dresses, shoes or coupons for wedding outfits. Everyone pulled their weight to help the bride.

There was not much to do in the blackout so making rugs, clothes, curtains, embroidering table linen or knitting for the bride's bottom drawer were the main occupations during the winter.'

'A pig club was set up for the area around Woolhope, giving cottagers the chance to keep and kill annually their own pig. Strict control was kept over the distribution of the pig food, and a member of the club was chosen to go round the area with an official to make sure there was no cheating.'

DIG FOR VICTORY

'At the beginning of the war there were posters everywhere, including one entitled "Dig for Victory", with a huge booted foot resting on an equally huge spade. Everyone who had a piece of land or garden, however big or small, was expected to have a go and produce as many vegetables as they possibly could! This was no big problem to country dwellers as most had a kitchen garden, as it was called. Likewise, the town and city dwellers also did their bit on their allotments.

Well, at Yew Tree House at Dilwyn we were all roped in to help. Dad grew mostly vegetables anyway – with six mouths to feed (and little did he know that there would soon be ten mouths to feed, when our cousins plus evacuees were living with us) he said he would rather see a cauliflower on his dinner plate than look at a flower in a vase! So set to work we did. Dad always did the digging – by hand (no cultivators then), and I bet his back ached! He dug most of the garden "rough" in the autumn, with a good dollop of manure at the bottom (the real stuff) and left it to let the winter weather break the soil down. I say "most" because there would be areas where the winter greens were growing – Brussels sprouts, savoys and the like – also he would leave the parsnips in the ground, because with "a bit of frost in them they were always sweeter," and he was right.

So, come spring, the winter-dug soil would be very easy to work. All it needed was a rake to level it and it was ready for planting. This was where we came in. Dad would put down his garden line and make the seed drills (or rows) with the hoe, then under strict instructions from him, planting would begin. Planting potatoes was my favourite, although I had to do this carefully – spurts upwards and placed precisely with the same space between them. Woe betide me if I didn't, I would just have to start again!

After all that, Mother Nature would take over, and it was a matter of keeping the weeds down (no mean task) and thinning out the seedlings as they became big enough. Then, when they were tall enough, "sticking" the peas and beans – Dad would have cut the sticks long before from the hedgerows (his own, I hasten to add!) and hopefully they would last several seasons. Also, if it was a dry time with not much rain, out would come the watering cans, and the water which had been stored in the butts (or tanks) was used to give everything a drink.

One job I absolutely hated was when the caterpillars appeared on the greenstuff, and we kids would be put to work to pick them off – ugh! Also when the green, black, white (or any other colour) fly cared to show themselves, we would be armed with a bucket of soapy water and an old bicycle pump, and sent to spray them – we enjoyed doing that – and of course we had a bit of fun spraying each other (when Dad wasn't looking). Come to think of it, why are all these poisons used as sprays nowadays when such simple methods were used to keep pests at bay, and very successfully, I might add, all harmless to humans, birds and animals.

It was really exciting watching everything growing to fruition. Dad used to say there was "no better sight" than a well-tended garden full of vegetables and fruit. How we would look forward to when the first crops were ready – broad beans to eat with home-cured bacon, or sweet new potatoes and peas to have with the Sunday joint (which during the war was so small one could hardly see it when it was cooked!). However, having all those lovely vegetables certainly helped to stretch it. My favourite was (and still is) kidney (or stick) beans.

Come harvest time, the main crop potatoes would be dug, with us kids picking them up and, as we did so, sorting the seed sizes (for next year's crop) from the eating sizes, which were then carefully stored in the cellar along with the carrots, beetroot, etc. Then would come the grand clear up – waiting for the right day to have a bonfire, ie when there was a calm day with no wind (so as not to annoy the neighbours – or Mum, especially if she had washing on the line!). I just loved the smell and the crackle of the fire, as the waste was burned.'

WARTIME FRUIT PICKING

'I first visited Herefordshire in 1943 with a group from my school in Middlesex, to camp on a farm in Putley and pick fruit. We arrived at Ashperton station and then had to walk to Mr Robert's farm, though our luggage was taken in a farm truck. Our accommodation was in bell-tents, already pitched since we were following a group from the boarding part of our school which was evacuated to Tregoyd and Llan Thomas near Hay. We ate in a large marquee, and washing and toilet arrangements were under cover. We went in August and picked Pershore Yellow Egg plums followed by Worcester Pearmain apples. As I remember, the orchards were large, because besides the 30 or so St Helen's girls there were also members of Olly Taylor's large gipsy family all picking away, as well as two Italian POWs – one knew where they were for they continually sang snatches of opera. On our time off we explored the local lanes, attended services at Putley church (very high church it was then), even walked into Ledbury where I bought a splendid driving whip for my father's pony and trap from a saddler in New Road. On wet days when we could not pick, the lady from the village shop lent us vast quantities of Women's Weeklies to read.

When we arrived at Ashperton station on our departure day we were each given a chip of Worcester apples to take home – coals to Newcastle in my case since I lived on a farm with orchards, though mainly cherry, of its own. The camp was repeated the following year, especially enjoyable then as it was V-bomb time in our home territory.'

WAR IN THE VILLAGES

'Wessington Court became an auxiliary hospital run by the Red Cross and wounded soldiers were sent there to recuperate after battle. A few ladies got together at Woolhope and organised a Saturday night social and invited those "boys in blue" as they were called, and what fun we had. I remember one night we were all dancing, when suddenly the band stopped what they were playing and started to play the "tune of the day" which was *There is a lady sweet and kind*. What had happened was that the Matron in charge of the soldiers had just walked in the door!'

'The beginning of the war brought great changes to the village of Putley. Evacuees from a school in Birmingham had arrived on 1st September bringing with them their own teachers, and had joined with our school. They were billeted in the village; I had three sisters and I still hear from them. They looked very sad on their arrival carrying their gas masks, missing their mother.

The men of the village were called up for service in the army and air force, the women for nursing, fire service and working on the land. There was double summer time, to give more daylight hours, but we still had to be careful with the blackout.

A school of 45 boys from Birmingham stayed at the parish hall to help with the harvest during their holidays.

Land Army girls were billeted at Ledbury and their services were called on to work the farms. There was also a prisoner of war camp so we had Italians and Germans working in the village. In our spare time we knitted socks and gloves for the services, and the WI also made jam at the parish hall and sold it to "Ledbury Preserves".

During this time the church bells were silent, only to be rung to warn us of an invasion. It was great to hear them on 8th May 1945 to announce the end of the war in Europe. All the servicemen and women returned home except for one air force boy; he was only 20 years old.'

'The whole of Colwall took in evacuees. A particular Jewish family were here for six years, and the son still visits to sit on the hill where his parents sat. A large house was turned into a wounded soldiers' hospital and the more active patients would walk around the village. The grounds of the private school were given over to growing food. There was much make do and mend, with old clothes being cut up and recycled – a prize was won at the flower show for a pair of children's trousers made out of an old shirt.

There was a dogfight over the hills one night, when the air raid wardens were at a meeting. Four bombs were dropped. One killed a pony in a field. At one house the sitting room door opened and closed twice, terrifying the schoolmistress who was boarding there at the time. The cinema was very popular during the war, when all Germans were booed and Allied planes etc cheered!'

BUILDING AN AIRFIELD

'Before the war, Shobdon airfield was shown as a lake and marshland on all maps. It was decided to develop the area as an airfield during the war, and thousands of tons of gravel were brought from the local quarry at Aymestry and deposited in the marshes. When the

201

runway was dug, the trench was deeper than the digger doing the work; only the smoke from the exhaust was visible above ground. It was originally intended to have two runways but the ground was so unstable that only one was constructed, for light aircraft use only.

Many prisoners of war were brought into the area to help with the construction work. The biggest claim to fame was that the glider pilots at the battle of Arnhem had trained at Shobdon. The reason that Shobdon was selected for gliding is that the steep hill provides a large amount of natural lift, and the Radnor Hills just beyond Byton provide natural "wave" lift. The RAF were billeted in the Nissen huts around what is now the housing estate called The Birches. The air raid shelters still exist in the adjoining woods. The hospital is now a private bungalow. The local girls looked forward to Saturday nights at Shobdon's own cinema (on the airfield) – and to the nylons and chocolates from the airmen!

South Wales miners were billeted just outside Shobdon, at Uphampton, to be re-educated as forestry workers. They were all dressed in brown trousers, boots and donkey jackets. The local children idolised them because they gave away sweets and organised Christmas parties for them.'

BOMBS AND AIR RAIDS

'In 1939 all the schoolchildren in the Bargates at Leominster were allocated a house to be evacuated to should the air raid siren go off. We stood, three children to a house, on the doorstep – sometimes we were rewarded with sweets and biscuits by the lady of the house. We realised how lucky we were that this drill did not take place very often during school hours.'

'My father built an air raid shelter at our house at Hampton Bishop. As we were not given them in the country, he dug a huge hole in the garden, shored it up inside with boards and made steps to go down into it. He covered the top with zinc sheets, then turf on top, and inside went a table and chairs, a food safe, tinned foods, a spirit stove for heat, food and water for the tea etc, and a Tilly lamp. Each time the shelter was used, one of us was allotted the job of restocking it for next time.

I worked at a munitions factory as a Civil Inspector of Armaments. One morning, just as we were going on our shift and the night workers were going off, a stray German plane dropped its bombs on part of the factory and house, and many people were killed. We ran for shelter in long grass in a field, and saw what we thought was an RAF plane chasing it. Then suddenly we saw the swastika flag on the tail! My luck was in that day.

We had neighbours from all around us sharing our shelter in the garden, and we used to play cards and snakes and ladders till the all clear went. We always carried tin hats and gas masks to work. I once forgot to leave my signet ring at home, and when I got to work I realised it was still on my finger so I put it on my wedding finger and turned it round (only wedding rings were allowed to be worn at work). Unfortunately my ploy did not succeed and I was suspended for four days.'

'On 10th April 1941, three bombs were dropped at Llanycoed, Dorstone. The cowshed was hit and cattle were killed, and a nine month old baby lying in his cot miraculously escaped being killed. Local people walked to Llanycoed with food and help for the poor saddened family.'

'At Withington, one stick of bombs was dropped in the area by a German plane trying to lighten its load before fleeing homeward. The first bomb dropped at Burley Gate, and so on in a straight line through the back of the village to Ocle Pychard, where a calf was blasted into a tree. It was the only casualty. One bomb dropped on someone's outside lavatory, which collapsed, but the bucket and seat was, thoughtfully, left standing!'

THE ROYAL ORDNANCE FACTORY, HEREFORD

'Two of my sisters were sent to work at the Hereford ammunition factory. One worked in the offices and was given a wheelbarrow full of sand and a spade as she was to be one of the firefighters if there was an explosion or air raid! The other sister worked in the shell shed filling the shells. She didn't mind that but she hated the mob cap she had to wear to cover her hair and the long overalls down to her ankles, made of a kind of thick rough calico, and the rubber shoes – she loved glamour, and that was far from it. Their hours were long, leaving home at five o'clock in the morning and not arriving back until seven o'clock in the evening. Mother was always up at four to get them off and dinner was always waiting for them when they returned.'

'I was Deputy Head Warden of the St Martin's ARP group from 1938 to 1946. On 27th July 1942, at approximately 6 am, a single German bomber circled over the Royal Ordnance Factory and dropped two 250 kg bombs onto a transit shed. One exploded, killing

19 personnel and injuring many more. No official number was given at the time. The other struck a girder and was deflected through the large open doors of the transit shed at a low angle. Striking the ground, it continued some 100 yards, passing through the wire perimeter fence of the ROF into the house of the Superintendent of the ROF Police nearby, killing all but one of the occupants.

I was on my way to Norton Avenue ARP post when the bombs exploded. I noticed that they were on the extreme south-west of the ROF and could have dropped on a small hamlet called the Moorlands, which would be the responsibility of my ARP group. Arriving at the scene, the Superintendent's house was just a heap of debris and when I called out, somewhat hopelessly, "Is there anyone alive?", a voice replied from out of 14 ft of rubble. The house nearby was only slightly damaged and the occupants were in their air raid shelter. Finding a usable telephone was difficult, but the Hereford ARP Rescue Team were soon rescuing the survivor. He was taken to hospital and found to be clear of any injuries.

During this time, I received a message from ROF ARP "that they had noticed that an unexploded bomb had passed through the transit shed towards the Super's house". I consulted the rescue team. They decided to carry on, but on seeing the crowds of onlookers I sent for assistance from the ARP Controller (the Chief Constable). He sent a detachment of infantry to move them to safer areas. Our wardens and a special constable were not able to close the incident until four o'clock due to the difficulty in making sure we left no traces of human remains over the very wide area. There was no unexploded bomb.

The heavy machine-gun raised platform in the centre of the ROF was not manned at the time, so I was told, the crew having been "stood down" due to the inactivity of the Luftwaffe in this area.

An elderly lady interviewed at Hillside had actually been inside the ROF at the time of the bombing. She was told that all the people killed were outside the factory area.'

'My father was a fireman at the Royal Ordnance Factory, Rotherwas during the Second World War. We lived in a row of firemen's houses at Rotherwas, during the time of a major bomb explosion at the factory, on 30th May 1944. A fire started with a large bomb and spread to other bombs, mines, and an incorporator filled with explosive. My father, Mr John Francis Jenkins, a fireman on duty at the time, was awarded the British Empire Medal for his great courage and devotion to duty, along with many other firemen and officers. Many of the workers on duty received commendations for their brave conduct.

My father and his mate were working on the bomb and others adjacent, when the first explosion occurred. This knocked him over backwards and he was badly cut about the head. His mate on the branch, Little, was very badly injured, so my father helped to get him out and take him to safety. The second explosion occurred whilst he was so engaged. He was instructed to evacuate the firemen's quarters and was later taken to hospital but returned after treatment, and again reported for duty.

My sister remembers my father arriving home to see if everything was all right. All the families had to take cover in underground shelters. I can remember my mother telling me about rushing down the garden path with my sister and brother, taking them to safety, and then having to come back for me, asleep in my cot upstairs. When it was all clear to return to the house, my christening clothes, and outfits for my brother and sister, all laid out ready for my christening, were covered in glass and debris. All the windows and doors had been blown in from the force of the blast.'

A CHILD'S WAR

For some children war brought upheaval and separation from their parents, as they were evacuated from the towns and cities and sent to safe haven in the countryside. The experience could be quite an eye-opener for both the evacuees and those who took them into their homes, but it forged some friendships that have stood the test of time.

THE FIRST DAY

'It had seemed to be a normal late summer Sunday. My aunt and uncle were with us for their annual holiday from London – a visit we all enjoyed. Mother had the lunch underway, but everyone was waiting to hear a special broadcast by the Prime Minister at eleven o'clock.

The grown ups were all very serious, and phrases like, "It is too soon to go through all that again" and, "What if Harry (my uncle) has to go back to sea?" floated about together with the buzzing of bees and the occasional fly.

Then there was Mr Chamberlain, his voice sad and serious, telling the world that there was now a state of war between Britain and Germany. I hopped about, with my four year old brother, telling everyone that we were not pre-war, having heard the phrase so often from those whose lives had been so rudely altered by the First World War.

The day wore on, but even as an eleven year old, I felt the stirrings of fear for the future.

My uncle decided to return to London to set in motion the evacuation of his office from the City, because there was fear that the Germans might bomb London right away. Then I remember my gas mask in its cardboard box and the stories of gas attacks during the last war and all those newspaper pictures of German soldiers with guns and ugly helmets marching into other people's countries. Suddenly life did not seem quite as secure and carefree as it had been yesterday.'

DARK DAYS

'When war was declared in 1939, I was seven years old, and of course, didn't quite know what it meant. My parents' generation knew exactly what it was all about, having already had one war during their lifetime. They faced this one with fear and trepidation, knowing that at least one of their children would be called up to fight for their country. Both my mother and father had lost a brother in the 1914-18 war, so they must have been very scared for the future. I vividly remember Jim Preece coming to the butcher's shop with a poster commanding us to black out all windows, or any point which may show a light during the hours of darkness (any such light would attract enemy aircraft). So there was a rush to buy black fabric to line all curtains, and Dad made a wooden frame with special blackout paper stretched over it – the paper, as far as I can remember, was two sheets of thick brown paper, with a kind of black tarry substance sandwiched between. This frame was for the big shop window. After dark, when all blackouts were in place, someone would "do the rounds" to see that no lights were showing. It must have cost a fortune for big houses with dozens of windows, and I expect the manufacturers and drapers did quite nicely supplying the fabric! Oh well, it's an ill wind.

Of course it was impossible to black out the church, so all services were held in the school – we thought it was a real novelty! There was always a big congregation; I suppose in times of worry and stress people tend to turn their thoughts more to the Lord.

Dilwyn formed a platoon of the Home Guard and they would patrol in certain locations each night. Also they would (as we called it) "play wars". I can remember times when they were hiding from the "enemy" in the hay-barn at Yew Tree House, and a group of us kids crept up on them and "shot" them with our home-made guns (pieces of stick, really!). We thought this a great game – though it was all very serious to the village men.

Dad was an ARP Warden (Air Raid Precautions – though some bright person soon thought up an alternative name: 'Anging Round Pubs!). His duties, mainly, were to patrol the village looking for any chinks of light coming from windows etc. Very often he would have to issue a warning to householders who were a little careless, "Put that light out – or else!"

Meanwhile, with our dear brother "at the front", it was left to the rest of the family to hold the fort here at Dilwyn! My eldest sister, Eleanor, had to learn to drive the butcher's van in double quick time, so that the meat could be delivered to the surrounding areas. Of course, my elder sister, Margaret, and I were at school, but as soon as we arrived home we were roped in to help with the deliveries. We would walk the village with huge wicker baskets (well, they seemed huge to me) loaded with meat for the customers. Although, as the war progressed the meat ration for each person became smaller and smaller – so this rather lightened the load. The smallest ration I remember was tenpence worth of meat per person, per week! Dad had the darndest job to make *that* go round the customers. We would often end up with nothing for ourselves – or perhaps if we were lucky, an ox-tail between ten people (the evacuees were with us then). But, we were all extremely lucky, and we survived – not like many thousands of other poor people who did not.'

COMFORTS FOR THE TROOPS

'At the outbreak of war, Broxwood school was asked by the various voluntary services to knit comforts for the troops. We used to attach our names to the finished articles, and through doing this I received about a dozen letters of thanks from various boys (and girls) in the Forces. They, and especially the badges which we received after knitting so many clothes, are my most treasured possessions today.

The letters mention beautifully knitted balaclavas, socks, sea-boot stockings, gloves, pullovers and scarves. They are dated between 1940 and the end of 1943, some envelopes bearing twopence-halfpenny stamps. They are mostly from merchant seamen, airmen and WAAFs, all recipients being really grateful for the lovely warm garments they had been given.

One letter was from a Lieutenant Commander in the Royal Navy, and he concluded it as follows:

"I hope that you and your schoolfellows and all the children in the world will, when this is over, have a cleaner and happier world to grow up in, and that such a shadow will never fall across your lives again." '

WAR BECAME THE NORM

' "Do you want any gum, chum?" was a regular greeting to a child who shopped with her Mum in wartime Kington. Country children just blushed and looked wide-eyed at the servicemen, who looked like Father Christmases in uniform! We accepted the gum, and all the other goodies proffered by American servicemen at the Kington base. There were American boxes, opened with such excitement and every item cherished – even the box, which would last until the cardboard fell to pieces.

Then there was the party, looked forward to for weeks, and from some old chest a party dress would appear and we'd be taken to the Camp to be mixed in with many other country children – oh, the noise and confusion! and oh, the number of children. What did we eat? Very little at the party, from what I can remember, we were completely overcome with awe and wonder at the splendid entertainment offered by the men.

Evacuees coming to the area were another mystery to the children, we felt they were sad and lonely, with different habits as well as different speech. Mothers talked a lot about the overcrowding, the bed-wetting, and the coarseness of those who came, but to us children – to whom nobody explained what and why and when – it was just part of life in a country school.

Then came the end of the war – what were they all celebrating? Younger children didn't know. For all our conscious lives we had known war, it was the norm – and not too bad in rural Herefordshire. If anything, it was the end of the war which brought the problems, in the shape of new beginnings – and fathers!'

'A whole new vocabulary was born during the war; we probably didn't know what half the expressions meant. "Fifth Columnist" was one I remember. We once attended a special service at the Methodist chapel at Huntingdon. It was a fine warm evening with an overflow congregation so the service was held outside. In front of us sat a lady who had very bright red cheeks, very frizzy yellow hair and a remarkable bright green hat – she joined in the hymn singing with tremendous gusto. My young sister looked at her in astonishment for some time before she tugged my mother's sleeve and said in an audible whisper, "Mum, is that a fifth columnist?" '

WHERE'S THE CHIPPY?

'I can remember very vividly the day I first came to Herefordshire. It was 2nd September 1939. War was inevitable and with a feeling of dread of the unknown I was accompanying my class of 14 year old girls from the biggest slum school in the centre of Birmingham. The girls were allowed to bring their younger brothers and sisters so that they could keep together as families. If I was feeling nervous, you can imagine the stark fear hidden under the famous cheeky "Brummie" veneer. At their most cheerful, they regarded it as a great adventure. The only grass they knew was that in the local churchyard or further afield in a small park. Most of them had never seen the sea. They lived in back-to-back houses with no water or toilet facilities. Their bathroom was a tin bath filled from water supplied from a tap in the communal courtyard and heated on the kitchen fire.

Their faces shining with an extra scrubbing from Mum, they arrived at school at 9 am. First, their emergency packs had to be examined. One girl in my class, Ellen, followed by Frankie, Stephen, Olive, Henry and so on down to five year old Annie – stepped forward first. Her freckled face shining with pride, she produced her parcel – a newspaper roll. Inside was the requisite food for the day, a mountainous pile of thick sandwiches, plus her gas mask, a new pair of brightly striped pyjamas, a toothbrush, a flannel and a change of underwear. "What a lovely pair of pyjamas," I remarked brightly, "Your mother was kind to buy new ones." "Please, Miss, what are they for?" asked Ellen. "Oh, perhaps you usually wear a nightie to go to bed?" I ventured. "No," came the blank answer. Of course she did not. I remembered the struggle I'd had to get the girls to strip off on the great day in needlework class when we'd finished the navy knickers and gingham blouses which were being introduced as a uniform for gym lessons – and I'd discovered those girls had been sewn into their underwear for the winter months!

Next came Frankie. Where was his parcel? "'Er's got it," said he, pointing to Ellen. One parcel for the whole family! I prayed for understanding hostesses at the end of our journey.

We marched in crocodile up to Snow Hill station, followed by anxious and vociferous parents. To the accompaniment of tearful

209

farewells and last injunctions to "do as yer told", the train eventually steamed out of the station.

As we left the smoky city and green fields began to appear, there was a silence. Then – "Cor, Miss, look at those apples, they're growing on trees" – "Where have the shops and houses gone?" – "Where are we going to stay?" The sun shone, faces became grimy, food parcels disappeared, and then suddenly the train stopped at our destination, Ledbury. We were met by kindly hostesses anxious to meet the families they had been allocated. In a very short time the children disappeared – "Fancy, Miss, we're going to live on a farm!" The great adventure had begun.

The next day we all gathered at the church. War had been declared. There was a feeling of fear, depression and sorrow among the adults in the congregation.

Monday dawned warm and sunny, and to the delight of all we were told that school was to be abandoned pro tem, and we were delegated to help the farmers pick their crop of hops. Within days, the children looked sunburnt and were entering into the spirit of Harvest, but sadly before the month was out it had all ended and every child had returned to the smoky city.

"Well, you see, Miss, there ain't no fish and chip shop, and they don't change the film on Wednesdays at the flicks," said Ellen.'

'When war broke out the evacuees came to Mathon, and anyone with a spare bedroom was compelled to take some in. We had a young mother with three children under five years. On arrival the first question they asked was, "Where's the pub and the chip shop?" On being told the pub was two miles away and the "chippy" was the other side of the Malvern Hills, they nearly returned to Birmingham.

One day when ours had been with us for several weeks, I had to go out and on returning in the late evening was surprised to find the house in darkness and not a sound to be heard. On entering the living room I found one terrified lady with three sleeping children huddled in a corner. I had filled and trimmed the oil lamps before leaving but it hadn't occurred to me that she hadn't a clue how to light them.

The eldest little boy was quite a chatterbox. One morning when I was dishing out the cereals for breakfast he looked up at me and in his Brummy accent said, "Where do ya keep getting the food from, lady? Ya never goes out but ya keep on finding it." I had to explain that my groceries were only delivered once a fortnight so I had to get in a supply to last.'

SO FAR FROM LONDON

'It was in 1941 that I first came to live in Hereford. I was eight years old, and with the rest of my family, mother, father and two year old brother, came from the hubbub of war-time London. We moved to rooms in a Herefordshire farmhouse, and so began a very different sort of life. We were used to holidays at the seaside, and perhaps day trips to places like Epping Forest, not too far from our previous home, but we knew nothing about the countryside.

Some of the things I noticed: the earth was brown and I had always thought of it as black, and I was quite convinced that all the animals in the fields were going to chase me. The only animals I had seen, apart from cats and dogs, were in the zoo!

Of course I had to go to the local school, and I remember that I found it very difficult to understand the local Herefordshire accents of the other children, and they found my London way of speaking equally strange.

My mother must have found it very difficult to cope with the housekeeping, having to put up with oil lamps and an oil stove for cooking. There was no hot water, and the iron had to be heated up on the fire. I used to collect wood for my parents, to light the open fire, and I well remember getting stuck in the mud in a gateway whilst doing this. There was no bathroom, only a pump outside, and an outside lavatory. After having all the conveniences, it was very different for us all.

Another thing I missed was the town transport. In the country there were few buses and no trains, so there was lots of walking, to school and for shopping and so on. I soon got to enjoy some of the aspects of life on the farm, though, and used to help to collect the eggs, and sometimes went on the milk round. It all seemed so very far from my old life in London.'

GOOD AND BAD

'We took in one evacuee at Hampton Bishop, and she was a naughty one, always into mischief. She set fire to newspapers on the table, and rode my brother's bicycle into flood water in the garden where she nearly sank in the mud and drowned! Her mother worked on nights at a local old people's home and was lodged elsewhere, but while my mother was helping feed other evacuees this woman used her daughter's bed in our house! My mother didn't know until she was told by a neighbour.

My mother used to help a lady at Tupsley who had opened her

house to about 30 evacuees. Some were very good, others naughty, but they were all sorry to go home when the time came.'

'We were on a camping holiday in North Wales with some friends when, over the portable radio, we heard that a state of war existed between Great Britain and Germany, and that all old people, mothers with young children, and children of school age were to be evacuated from the danger areas the following day; also that all windows were to be blacked out. We slept little that night and were up and away early next morning for home.

We had previously been warned that we were liable to have four evacuees billeted in our house. We arrived home at Pembridge in the early afternoon and then began a rush around for blackout material and making up beds for the expected evacuees. Kington was the distributing area and we expected busloads of children hourly and made several trips to the Institute to meet them. However, about 11 pm the bus arrived and there was more delay while the children

Evacuees like these four from Liverpool, in a garden at Pembridge, began arriving in the villages immediately war had been declared. The experience was not always a happy one – for evacuees or local families – but in many cases friendships were formed which have lasted over half a century.

and others were sorted out and each given two packets of biscuits and a half-pound slab of chocolate.

We reached home about 11.30 pm with four sisters from Liverpool, ages six to twelve. After a hot drink and some food they were bundled into bed, half asleep and too tired to be washed. They were very good children and, although they came from a poor home (nine children, and Father unemployed for six years) they were nicely brought up. We had them for three years, and then they had the option of going to a new home or returning to Liverpool. They decided on the latter course.

The three years they were with us were hectic in the extreme, especially on Sundays when all the relatives came to see the children. They arrived about 11 am and did not depart until after 5 pm. Soon after the children arrived we were asked to take two teachers in the cottage. They looked after themselves but I promised their dinners.

Sometimes on a Sunday we were 13 or 14 to dinner, and then early tea was provided before the visitors went away. After my husband had been on Home Guard duty all the morning, he helped me to wash up and then get tea. Eventually we had to limit the visitors to not more than four. The enormous parties were really too much and the food situation was very precarious and not improving.

This experience is typical of all the Pembridge folk who took in evacuees; it is certainly a holiday which the children will never forget.

Later, we had a German girl from Cologne for three months, through the Save the Children organisation.'

'People came from London to settle in Eardisland during the war, and children from poorer families in Bootle, Lancashire were sent to be given shelter in the community. These children were expected to arrive one evening at seven o'clock but finally turned up, filthy and tired, at ten o'clock when they had to be found temporary homes in the village. They must have felt almost as strange as the German prisoners of war who worked for board and lodging on the local farms, or the Italian schoolmaster POW, who experienced great difficulties with the language! However, the prisoners relaxed by giving concert parties to their employers and the children of the village, so their stay in Eardisland must have been reasonably comfortable; indeed, some married local girls and settled here!'

'When war was declared many evacuees from Liverpool came to the Kington area. My husband and I had two girls, aged eleven and 13, billeted with us. They arrived at about one o'clock in the morning and, what with the blackout and strange people and places, it must have been quite frightening for them.

Although we lived only a few yards from Huntington school, the children had to walk about two and a half miles to Mahollam school where the evacuees had a classroom to themselves. Their head teacher had come with them.

They stayed with us for nearly two years and went back to Liverpool when the bombing had eased somewhat. Both girls have kept in touch ever since and have never failed to send a Christmas card every year.'

GOING HOP PICKING

'During the early part of the Second World War a dramatic change happened in my life; two cousins, who lived in Eastbourne, were hurriedly evacuated to my home in Hereford. The two boys had been booked to sail with other children to America for safety but the trip was quickly cancelled when *The Bonaris* was torpedoed and sank, and they were sent to us. Suddenly from being a lonely, shy only child I was one of a family – I now had two brothers about my own age. It was wonderful, we walked, explored, swam, made dens, and made friends with a lot of children that I had never met before.

My mother, not quite so thrilled with her bigger family, and faced with an extended school summer holiday, "to help with the harvest for the war effort" took us hop picking. This was a different world from hop picking today. The hops were grown up wooden poles and we picked the hops into a crib made of hessian with wooden supports at each end.

It was here that we met Mr Izzard. Mr Izzard's word was law; word spread like wildfire if he was coming. He was a tall upright man with a walrus moustache and to us children seemed very old. He walked round the hop yard and brought us the poles covered with hops for us to pick. When we had picked all the poles in our "house" he came and moved us to the next one. There were two other men and two Land Army girls helping there. We knew them by their Christian names but not Mr Izzard!

Twice a day the men would come to "bushel up". They arrived with a large sack and a basket which held a bushel of hops and measured what we had picked – you had to watch Ben because he pushed them in with his elbow, or so people said.

Twice a day too a milk churn of scalding hot tea was brought round and since tea was rationed it was very welcome. Everybody rushed off with mugs, cups and jugs to get their share.

There were other diversions too. A shout would go up that somebody had found a Hop Dog – a large beetle-type of thing – and we would all dash off to see it. Then there was the strike (which was a tradition every year) when the price per bushel was fixed, eightpence that year.

The Red Cross had the next crib to us, and there was a steady stream of people with an hour or two to spare who came and picked for the Red Cross to help the war effort.

At the end of the two weeks we had to queue up to collect our pay, but worth more than that a few extra rations we were allowed as well.

Wild hops grow in a hedge near my home and every year I gather a few. The lovely smell of them takes me back in time to those wonderful long sunny days in the hop yard.'

FRIENDS FOR 50 YEARS

'I was six years old when the Second World War started, and lived with my mother and father in Ledbury. I had no brothers or sisters, there was just the three of us.

Then came the mention of evacuees – who were they and what were they like? We were to have one, would it be a boy or a girl? I very soon found out when Joan arrived on the scene. Joan came from a large family in Ladywood, Birmingham where four terraced houses shared one toilet etc which was situated in the back yard.

This little girl was twelve months older than me and half my size, with a very thin little face with glasses. One of the first tasks Mother had was combing the nits out of Joan's hair onto newspaper on the kitchen floor. She counted them daily then gradually they got less and after several weeks they had gone. When Mother scrubbed her in the bath Joan was very shocked to see her nails come clean, she thought they "was olluz black". She did not know that apples grew on trees and thought they came out of the ground. Gloves had never been seen before so we gave her a pair of mine, consequently she paraded down the centre of Ledbury with hands splayed out either side. The brightest of necklaces was worn and even a smart, big as she could find, handbag was carried.

To go to bed at seven o'clock was unheard of – Joan always went with her parents to the Beehive pub and sat on the step outside until 10.30 pm when they returned home.

Joan and I shared everything together and when the first Christmas arrived she did not believe in Father Christmas. Instead of mother and father telling me this was just fantasy, there was a stocking at the foot of each of our beds. She just could not believe it, and wrote immediately to complain to her mother that Father Christmas never visited Barker Street in Birmingham. What joy Christmas gave to her and what a pleasure it was to see her little face.

The two of us had separate bedrooms but as the days went by the friendship grew and we became closer. The time came to share a double bed when the German aeroplanes flew overhead on their way to bomb Birmingham. We lay close together praying her mother and father would still be alive in the morning. She had a brother serving abroad in the forces and there was a special prayer for him. These particular memories are the most vivid of my childhood. Thankfully they were all all right and survived.

Joan's mother and father used to travel to Ledbury by train but father was the one that came more frequently and always brought bottles of beer with him.

My father was in the Home Guard and we were used to him carrying a gun and going for practices on the Ledbury Tunnel.

Father had a large map on the dining room wall with coloured pins which were placed wherever the battles were taking place. Even as small children we felt we were part of the war.

As the war drew to a close the time came for her to return home. What a gap there was for us, especially me. It was also very strange for her. From the age of six to eleven years is a long time in a young child's life.

We always kept in touch and when Joan started work she would stand at a machine and wait for buttons to land on cards in a factory. She was earning £5 per week. I was working for a firm of solicitors and earning ten shillings and sixpence per week and also having shorthand and typing lessons which Father was paying for. This seemed so unfair to me but Father explained the monotony of the job which Joan had, but I still thought it wrong.

Being an only child it was nice to have Joan to be my bridesmaid at our wedding, in fact the only one.

Joan and her husband spent regular weekends with us all as a family, the most recent being to my grandaughter's christening.

Nobody wanted a war and nobody wants a war again, but there were so many friendships made and this was one that has lasted for over 50 years.'

DOING OUR BIT

Those who remained at home still did their bit for the war, whether it was as a member of the local Home Guard spending night after night on watch for the enemy, or in the Women's Land Army helping the farms to produce the food so badly needed as the war dragged on. The land girls did not always have a happy time of it, having to contend not only with a completely new way of life and heavy manual labour but also sometimes with a less than sympathetic farmer and his men!

IN THE LAND ARMY

'Many town girls who joined the Women's Land Army were sent to an agricultural college for six weeks to learn about the various and numerous jobs that have to be tackled on a normal farm. But life on the farm was very different to the college.

Rise at 6.30 am – light the candle – wash in cold water on the wash-stand – visit the privy 20 yards away from the house, whatever the weather, and often in darkness. What a shock after the convenience of city life!

Thirty cows to be milked and only two hurricane lamps for light in a long cow-shed. Carrying all the milk in buckets to the dairy where they were lifted high above one's head to trickle the milk over the cooler. Then the 17-gallon churns were rolled to the milk stand for the lorry to pick up and take to the factory. If the milking engine broke down, milking was done by hand, and if the cows objected their legs were restricted by their own tails to prevent them kicking the milkers!

Cleaning out the sheds was done by a shovel and broom, and when the cess pit clogged up, it was the land girl who got down inside to bale the slurry out by the bucketful – the farmer being too fat to get through the man-hole cover!

During the day field work went on with the seasons. Sometimes with a tractor, sometimes with a horse. The tractor started by turning the starting handle, but harnessing the horse was much more tricky. Getting their collars on was a major achievement, as they raised their heads to avoid it, and during the rest of the harnessing one hoped to escape being trodden on, bitten, or squashed against the

Elisabeth Lane joined the Women's Land Army early in the war. It was a hard life, particularly for city dwellers, but essential work at a time when we needed every bit of food that could be produced.

wall. However, once backed into the shafts of the cart they were raring to go.

Hoeing and 'singling' mangolds, swedes, etc was always done by hand. Many days were spent walking up and down the fields. After the hay was cut and dried, it was forked up into cocks and later pitched onto the carts and carried to the rick-yard where it was built into ricks, or stacks. The corn was cut with a binder that threw out the sheaves, which then had to be picked up by hand and stood up in stooks. Eight sheaves to a stook. When they were dry the sheaves were loaded on the carts, sometimes so heavy the horse strained to lug them from the fields. The corn was also built into stacks. Later, all the ricks were thatched to keep out the rain.

During the winter the threshing drum – a huge, noisy, dusty contraption, driven by a belt from the tractor – would visit the farm to thresh the corn from the sheaves. The sacks of corn which weighed over two hundredweight were carried up to the barn lofts by the threshing men. A gang of hostel land girls would travel round with the threshing drum all winter.

Land girls were paid 42 shillings for a 45 hour week, half of which went back to the farmer for board and lodging. Overtime was one shilling and a penny per hour. One week during harvest time I remember working 18 hours overtime, making a 63 hour week!

I worked as the only land girl on two different (in many ways!) farms during three years. As I was a city girl, and joined to avoid working in a munitions factory, four brothers and a fairly outdoor life stood me in good stead. I attended an agricultural college for six weeks.

Arriving at my first job straight from college I was expecting to be met by the farmer and at least a car, but it was his wife who came, and we set off on the bus! More shocks at the farm. No electricity, one tap in the kitchen, double-throned earth closet, and no handle to my bedroom door – only a bent nail to stop it blowing open! Candles to go upstairs with, and a jug of cold water for washing. I was terrified when spiders crawled over me during the night, so went home and cried, saying I wouldn't go back. But having left my father's farm, he didn't have much sympathy and said, "Well, *you* wanted to go, so now you must make the best of it." So I did, and never complained again.

The farmer used to undress downstairs by the fire, and in the morning, after knocking on my door, said, "Don't get lighting any candles till I've found my trousers!" He then threw sticks on the fire saying the kettle boils quicker on sticks, put tea in the cups and poured on boiling water. It tasted awful and the leaves floated on top! There was a fly-sticker fixed to the low ceiling coming down into the centre of the table. It stayed there all winter, being replaced the next summer, and as it dried, the flies fell off, so when we had blackcurrant jam I didn't have any!

We had hurricane lamps in the cow shed, and one old chap called

219

"Cloggy Dick", a Scotsman, to help. One day when the farmer went to market he asked me to collect the eggs, as he suspected CD was taking them. I kept watch in between working and when I heard a hen cackle I would go to get the egg. Imagine my surprise to find the egg had already gone! I was so incensed that I went to CD's jacket and found the egg in his pocket. I took it out and into the kitchen. What do you think? When the farmer returned home, CD told him he'd have to watch out as there was a thief about!

After I'd been there for three months we had the pig killing. This was a dreadful experience because they never told me what was actually going to happen. The pig was just bled whilst being held down by three men and squealed its head off. After the singeing I was detailed off to fetch buckets of water, and each time I returned the pig-killer would flick nasty little bits at me or try to put things in my pocket, so I warned him if he did it again I would throw the next bucket of water over him and that is precisely what happened. I fled. The farmer said afterwards I went over the muck yard like lightning, so fast my feet didn't get stuck in the mud. I got into the house from the front and stayed there. Some hours later when all was quiet I went outside to get water to wash my hair, and suddenly the pig-killer appeared, lifted me up, and put me head first into the water butt! What a day!

I was 21 whilst I was there, which as far as they were concerned was a non-event. Only the miserable old cowman wished me a happy birthday. Thank goodness I had had a lovely family party the weekend before. I used to cycle five miles to catch the train, and dreaded the ride back on dark winter evenings because I had to stop to open two gates. When the dynamo on my bike went out I felt sure, as I was struggling with it through the gate, that someone was going to grab me!

Across the fields lived a very shaky old farm worker who couldn't read or write. Once he asked me to go one night (across three fields in the dark with a torch) as he knew a woman who would marry him if he could let her know his wife had died. Rumour had it that he locked up all the food in his cottage and took the key to work and his late wife got frailer and frailer until she died, but I didn't know that at the time. Anyway, I did write the letter for him and read her reply saying she would come! After I had left I heard they did get married, and often wondered if she fared any better than the first wife.

After being there nearly a year another land girl unexpectedly appeared – nothing had been said to me. She was quite nice but the farmer's idea was to have her help his wife in the house most of the time. At this, I told him we must share the inside and outside jobs equally, but he said if I didn't like it I could go. Which I did.

After a month at my new farm he wrote asking me to go back – but no fear! I was now at a very different farm which was so much nicer in every way.

Here the farmer's wife had spent time preparing a nice room for "our land girl". Still no running water or electricity but everywhere spotless. At seven o'clock in the morning she could be seen polishing the floors, on her knees, pushing a candle ahead of her. She was also an excellent cook so I was feasted as if rationing didn't exist. Unfortunately the farmer didn't have very good health, taking numerous tablets daily, so it was left to me to start the tractor by turning the starting handle, which often "kicked" and could be very painful to one's thumb. We spent much time changing tractor wheels as the spade-lugg wheels were not allowed on the road.

Milking and farm work went on with the seasons, and I was allowed to plough turf, which apparently was a special privilege. I also worked with horses, and would have to spend all day spreading basic slag, which came in hundredweight sacks, though only as big as sandbags. I would have to take them off the trailer and put them in the spreader, then walk up and down the field leading the horse. I don't know which was worse, trying to avoid him treading on my foot as we turned, or him biting my hand! I was only just five feet tall and harnessing the horses was a real nightmare. As I tried to get the collar on they would raise their heads high in the air so it was a case of pushing it on quickly as they brought their head down again, and sometimes, third time lucky! I often tell the Young Farmers round here that they don't know what really *hard* farm work is!

Hearing that the son of the farmer next door was ill in bed, I decided to visit him one evening. His mother showed me upstairs and brought up a tray of tea. When it was time to go, I went down and she said to me, "Would you like to be a farmer's wife?" To which I replied, "Oh no, it's far too much like hard work." At that she said, "In that case don't come here again after my son." I could hardly believe it, and had to send him a note of explanation.

Once when the farmer's wife had to go to hospital I had to nurse her husband who was also in bed ill. It was quite embarrassing having directions from the doctor, and answering queries about his bowels, etc. However, he complimented me later on how well I'd coped. All in a live-in land girl's life!'

'I first wanted to go to Hereford when I was a young girl at school in London. This beautiful agricultural town was fixed in my mind when I learned about it doing a lesson on farming. Finally the chance to escape to the countryside came when I heard about the Women's Land Army. I was a Londoner and I wondered whether I would tolerate life on a farm. But I was only a *little* doubtful, for I knew in my heart that this was the life for me.

So there I was travelling down on a train to Herefordshire, a girl of 17, not knowing quite what to expect. "Well," I thought to myself, "I can always go back home to the smog if I do not like it."

The Land Army sent me to a dairy farm at first. The farmer and his family made me feel very welcome and comfortable. Mrs Rogers took me up to my bedroom. It was very different from what I had been used to at home, but I liked its cosiness.

Next morning Mr Rogers called me at six o'clock and said I could start by cleaning out the cow shed. Then he would teach me how to actually milk the cows. I was very nervous at first, but after a while I got the hang of it and eventually I could milk as efficiently as he could.

When haymaking time came along I was allowed to go milking on my own because Mr Rogers was needed elsewhere. Now I had the opportunity to prove I could manage on my own. The milking at that time was done by hand which did not disturb me, but I was a bit dubious of the bull in the next stall. So I sat down very gingerly with my back to him, praying that he would not move while I milked the cows. However, all I had to put up with was the occasional slap in the face from a rather dirty, unhealthy tail.

Other jobs were not to be so exciting, I was to find. Before Mr Rogers went to the town, he showed me how to spread manure. I took one look at the fork and smiled to myself. Here I was, on my own, spreading muck in a rather isolated field. "If my mother could see me now," I thought to myself, "she would have a fit."

Eventually I learned quite a lot and I was very happy and contented to work on the farm, even though one was expected to get up so early in the morning.'

THE HOME GUARD

'The Home Guard did great work at Fownhope, their members drawn from every section of the community. Occasionally there was a noteworthy episode. One night a German airman, armed, was reported in the vicinity. At once the Home Guard erected barriers across the road and searched the woods. He was not caught, but subsequently a report was received that he had been spotted and taken prisoner near Gloucester.

Many of the members of the Observer Corps were British Legion men. The observation post was set up in Whiterdine and at every hour of the day and night planes were spotted and their course plotted. The men who manned the observation post and the Home

Guard were hard worked and many of them elderly, but they cheerfully sacrificed all their time to doing their bit for the village.'

'My younger brother was too young to join the forces but he did join the Home Guard at Colwall. The sergeant lived near us but had no telephone, so at night, if there was a call out, we got the call. One night in the early hours the phone woke us and my brother dressed quickly and went to rouse the sergeant. A German plane had come down on the Malvern side of the hill and the Home Guard went to help find the airman – successfully.'

'Once during the war the church bells at Huntington rang. The Home Guard raced to their meeting place only to find it had been a false alarm. Two lads had been searching for an owl's nest in the church tower and had accidentally tolled the bell.'

'We always went up on Linton for Home Guard all through the war because you could see Gloucester, couldn't you? We had a lookout post there and so many had to do time up there like, two or three of us at a time. Once we reported two parachute troops dropping from a plane over Gloucester. And of course they all got upset and worried and old Colonel Ling from Bromsash House went out with a rifle and he shot his foot.'

'During the war Charlie was a member of the Home Guard at Clifford. They were instructed by the Military Police who were stationed at The Moors; patrols were sent out on exercises on Merbach Hill, which incidentally had a "V" cut in the fern for the duration of the war, the patriotic spirit very evident in the locality.

On one occasion they had been given live ammunition, and one over zealous member of the Home Guard challenged the local bus, brandishing his gun. The bus driver soon reported this incident, which had terrified his passengers, to the bus inspector!

It was the duty of the ARP warden, when hearing incendiary bombs dropping, to count the number of whistles they made on landing and next day to go and check to see if he could find the number of unexploded bombs to tally with the whistles counted.'

NURSING THE CASUALTIES

'When war broke out in 1939 I was working in service at Ledbury Park for £12 a year. The grandchildren of the house were evacuated from London with their governess, and later part of the house was shut off to house evacuees.

Eventually I left Ledbury Park and went to Birmingham to the Women's Hospital as a student nurse. The air raids became very severe and we had to sleep on camp beds in the basement; the matron and 22 fire service men were on duty every night. It was very distressing when visitors told patients that they had lost their homes and often members of their families. It was sad to leave the hospital and find houses flattened, furniture hanging from upstairs rooms with people sorting through rubble which once had been their home. After one heavy raid we had no water supply, so planks were put across craters outside which enabled us to take tea-trolleys etc with buckets and jugs to a nearby nursing home to get water to flush all toilets. The hospital was then closed and patients transferred to Worcester.

After returning to Sollershope my next war work was at the Hereford Ammunition Factory. I was there when it was bombed and I can still see the German pilot grinning at us as he came out of the mist to drop his bombs. Later in 1942 I obtained my release from the factory to go nursing again. I joined the Civil Nursing Reserve and did a fortnight's intensive course at Hereford County Hospital where we slept in one of the huts. I was posted to Barnsley Hall Military Hospital near Bromsgrove. Most of my time on day duty was in the theatre where we had to sterilize everything including needles and syringes in pure lysol; bandages, gloves, gowns etc were packed into biscuit tins and put into a sterilizer called Bertha. Often we would be operating for three whole days running when we had convoys of 100 or so men to deal with. Days on the theatre were very hectic, having to scrub down the theatre after each surgeon had finished with his casualties. Every now and again nurses were transferred to night duty for a well earned rest while others took over. The convoys at first were from the European war but later we had others who had been prisoners of the Japanese. Nurses at this time had to clean the wards, polish the floors, sterilize bedpans for use again as well as looking after the patients. Walking patients wore hospital blue suits.'

VICTORY CELEBRATIONS

At last, the war was over, first in Europe and then in the Far East. We celebrated formally and informally, in towns and villages across the county.

MUSIC IN THE STREETS

'When the war ended, parties were held out in the open air at Eardisland and people danced to the music of a record player placed on the river bridge. Even the members of the Women's Land Army, many of whom lived in a hostel at Kingsland, were allowed time away from their agricultural duties to join in the lively celebrations; eating, drinking, laughing and dancing around the village streets.'

'I well remember the night Victory in Europe was declared, everyone at Holmer got up in the middle of the night, lit a fire in the street and danced around it. The street party celebrations afterwards were marvellous.'

'At the Victory celebrations at Hampton Bishop, a tea was held for all the children in the village, with sports after, and each child was given a mug.'

'For VE Day at Leominster we had a street party with trestle tables laden with jellies, cakes and sandwiches, mainly supplied by the many English and American soldiers who were billeted in the six larger houses in Etnam Street. We had sports, carnivals and dancing in the streets. The Corn Square was also packed with hundreds of people celebrating the victory. Victory over Japan came later and was celebrated in an even greater manner.

On VJ Day all grammar school pupils over the age of 14 were invited to a special party held in Batemans Buildings, which were located in part of the present bus station area. We were given a splendid tea and waited on by the GIs. I remember especially the ring doughnuts covered in sugar. We each received a present of a book, candy and chewing gum. The Forces Dance Band played while we ate our tea.'

HIGHDAYS & HOLIDAYS

MAKING OUR OWN ENTERTAINMENT

In the days before television, and even before radio, we made our own entertainment either within the family or in our own town or village. The amount of local talent that could be pressed into action for amateur dramatics or concerts was often impressive, and everybody thoroughly enjoyed watching their friends and neighbours 'tread the boards'. We would walk or cycle miles for a dance, often after a long day's work and faced with the prospect of an early start on the farm next morning.

PLEASURE FROM SIMPLE THINGS

'In the early days at Pembridge there was little in the way of organised amusement. The men worked hard, their hours long and there was not much time left for fun and games. They got pleasure from simple things such as part-singing, glees etc, where one would conduct with the help of a tuning fork. They used the tonic sol-fa.

Practical joking was a popular pastime, and small pubs or cider houses in the country districts provided meeting places for the young and rowdy elements in the community. Sometimes a solitary roisterer on his way home would get a sobering shock on a dark night by seeing a ghostly face glinting at him through a hedge. In more sober moments he might have realised that a hollow turnip with holes for eyes and a candle inside makes a good ghost!'

'In my early childhood at Colwall in the 1920s we had no radio and in the evenings Father often read to us. He played the autoharp and we would sing hymns and songs to his accompaniment. We were encouraged to entertain ourselves and at Christmas we "put on a play", which sometimes we had to repeat when the neighbours were brought in.'

THE DRAMATIC ERA

'In the years before the First World War at Eardisland, Miss Jenkins could recall wonderful children's concerts, especially having participated herself in a mime when the girls were required to shave the boys. Another highlight of the dramatic era was when Mr Harvey used to visit the village with his concert party and would call at The White Swan to borrow corks with which to blacken the faces of the actors so that they could perform the minstrel songs. Another villager, Mrs Nancy Price, remembers being in the Swan when the actors put the corks up the chimney and rubbed them in soot for the blackening ceremony.

Children's pastimes were organised to raise money to buy cocoa to supply nourishing hot midday drinks for the schoolchildren. Local farmers donated the milk.

Other pastimes took place at the Old Smithy; this building was used as a working forge until Mrs Clowes of Burton Court leased it from the Levick Trust in order to use it as a meeting room for the WI. Apparently, the members found the room rather cold, despite a cheerful fire, and they had to wash up in tin bowls, disposing of the water by hurling it outside. These conditions, however, did not dampen the enthusiasm of the intrepid ladies.

The Old Smithy also played host to the Airgun Club and the Men's Social Club, although some activities were more spontaneous, such as on the night of a village dance, when one gentleman broke into a lady's bedroom and then leapt into the hall wearing her nightgown causing hoots of laughter all round!'

'In the 1940s Mrs I M Hayes who was the postmistress at Much Marcle, near Ledbury, produced many successful concerts. The venues were Much Marcle, Fownhope, Woolhope, Gorsley, Putley, Dymock and Kempley. The backstage and wings travelled with us from place to place, prepared and sized by Mrs Hayes and Mrs Sadley, a member of the cast. Mr Roy Beavan, brother to Mrs Hayes and an artist, came over from the RAF station at Credenhill to paint the village scene in oils. When the curtains were drawn, the audience were thrilled and amazed to see their village facing them. A generous amount was collected in appreciation of Mr Beavan's work and he promptly returned it with thanks and it went to the Red Cross.

One of the most popular items was "O 'Enery, O Sarah", which the late Mrs Munthe (the author, from the historic house Hellens at Much Marcle) said was good enough to put on in London. One coach firm sent in their bill, which read, "No charge – congratulations on an excellent performance."

Homme House, owned by the Money-Kyrles, was used by the Red Cross as a convalescent home for the war wounded, who were called "The Blues". We had a request asking us if we would go and entertain the Blues who would be flown over from Dunkirk. We certainly managed to cheer them up!'

A CHOICE OF ACTIVITIES

'Orleton people have always enjoyed a choice of activities in an ex-army hut which acted as a parish hall for many years. There were whist drives and dances, the WI from 1937, the Young Farmers Club from 1943, the Choral Society, Girl Guides and Scouts, cricket and football teams, and an excellent tennis club used a court at the vicarage. A flourishing church choir existed under the leadership of the Rev Lewis and his wife. Craft classes such as basketmaking and car maintenance were held in the old school. A village band played at festivals in church and for other special events. Travelling groups like Madame Landerdale and Harry Matteau paid visits.'

'In the past the social life of most people was bound up with that of the whole community. There was no television and in most cases no ready means of transport to the nearest town. So people stayed at home and joined with the rest in making their own entertainment. All kinds of clubs and societies flourished.

A Men's Club was first held at Bodenham Hall Cottage and later in a room at England's Gate. Young people's clubs have run continuously in the village, and have included a Boys Club started in 1944, the Girls Friendly Society and the Girls Club. In 1949 these were succeeded by the Youth Club which had 30 members. The first Bodenham Girl Guide Company was started in 1927 and met in various places, including a room over the vicarage. This was followed by the Brownies, both still in existence. The Young Farmers Club was started in 1945 by Mr Weyman-Jones of Bodenham Court.'

'There were local concerts, whist drives and dances at Colwall, cricket and football matches. The flower show was the main event of the year with a fair, fortune telling etc always held on the last Thursday of July. There were two tents, one for the "Cottagers" and one for the "Gentry". At Christmas there were Sunday school parties with sandwiches and slab cake eaten from trestle tables. Presents were given to children. Families visited the pantomime at Malvern Theatre where Midland Red buses were always waiting to take people back home.

There was a girl's club for the over fourteens and amateur dramatics. Once the girls formed flags of the world dancing with ribbons. There was a Band of Hope run by the Miss Ballards, where

230

hymns were sung and lectures on the demon drink given (they didn't know about the home-made dandelion wine).

A men's club met in the Church Institute where whist and billiards were played. The two clubs helped each other, the men moving chairs etc and the girls providing refreshments. There was a racecourse and a golf club in the village for the better off, and entertainment of another sort provided us locals gathered to watch traffic hold-ups on the steep hills and bends on the way to the races. Few people had cars, just walked or biked, but the bus service was better than now. Living inland, many children would not see the sea until they were older. Bonfires on the Malvern Beacon were a local feature, dating from 1588 when the Armada was sighted, then on occasions such as Coronations, Royal Jubilees and weddings. There were processions at Hallowe'en up the hill from the Wyche Cutting to find the witch – one year 1200 people took part.

The Queen and Duke of Edinburgh came along Chase Road, Upper Colwall following a visit to the British Camp in 1953. The road was surfaced specially!'

THE VILLAGE 'HOPS' AND THE CINEMA

'In the early days of the cinema at Kington, the film frequently broke down and then there was a time of chatter and orange peel until the cheer went up when the film restarted. Bombing the people down below from the balcony with sweet papers and orange peel was great entertainment!'

'Dances were arranged by Joe Clifton, Rhys Harding and Flo Powell at least once a week in the 1930s at Clifford village hall. The Diamond Players were a Hereford based band who came to play at local hops.

Living so close to Hay on Wye, most folks went to the pictures at the Plaza once a week, sixpence a performance. They often walked home in the dark, and there must have been many more people on the roads after dark in those days.'

'Never missed a week but what we went dancing in summer – village halls, one and sixpence. Harry Jones's band used to be all the go in them days, Harry Jones playing the piano, Bob Tayton playing saxophone and somebody else on the drums. Always had dancing competitions every year. I danced at the Shire Hall, Hereford in the competition. It sort of broke up during the war, like. We used to go to every place and get a prize like every time we had a chance to. I used to be dancing till three o'clock in the morning, then milking

231

cows at six. Father would be shouting up the stairs, "I'm glad you boys are just moving" – and we was only just about getting in! I had a twin brother, look, we was always two together like; we was never apart. He married the same day as me; we married two sisters.'

'The young people of Aston Ingham had to travel to neighbouring villages for dances. The young men thought nothing of walking several miles after work to a dance, walking back and then being up at four o'clock to harness the horses ready for another day's work.

For a long time the village boasted a very good drama group known as the St John's Players. Productions attracted audiences from a wide area, but sadly the group finally disbanded.'

THE CONSERVATIVE BALL

'In the 1920s a Conservative Ball was held in the Shire Hall every year and Granny and Grandpop would go. The ladies had a dance programme with a pencil tied to it and the gentlemen would book their dances ahead of time. The waltz, lancers, square dance, quickstep or barn dance were danced.'

THE COMING OF RADIO

'Mr E Jones was the first man to make a wireless set in Fownhope in 1919. His mother would not have it in the house in case it blew up, so they listened to it outside in the shed.'

'If we could be transported back in time, I think the silence about the house would be very noticeable. The wireless set, if the family had one, was a big piece of furniture in the sitting room, manipulated by Father. My father was a radio pioneer and in the early 1920s I remember the excitement of hearing "2LO calling" through huge headphones to which one of my ears was pressed. I also remember my mother looking at the jumble of wires and saying helplessly, "I thought this was called wireless!"'

'Entertainment was home-made; only the piano at one time, and a gramophone with a large horn which needed winding up before and during the playing of a record. The first wireless we had was operated with a wet and dry accumulator. We would listen to the news, "In Town Tonight" and a concert or talk, then turn it off in case the accumulators expired before they were changed once a fortnight by the paraffin man.'

A SPORTING LIFE

There was sporting activity to suit everyone, from cricket to football, from following the Hunt to playing golf.

HUNTING, SHOOTING AND FISHING

'The North Hereford Hunt was formed early in the century and the hounds have always been kennelled in Bodenham. Closely allied to the Hunt is the Pony Club which has thrived through the years and is still in existence. It came into being in 1951 at the kennels and has been supported with enthusiasm. Its objects are: "To encourage young people to ride, to enjoy all kinds of sport connected with horses and to instill in them the proper care of horses."

Another popular pastime was fishing in the river Lugg for grayling and trout. The Fishpools situated about halfway between Dinmore station and the village were used for the raising of young fish to restock the river. The club was disbanded in 1924 when parts of Hampton Court were sold, and after the Second World War the Birmingham Anglers' Association leased stretches of water. Cricket has long been a favourite form of sport, it lapsed during the war and restarted in 1952, playing in the Ketch meadows.

For a long time the Air Rifle Club has flourished, and with many successes and after several changes of name, survives as the Rifle Club, meeting now at Bodenham Manor.'

WINTER AND SUMMER

'Aston Ingham seems to have had a go at a great many different sports, all of which have had their day and been replaced by others. A golf club flourished at the turn of the century with an annual subscription of five shillings. The course was ploughed up at the start of the First World War. A football team was formed when a Mr Bourton said he would give ten shillings if ten other men would do the same to start the club. The original transport was by coal lorry, which was renowned for its unreliability. On one trip to Gloucester it broke down so many times that a tramp on the road kept overtaking it and arrived in Gloucester before the players. It was an understood thing that the team never arrived home on the same day as the match – their liking for liquid refreshment saw to that!

233

Following the Hunt was another pastime for many. The land was covered by the Ledbury Foxhounds until 1914 and the Rector always provided tea at the end of the hunt.'

'In the 1930s Mr Tom Wood, headmaster at Eardisland school for 40 years, lived at the school house and captained the Burton Court Cricket Club. The matches were played in these lovely surroundings with spectators enjoying the shade of the lime trees. The staff of Burton Court provided teas for the cricket teams and these facilities were used until 1948. In addition there was an enclosed area for two tennis courts and a bowling green, so the recreation ground near the village hall has followed something of a tradition in being used for cricket and the Eardisland Bowling Club.

Winter sports were somewhat less organised; in 1947, after heavy snow falls the river Arrow froze over and the villagers skated on it – holes had to be cut in the ice, however, to allow the resident swans to drink! The resulting thaw caused heavy flooding, the only dry patch near the river being on top of the bridge.'

'Madley has a fine tennis club, with four splendid en-tout-cas courts and a clubhouse. This is unusual for a village, even today. In the 1920s only one person in the village knew how to play tennis. She was Mrs Dry, the wife of the schoolmaster, and she decided to

Pembridge football team pose proudly in their strip in about 1920. Most villages made their own entertainment in the form of sports, clubs and societies in the days before television.

234

start a club. It began in a rough meadow with makeshift equipment, and she taught the farmers how to play. Eventually they improved the ground and progressed to two courts and a clubhouse. This they built themselves, mostly from wood. The floor was of railway sleepers, a much used material in those days, and the roof was covered with a tarpaulin. As time went by they built a second, much better pavilion, but right from the start there were always teas!'

'There was a village cricket team at Shobdon in 1921, but no football team. In the early to mid 1950s the village cricket team was renowned for its skill. Hereford refused to play us, and there is a press cutting from the national newspapers about the village side that bowled the opposition out for nine, and another for two. Games were played on the field opposite the church, on a very dodgy wicket.'

THE RIVER WYE

THE GENTLE GIANT

'Splash! As another part of the river bank slides down into the river bed, the pace of the impressive river constantly changes. Sitting on the bank on a warm sunny day with the water quietly passing one by, one forgets the tremendous power of the water underneath, pummelling against the river bank and taking away with it particles of soil. Even a church at Whitney on Wye succumbed to the power of the Wye as its foundations were eroded and it was carried away to be deposited all along the river.

The majestic swans paddle serenely against the current, dipping their long necks beneath the surface to forage for small fry and water insects. They run and flap lifting their weight off the water, their necks outstretched, straining with the effort to gain flight. They fly in their renowned V formation over luscious green meadows, which support the world-famous Hereford cattle, over apple orchards and hop fields.

The river, as it begins its journey through Hereford, is watched over by the Black Mountains before it meanders its way quietly in front of Hereford Cathedral.

Here Hereford bustles along, going about its business unaware of the never-ending, never-faltering, constant flow of life beneath the bridges; another world which takes very little notice of the surrounding mayhem. The only time the outside world really notices the river is when it is angry and full flowing, flooding across land and roads and making its presence felt.

The salmon that come up the river have an amazing calling to come back to the head of the river where they were hatched to spawn, defying man to get there. The small fry then have to make an incredible journey down the river to go out to sea to grow and develop before they return.

Fishermen will try to tempt the salmon to take their bait whether it be fly, prawn, minnow or worm by teasing them until they snatch at it, as a salmon returning to spawn does not eat while in the river. Miss Davey, who came to the Winforton Fishery as a guest of Sir Thomas Merton in the late 1930s must have told an amazing fishing yarn for the rest of her life after she caught the largest rod-caught fish ever recorded on the river Wye of 59½ lbs. She must have felt she had a whole rugby team pulling against her on the end of her line.

During the calmer, warmer summer months the river becomes popular for canoeists who come from near and far to enjoy the scenery. Normally they paddle quietly downstream, but once a year the river has a very busy couple of days when there is lots of shouting and commotion as the raft race takes place from Hay-on-Wye to Chepstow. The fish must panic and dive to the river bed until they have passed but then life returns to normality and the racers have helped various charities. Even when the river is low during the summer it will occasionally remind us of its inner power and strength, so one should always hold respect for the gentle giant meandering its way from Plynlimon to Chepstow and out into the Severn estuary.'

THE CARROTS FISHERY

'The Carrots Fishery in Hampton Bishop has always been considered to be one of the finest salmon fisheries on the Wye, which, in itself, is considered the finest salmon river in England.

Arthur Hutton in his book *Our Fishing Diary, Hampton Bishop 1908-1933* describes the salmon fishing of those days in detail. During 26 years of fishing, he and his friends caught 3,807 salmon and grilse weighing 66,690 lbs – an average weight of just over 17¼ pounds per fish.

In 1900 salmon disease (ulcerated dermal sclerosis) broke out in the Wye, and salmon were brought in from the Rhine to replace diseased fish. They have a bluish colour on the back, and their progeny can be recognised in the Wye today. It broke out again in the 1960s, and this, with water pollution and netting of salmon, caused considerable deterioration in the number of catches, particularly in the opening run of big fish. Now poaching, with poachers coming from all over the country, has decimated the number of fish caught. To the poachers, a short spell in prison is outweighed by the financial gain.

There have always been very cordial relationships between the owners of the fishery and the Hereford Anglers Association. The National Wye Championship coarse fishing competition, and many other coarse fishing competitions, take place over this stretch of water. The Hereford Anglers once rented a stretch of the river Lugg, rich in coarse fish, grayling and trout, from the Church Commissioners, which ran through our common land to Mordiford. Unfortunately the Birmingham Anglers purchased it.

Having been a fisherwoman for 60 years, I used to come up from London for holidays and weekends to fish the Wye for salmon, and I caught my first salmon at Clifford – weight 19½ pounds. Since then we have had the pleasure of fishing the Carrots water as guests. We now live within a stone's throw, and watch the height of the water from our bedroom windows.

When we first saw the Carrots, salmon would be rising and jumping every day; now, unfortunately, it is a very "dead" river. Hopefully it will regain its fame.'

ROWING ON THE WYE

'To Herefordians, the river Wye is very special. For the anglers who fished their expensive stretches of bank in search of fine salmon and the kids who dangled bent, bread-baited pins off the Victoria Bridge, the river always had an excitement all its own. As a child I loved to look at it almost every day to see how different its moods were, the currents and deep eddies under the overhanging banks, the colour of the water when snow up in the Black Mountains had melted and the noise it made in full flood spate.

The medieval Wye Bridge was just above the entrance to Hereford Rowing Club, which I joined as a junior aged 14. Boatloads of us would row about four miles upstream to the Camp Inn at Breinton. We'd stow our boats and clamber up the steep bank to the pub at the top for a picnic, glass of shandy and the glorious views. This was one of the few safe swimming spots too, since the Wye was then, and is now a river demanding respect from those who use it.

The Rowing Club was great fun. There were regular races, with single and double skiffs, and eights which practised all the time. The annual Regatta at Whitsun Bank Holiday was famous far and wide amongst the rowing fraternity and there was great rivalry amongst the crews from Leander, Ross-on-Wye and Monmouth. We in turn competed at their Regattas and usually went up to Henley. It was a time of non-stop parties and I made many friends here.

On the bank opposite the club I remember a commercial boatyard owned by the Jordan family. They hired out boats for fishing and punting and in the 15 years before the war they had a thriving business. Sadly, like so many other things, this changed after the war and the yard closed.'

ROYAL OCCASIONS

Jubilees, coronations and weddings were celebrated with enthusiasm by Herefordshire's towns and villages, just a few of which are remembered here. George V's Jubilee in 1935 may well have caused Herefordshire's very first major traffic jam!

1935: GEORGE V'S SILVER JUBILEE

'At the Silver Jubilee in 1935 there was a celebration at our village school near Hereford, with two wireless sets on tables in the school yard. We listened to the broadcast and were presented with a commemorative cup and saucer. Most schools had mugs.'

'I well remember the celebrations at the Jubilee. It started with a pageant processing through Colwall. There was a tea party for the children and I still have the mug I received. In the evening we all went on the hill near the Wyche Cutting to see all the bonfires that were lit all over the countryside – the excitement was immense. We thought of those bonfires being lit to warn of the Armada! So many people in cars had come to the hills, which was an excellent viewing point, that a huge traffic jam occurred. Well after the bonfires had died down, we stopped to watch. A ribbon of cars stretched round the hills as far as we could see, and that was a good long way as the cars had their lights on and were quite visible. It was all very good

Our King and Queen.

PEMBRIDGE.

Silver Jubilee

1910 — 1935

Record of Celebrations.

Souvenir.

LEOMINSTER PRINTING CO. LTD., DRAPERS LANE. LEOMINSTER.

Towns and villages throughout the county celebrated George V's Silver Jubilee in 1935 with a day of activities.

humoured with horns sounding and lots of laughter. Eventually it was cleared and we walked the mile home, fortunately downhill.'

THE ABDICATION

'I remember that at the time of the Abdication crisis in 1936, the head teacher sent us home early from school at Huntington to tell our parents that the King was to speak on the radio at three o'clock. At our house the only wireless was a very primitive crystal set with headphones – one set only. My mother went into the front room to hear the announcement and when she came back to the kitchen she told us children that the King, Edward VIII, had abdicated because "he found the burden of kingship too heavy to bear". She did not add the rest of the sentence – "without the help of the woman I love". She would not have thought it proper that children should know about that sort of thing. With such a sheltered upbringing it's hardly surprising that even today the average eight year old could teach me a lot about the facts of life.'

1937: GEORGE VI'S CORONATION

'The Coronation of George VI was celebrated in great style at Hampton Bishop. At that time "The Field" (now a nursing home) was owned and occupied by a Mr Martin and his Portuguese wife and family. They took a great interest in the village and threw open one of their fields for the celebrations. A refreshment tent was erected and well used – and I'm sorry to say that by the end of the day, damage was done and reputations lost!'

1947: ROYAL WEDDING

'In December 1947 the wedding of Princess Elizabeth (now Queen Elizabeth) and Prince Philip was marked in Pembridge by a modest celebration in the form of a cinema show and teas for the children, followed by a dance in the evening. The expenses of the day were met by donations.'

1953: CORONATION OF ELIZABETH II

'On the occasion of the Coronation of our present Queen, Mr Donald Swabey, then living at The Green, and Mr Lister, who looked after the church clock, had to see that the flag was flying from the flagstaff which projected from Withington church tower. It must have been a hair-raising experience, with ladders tied together with string, and having to climb up via the bell ropes! However, they succeeded, and the flag fluttered bravely overlooking the village festivities to mark the occasion.'

GETTING AWAY

Holidays were few and far between for many families between the wars, who had to make do with a day out as a break from working life. For those who were able to get away from it all, seaside holidays on the Welsh coast drew some, while cycling was a very popular – and cheap – way of seeing the beautiful Herefordshire countryside.

PICNICS AND TREATS

'As a child in Hampton Bishop, we didn't have holidays as there was not a lot of money about, but we did have picnics by the local river or go to the seaside for the day, or perhaps two days, in the summer. We helped Grandad haymaking, for which we had sixpence to go to the May Fair. Also for a treat we used to go to see Hereford Races, which were run partly across Grandstand Road in those days, so it did not cost us anything.'

'A Bank Holiday treat for us children at Cradley was a walk into Malvern, a round trip of about eight miles, going up Cockshot Hill and the Worcestershire Beacon, and home on the road round the North Hill. At the top of the Beacon we ate our picnic, and hoped to see the donkey with his panniers carrying the ice boxes which would have ice creams. After lunch we went down the other side to St Anne's Well for a drink of crystal clear Malvern water and to listen to Blind George playing his harmonium. We were allowed to spend our money at Pipers Penny Bazaar on the way home. Smaller children were very tired at the end of the long day.'

OFF TO THE SEASIDE

'We always had our fortnight's holiday during the first two weeks in September. Mother said she waited until 40 days after St Swithun's

241

Day, but I think it was because school started immediately after our holiday and it meant that during those long August days we had something to look forward to. We always went to Mumbles and had rooms in a large bungalow on top of the cliff overlooking Swansea Bay. We bought our own food and the lady of the house cooked and looked after us. We had no car, so travelled by train – our luggage being a large trunk sent in advance. Miraculously it was always there when we arrived. Our buckets and spades were left in the cellar of the bungalow each year. Strange – the sun always seemed to shine and we spent idyllic days on the beaches.'

CYCLE-CAMPING IN THE 1930s

'In the summer of 1935, when I was 15, I cycled from north to south through Herefordshire with my parents and three brothers, aged 13, 14 and 17. Like the majority of families then, we had no car and all our summer weekends, and my father's annual fortnight's holiday from the Sheffield steelworks where he was employed, were spent cycling and camping, highly organised by my father, who must have been one of the world's best packers of luggage. We travelled on two tandems and two single bikes. All the equipment – lightweight tents, sleeping bags, blankets, food, clothes and cooking utensils – had to be carried in saddle and pannier-bags or tightly rolled and strapped to the carriers. The problem of spare clean clothing was solved by posting on from home large parcels (at one shilling a time) to be collected at post offices en route. Dirty clothing was packed in the reversed wrappings and posted back home.

The greatest bugbears were headwinds and overnight rain, which meant wet and heavy tents and harder cycling. However I don't remember any wet starts on this holiday and the roads of Herefordshire seemed both gentler in their gradients and freer of traffic than the familiar Peak District hills near home. We belonged to the Camping Club and used their lists of accredited camp-sites, usually on quiet farms, very different from the large motor-camps of today. An overnight stay cost sixpence or a shilling per tent. Once arrived, each member of the family had an allotted task – erecting the tents (one medium-sized and two small), going to the farm for water in folding canvas buckets or for milk in a lightweight aluminium can, or starting up the primus stoves for cooking the evening meals. Cotton palliasses had to be filled with hay or straw from the farm. By 1935 several years' practice had made us all pretty slick at this routine, though exhaustion and hunger at the end of a long ride (anything from 40 to 80 miles) could produce frayed tempers.

After crossing the Peak District and the Cheshire Plain we came into Herefordshire from Shrewsbury and camped for a night near Leominster. Next day we cycled to Hereford where we went in the Cathedral and marvelled at the Mappa Mundi and the Chained Library. My parents were devotees of the old Ward Locke Guides, so we knew in advance what places and objects of interest to look out for. I remember pausing beside the Market Hall in Ross (a difficult thing to do nowadays!). At Symonds Yat we looked down on the famous view from Yat Rock and went on a boat trip on the river. We must have camped not far away, for I certainly don't remember lugging our laden bikes up those mighty gradients.

From Symond's Yat we had to make an unwelcome diversion from the planned route. One of the tandems had developed a mechanical fault which meant going down to Newport in search of some vital spare part. This was a nasty shock, as my father had planned to avoid all centres of industry. But we survived and went on to spend several days at Manobier before cycling up the Welsh coast and back by Barmouth, Llangollen, Cheshire (where I read my School Certificate results in the paper), Derbyshire and home to sooty Sheffield. I remember those halcyon days of the 1930s whenever I drive into the traffic hazards of Ross-on-Wye to do my shopping.'

THROUGH THE YEAR

Every year brought its familiar round of festivals and events. Some are still celebrated today, such as Oak Apple Day at Fownhope, while others have long since disappeared from our calendars – Empire Day, for instance, once celebrated by every schoolchild on 24th May, has gone the way of the empire it represented.

EMPIRE DAY

'When I was at the Girls High School in Hereford, before the Second World War, Empire Day was a very important event in the school calendar. Those were the days when the largest portion of the world atlas was coloured pink, representing Great Britain and all of her Dominions and Colonies.

The date was 24th May, and the organisers must have prayed for a fine day. We were told beforehand to wear daisies on our tunics, because the centre of the daisy represented the Mother Country, Great Britain, and the petals were her possessions, the Dominions and Colonies. After assembly, all 300 of us were marched two-by-two to the Castle Green, and there were joined by all the other city schools, duly marching past the various city dignitaries, the Mayor, the Bishop, and also the Lord Lieutenant of the County; the city band played *Land of Hope and Glory* which, when I was a new girl I very proudly sang, but when I was older I learned other versions of Elgar's famous chorus!

The ceremony ended with the playing of the National Anthem, when we all stood strictly to attention. Then came the good news from the VIPs on the dais – the remainder of the day was declared a holiday.'

'In Peterchurch the rector would come to the school on Empire Day and the day started with a service. After this a party was laid on with the usual sandwiches and cakes, and lemonade to drink, followed by games. This lasted all morning, then to our delight the rest of the day was a holiday, so we all went home. The great bonus of the day was the time spent away from school!'

OAK APPLE DAY

'In 1948 Mr F C Morgan read a paper at the Woolhope Club regarding the celebration of Oak Apple Day at Fownhope on 29th May, which included the following:

"The Fownhope Heart of Oak Friendly Society, 1876 was probably founded from the older society (Fownhope Amicable Society); the accounts for 1876 show a payment of ten shillings and sixpence for the box purchased from the old society. The members meet on Oak Apple Day, and when parading to church for the service at 11 am, carry their Club sticks on which are wooden oak apples. The ceremony is certainly picturesque for there is great friendly rivalry concerning the adornment of these with flowers. In procession the men on the right of each file carry their sticks on the right shoulder, and the men on the left have theirs on the left shoulder, thus displaying a double row of colours. Preceding all is a man carrying an oak bough with gilded apples, and another carrying the banner, and then the band. (In 1876, the Fownhope Brass Band was in existence and the musicians' dinner cost £1 2s 0d.) Arriving at the churchyard the members line up according to age and the younger pass through in pairs. After the service ceremonial calls are made at the vicarage, the doctor's and perhaps the houses of honorary members of the

Fownhope's Oak Apple Day celebrations, shown here in the 1950s, have a long history. The procession through the village by the Heart of Oak Friendly Society was a highlight of the day.

club, at which light refreshments are served. Later a return is made to the Club Room for dinner, with the leading spirits of the village at the top table, speeches with good humour follow the repast and the day ends with sports and other amusements. The dinner was revived after a lapse during the war years."

Oak Apple Day is still celebrated in Fownhope today.'

'In the 1930s at Peterstow it was the custom to bring an oak apple to school on 29th May. The boys had attached to this custom a threat that if we had no oak apple we would be chased and stung with stinging nettles. The evening of the 28th would be spent anxiously searching the hedgerows for oak apples. I was quite ignorant of the historic reason for the commemoration of this day (Charles II's escape from his enemies by hiding in an oak tree) and do not remember Mrs Lucas the headmistress ever explaining the meaning of the custom.'

THE MAY FAIR

'At the turn of the century the Pleasure and Hiring Fair held at Pembridge on 13th May was an occasion that was looked forward to for many a long day. People flocked to it from near and far, on foot, on horseback, in gigs, in horse brakes, in waggons, on donkeys. The early part of the day was devoted chiefly to business, the men and maids for hiring and the farmers and their womenfolk looking for workers. When deals were satisfactorily completed the remainder of the day was spent in pleasure and amusement, both of which were liberally provided. The whole village was en fete, and the pubs did a thriving trade, being easily spotted by the green branch stuck outside.'

'With the coming of the month of May, us children would be eagerly looking forward to the May Fair visiting the area. Weobley and Pembridge were our nearest ones, five miles away. The fairs never seemed to come to Dilwyn – perhaps the village was not big enough.

So, if we were very good and tried hard not to get into too much trouble, we would go to one or the other – sometimes even *both*. It depended on how well stocked the coffers were, we had to depend on our parents financing the outings as we were never given pocket money, except perhaps a pennyworth of sweets on a Saturday morning from Mrs Stewart at Dilwyn Stores, if we were lucky!

As far as I can remember, Weobley Fair was held on 8th May and Pembridge on the 13th (I can remember the 13th because Dad always planted his kidney beans on that date).

The big day dawned and we would go quite happily to school, knowing that we had a treat coming later in the day. All day there would be excited chattering about which rides we would, *hopefully*, be going on – I say hopefully because Mum and Dad's word was law, *they* dictated which rides we would take! So with school over, it was home for tea (not too much food – in case the excitement, plus the rides, made us sick!), then a quick "face and hands" wash and into our Sunday bests. After that it was a matter of waiting until our parents were ready – they had so many chores to do before they had a few hours off. If they couldn't manage to get everything done, Dad would usually stay behind – with hindsight he was probably thankful for a little peace and quiet.

At long last we would set off, usually with uncles, aunts and cousins – quite a gang we were. We went by Shanks's Pony with much leg pulling and hilarity, we didn't notice the journey, and with bright lights beckoning we were there before we knew it. To get to

246

Weobley we walked across the fields, where there was (and still is) a bridlepath at the top of Field's Place bank (on the "back way" to Weobley), and to get to Pembridge, we walked up Haven Lane, over the top and down into Luntley, then on to the village.

Having reached our destination, there would be the big decision: "What shall we ride on first". My favourite ride was The Big Horses – the roundabout with the beautifully painted horses, all named, with the twisted pole, mostly gilded, to hold on to! To my young eyes they were a magnificent sight, especially with hundreds of electric lights to enhance them. Mum would make sure we rode on an "inside" horse, because the ones on the outside of the roundabout seemed to go much faster, and she was afraid one of us would take a tumble! I think my second favourite ride was the Helter Skelter – climbing up the steps to the top of the tower, clutching a coconut mat almost as big as myself, then sitting on it and whizzing round in a spiral back to the bottom. I think Mum was a very wise lady not to give us too much tea. And, what about the Bumper Cars (or Dodgems), they were fun. Especially if one could get to drive – that was wonderful, that was! With the passenger hanging on for dear life waiting for the bumps. If I remember rightly those were the only rides we were allowed on. We were never allowed to go on the Ghost Train, in case it gave us nightmares. And we never did see the bearded lady! Instead, we could have a go on the coconut shy, the hoop-la and the like.

All these doings were interspersed with the grown-ups meeting and chatting with people that they had not seen since the last May Fair. This was the time when we young 'uns took a back seat, that is keeping quiet and waiting patiently for the pleasantries to finish. Oh, that was agony when we were dying to get on to see the rest of the fair. We dare not wander away, otherwise we would soon hear the sharp edge of the parent's tongue! Dad would inevitably get invited to go and have some liquid refreshment with one or two of his old mates, so he would disappear for a little while.

By that time we were usually as "hungry as hunters". So, Mum would treat us to sausage and bread (which cost one penny) and a brandy snap, all washed down with a drink of lemonade. No more rides after *that* feast – you can guess why. By then, we would have had enough anyway, and Dad would have rejoined us, so it would be time to call it a day and head wearily for home. We little ones were lucky, we were always given piggy-back rides by the menfolk. Oh so tired – but happy, and as we tumbled into bed a question was asked of Mum, "Can we go again *next* year, please?" To which Mum would reply, "All being well, if the tack holds good, and we are all alive and kicking"!'

'May 13th was the highlight of the year in the 1920s – Pembridge Fair and a half day holiday from school. Mother took us in the pony and trap. On one occasion there was a terrific thunderstorm and going along the Broad Road there was one almighty crash, the horse bolted, the trap tripped up and we all landed in the ditch.

The farmers always put up at Beavan's at the Court House. The horses were stabled and the visitors were given a warm welcome with tea laid on. The fair was laid out in the streets with the big horse carousel in the Market Square with a lovely mechanical steam organ.

There were stalls all along the street selling brandy snaps and toffee apples and monkeys on a stick. There were swings and helter-skelters and sometimes a Wall of Death. On one occasion the motor cyclist who rode round the inside of the wall had a sidecar with a lion (or was it a tiger?) riding in it. There were fat ladies, fire-eaters, sword swallowers and freak animals.

The favourite with small children was the roundabout of little horses, and in charge of this was a Mr Brewer, who had a hook on one arm in place of a hand and he used this very effectively to pull the roundabout.

People came from far and wide to the fair as Pembridge was always considered the best.'

FETES AND FAIRS GALORE

'In 1890 the parish church at Aston Ingham underwent extensive rebuilding and was temporarily closed for worship. In 1891, on 11th August, it was reopened amidst great celebrations, and every following year on 11th August there was a village fete. Trestles would be set up on the rectory lawn, all the farmers' wives brought their best silver and china, and the Ross Town Band was engaged to play, or a band from the Forest. The children had sports in the field known as Ellesmere and there was a dance at night in the school (which must have been pretty crowded) before the village hall was built. The event was held on the 10th if the 11th fell on a Sunday.

Neighbouring fairs were also a highlight. The Onion Fair at Newent was easy to reach because it was in cycling distance. Barton Fair in Gloucester was very exciting because the pony and trap was used. We little girls felt very grand sitting up beside Dad. This was always a day out for everyone. The May Fair at Hereford was only attended by a few lucky ones because of the greater distance.

In the village there was a Cherry Fair, held at the local pub to celebrate the cherry harvest. The local chapel always held a Whit Monday Tea for the parents and a May Tea on the Tuesday for the

Sunday school children. The highlight of this was handfuls of sweets being thrown for the children to scramble after.'

'Hay Fairs were held at Clifford in May and November. Extra buses were arranged and the last one home was at ten o'clock. This one was always very full and people had saved enough money for chips on the return journey. What fun it must have béen enjoying the whole evening out and the return journey round the houses, home together.'

'Important events in Huntington village were the twice yearly horse fairs – one on 18th July many years ago called the Cherry Fair, and one on 14th November. In the old days the November fair was a two day event with sheep and cattle and other commodities on offer as well as horses. Farm working horses, smart riding ponies, but especially unbroken Welsh Mountain ponies were brought here to be sold. Dealers would start to arrive at dawn to cast their keen eyes over what was on offer. Sometimes a dealer and a vendor would spend hours bargaining before the deal was clinched by the slapping of hands. At the end of the day horses which were to go long distances were fitted with halters and the end of the rope was tied to the tail of the horse in front. Thus they were led in single file to the railway station at Kington.

Traditionally the pony which realised the highest price of the day was ridden through the inn – sometimes causing considerable havoc! There is no record of when this custom started but villagers remember seeing it done. The first recorded fair was in 1403 but from about 1935 numbers dwindled until it finally ended in the early 1950s. The local school was about a mile from the village and on these special days the headmistress sometimes allowed the pupils to go to the fair during the dinner hour (it wasn't called "lunch" in those days). The excitement of buying a few sweets from the shop, listening to the arguments between men who had consumed too much alcohol, often caused us to exceed the time limit. The punishment was the cane across the palm of the hand. If the hand was withdrawn as the cane descended, then the offender received the cane on both hands. Only once did I have this punishment because the memory of the tingling in my hand was sufficient to deter me from being late again!'

'The Flower Show at Colwall was an exciting event at the end of July, because the fair came too. That Thursday afternoon, the village would be virtually empty with everyone viewing the flowers and vegetables in the marquees, watching the pageant or enjoying the

249

roundabouts, coconut shies and swings. The Second World War saw the end of this event. There is still a Flower Show, but it's not quite the same!

In September the streets of Ledbury were full of hop pickers who had arrived by train en route for the many hop yards around the town. The trains used to transport the pickers must have been the oldest that could be found and we would see the coaches parked in the sidings at the station. Later the Hop Fair took place in the streets.'

'There is always something going on in a village and Withington is no exception, although many of the old traditional celebratory days have disappeared. The highlight of the year for Withingtonians must surely have been the Withington and District Flower and Horticultural Show. This was started by the Thinghill Lodge of Oddfellows in 1925 and was to survive until 1990. Entrants and visitors would come from miles around to enjoy the fun, and maybe take home a silver cup or a prize. Not only flowers and produce drew the people, but many other attractions as well. A fair with swings and roundabouts and "curiosities", races of all kinds, a tug of war, and a carnival with decorated floats were but a few of the many entertainments on offer.'

'A big day for us was Bishops Frome Sports Day held at Cheyney Court, with a fairground with roundabouts, swingboats etc. Mother always showed butter and eggs, usually getting first prize for both. There was also a garden fete at the vicarage.'

HARVEST FESTIVAL

'The main event of the year at Sutton St Nicholas in the 1920s was the Harvest Festival celebrations. The service was always held at three o'clock on a Friday afternoon in early October. All the local farmers attended and all the workmen were given the afternoon off. The church and porch were beautifully decorated with huge sheaves of corn, and every householder sent their offerings of fruit, vegetables and flowers.

A huge tea was prepared in the school and all the villagers were welcome. A dance followed, with the lancers, gay gordons, military two-step and the polka. The men were warned not to swing the ladies off their feet in the Lancers but of course they did. Often their shoes fell off and there was a great scramble to return them afterwards. Some of the local comics did a turn in the festival – often hilarious. In fact, a happy, enjoyable village do.'

'Harvest time was an important festival in any rural community. At Eardisland children were sometimes absent from school as they had to help with gathering in the harvest, but on the great festival day *everyone* turned up at three o'clock for the church service, with the crowds overflowing into the porch.

After the service in the church the villagers walked to the school where a lavish tea was served. This was followed by a lively dance once the debris of the meal had been cleared away by willing helpers.'

ARMISTICE DAY

'On 11th November at Pudleston, a procession of parishioners and schoolchildren was led by the vicar and choir to the war memorial to honour the war dead.

At exactly eleven o'clock a two minutes silence was kept and we all stood with bowed heads. We sang hymns, which were the same every year as they were appropriate for the service. We all wore our red poppies and felt quite emotional. It was a very moving service which is still taken today, but is not remembered in quite the same way.'

CHRISTMAS

'At Christmas at Holmer we went carol singing, carrying lanterns. Holmer church organist Miss Maud Davies sat in a bathchair with the harmonium on the front and was pushed by the men. We had a lot of fun on those nights.

I remember walking from Clehonger to Hereford early one morning before Christmas with my mother and brother. We carried a clothes basket filled with dressed poultry for the Christmas market held in the Butter Market. Once there we rented a stall and displayed our poultry. The poultry buyers from Birmingham arrived about 8 am and Mother's poultry, which was always beautifully dressed, sold quickly. We then went Christmas shopping and returned home by carrier cart, "The Lady Queen", whose driver was also the village midwife.'

'The weeks leading up to Christmas at Pudleston were very busy. We children would get together to go round the parish carol singing. We were always welcomed and were given mince pies and a few coppers. We had our annual school Christmas party in the parish hall with a gift for all the children and a lovely tea.'

251

'On Christmas Eve Mother got one of her knitted stockings and put inside one orange in the toe, then filled it to the top with sweets and small presents to be hung on the bedrail for Christmas morning.

My brother and I put a nail in each side of the door jamb one year, with a piece of string across about one foot off the ground. When all was quiet, Dad crept up the stairs to hang up the stockings, caught his foot in the string and over he went. My brother woke and said, "We've got him!". I cannot say what Dad said, but we knew what he did with his hand.

On Christmas Eve we went in pairs or groups to each house in Weobley to sing a carol. Our reward was a penny or two – sixpence was a lot when £1 a week was a man's wage. We shared the money collected between us, tired but happy.

Christmas was a happy time; a sweet mouse, some nuts (which we put in a jar with salt until Christmas) and a jelly on the table. We had an old gramophone with one needle and two records, *The old rustic bridge by the mill* and *Climb upon my knee, Sonny Boy*. They both had cracks, then it was a rush to help it over to keep playing. We also played Hunt the Thimble.'

'Preparing for Christmas was an exciting time, chopping up the lemon and orange candied peel which came in big lumps with sugar in the middle, blanching the almonds by plunging them into boiling water and shredding the suet.

Father always enjoyed Christmas and his job was bringing in the tree and holly and mistletoe, but *never* before Christmas Eve as that was considered unlucky. One piece of mistletoe had to remain hanging in the hall till the following Christmas.'

Index

255